AMARNA

A GUIDE TO THE ANCIENT CITY
OF AKHETATEN

AMARNA

A GUIDE TO THE ANCIENT CITY OF AKHETATEN

EDITED BY
ANNA STEVENS

The American University in Cairo Press
Cairo New York

First published in 2020 by
The American University in Cairo Press
113 Sharia Kasr el Aini, Cairo, Egypt
One Rockefeller Plaza, 10th floor, New York, NY 10020
www.aucpress.com

Dar el Kutub No. 22301/19
ISBN 978 977 416 982 3

Dar el Kutub Cataloging-in-Publication Data

Stevens, Anna
Amarna: A Guide to the Ancient City of Akhetaten / Anna Stevens.—Cairo: The American University in Cairo Press, 2020.

p. cm.
ISBN 978 977 416 982 3
1. Tell el-Amarna (Egypt)
2. Egypt — Antiquities
932.014

2 3 4 5 26 25 24 23 22

Designed by Sally Boylan
Printed in China

Dedicated to the memory of our
dear friend and colleague Boris Trivan

CONTENTS

INTRODUCTION

The archaeological site of Amarna in Middle Egypt (figs. 1–3) survives as a testament to the extraordinary reign of Pharaoh Akhenaten, history's first reputed monotheist. Some 3,000 years ago, Akhenaten turned his back on most of Egypt's gods and devoted himself to the sole worship of the sun god Aten. At Amarna, he created a cult arena for the worship of his god—a place he called Akhetaten—"Horizon of the Aten." Here he built vast open-air temples, palaces, and a new royal burial ground, and watched as a huge settlement sprang up, which today survives as Egypt's best-preserved pharaonic city. Was he an idealist, individualist, or despot? Views on Akhenaten today are diverse. Regardless, his reign was a momentous episode in Egyptian history and one that still challenges us today.

Figure 1. A view across the Amarna bay, looking to the south. Photo courtesy of the Amarna Project.

This book is a cultural guide to ancient Amarna. We present Amarna to you with an archaeologist's eye, sharing insights on life at the ancient city obtained from over one hundred years of research, together with knowledge from local communities and heritage caretakers. It combines a guide to key monuments with stand-alone case studies drawn from ongoing investigations at the site, a historical overview of the Amarna period, and visitor information.

Beautiful tombs, busy with scenes of ancient life, a royal burial ground, and the footprint of a vast ancient city lie before you. Few heritage sites in Egypt offer such diversity, and nowhere can the presence of ancient kings and commoners alike be felt as acutely.

Who Was Who?

Many of the finer details of the Amarna period, including certain aspects of royal succession and family relations, remain much debated by Egyptologists—and some may never be fully resolved. A summary of the most commonly held views follows, but more information can be found in the readings listed in the Further Information section.

Akhenaten's Predecessors

Amenhotep III: Akhenaten's father, who ruled for nearly 40 years during the peak of Egypt's New Kingdom empire. One of ancient Egypt's most prolific builders, he is also known for his interest in the solar cult and promotion of divine kingship. He was buried in WV22 in the Western Valley, off the Valley of the Kings, at Thebes (modern Luxor); his mummy was later moved and hidden with other royal mummies in the Tomb of Amenhotep II (Valley of the Kings Tomb 35).

Tiye: Amenhotep III's chief wife and the mother of Akhenaten. Her parents Yuya and Tjuiu were from the region of modern Akhmim in Egypt's south. She may have lived out her later years at Akhetaten, and died in the 14th year of Akhenaten's reign. Funerary equipment found in the Amarna Royal Tomb suggests she was originally buried there, although her mummy was later moved to Thebes and is perhaps to be identified as the "elder lady" from the Valley of the Kings Tomb 35 cache.

Akhenaten and His Family

Akhenaten: Son and successor of Amenhotep III, known for his belief in a single solar god, the Aten. He spent most of his reign at Akhetaten (modern Amarna), the sacred city he created for the Aten. He died, of causes unknown, in the 17th year of his reign and was buried in the

Amarna Royal Tomb. His body was possibly relocated to Thebes and is often suggested to be the enigmatic mummy recovered in the early 20th century in Tomb 55 in the Valley of the Kings (KV55). Forensic evidence, however, suggests this individual died at too young an age to be Akhenaten.

Nefertiti: Akhenaten's principal queen. Little is known of her background, although she may also have come from Akhmim. There is no evidence that she was of foreign origin. Her last known attestation as queen is an inscription dating to the 16th year of Akhenaten's reign in quarries to the north of Amarna. Shortly before or after the death of Akhenaten, Nefertiti likely ruled for a short period using the name Neferneferuaten.

Meritaten: The oldest daughter of Akhenaten and Nefertiti, with the important title "King's Daughter." She is associated with such monuments as the Maru-Aten and North Palace at Akhetaten, and was probably a significant figure in the royal court. Later in Akhenaten's reign, she may have served in a consort-like role. Scenes in the Tomb of Meryre (II) at Amarna (North Tomb 2) show her apparently married to King Smenkhkare, with both of their names in cartouches as king and queen.

Meketaten: The second daughter of Akhenaten and Nefertiti, who died at Akhetaten and was buried in a side chamber of Akhenaten's tomb in the Amarna Royal Wadi. Her body was probably relocated to Thebes after Akhetaten was abandoned.

Ankhesenpaaten/Ankhesenamun: The third of Akhenaten and Nefertiti's daughters was married to Tutankhaten/Tutankhamun, and after his death may have married the pharaoh Ay.

Neferneferuaten-tasherit (Neferneferuaten the Younger), Neferneferura, and Setepenra: Little is known of the three youngest daughters of Akhenaten and Nefertiti. Setepenra disappears from the historical record in the latter part of Akhenaten's reign and may have died by this time.

Secondary Royal Figures

Kiya: A secondary wife of Akhenaten, who had the unique title "Greatly Beloved Wife." Little is known of her or her origins. In around year 16 of Akhenaten's reign, her name and image were removed from some monuments at Akhetaten and replaced with those of Meritaten and Ankhesenpaaten. She may have died at Akhetaten; her body was probably later moved to the Valley of the Kings, where some burial material in her name was found in tomb KV55.

Ankhesenpaaten-tasherit (Ankhesenpaaten the Younger): A little-known princess, daughter of Akhenaten and possibly Ankhesenpaaten or Kiya.

Meritaten-tasherit (Meritaten the Younger): A little-known princess, daughter of Akhenaten and possibly Meritaten or Kiya.

Coregents and Successors

Smenkhkare: Ruled briefly at Amarna, probably as coregent to Akhenaten. He may have been Akhenaten's son from a secondary wife, or his brother. In the Tomb of Meryre (II) (North Tomb 2), he is shown as king, married to Akhenaten's daughter Meritaten. His main monument is the Grand Hall at the southern end of the Great Palace. The mummy from tomb KV55 may be that of Smenkhkare, if it is not Akhenaten himself or another royal male.

Neferneferuaten: The name Neferneferuaten was used by a female ruler in the latter part of Akhenaten's reign. She was perhaps Meritaten, although most scholars believe her to be Nefertiti. Details of the reign of Neferneferuaten are obscure. She was possibly coregent with Akhenaten, perhaps after the death of Smenkhkare, or took the throne alone when Akhenaten died. It is also possible that she ruled as coregent in the early years of Tutankhaten's reign. In any case, she ruled only briefly and has no known monuments.

Tutankhaten/Tutankhamun: Thought to be Akhenaten's son, either by Nefertiti or by a secondary wife, perhaps Kiya. He assumed the throne, as a boy, after Smenkhkare, perhaps with Neferneferuaten as coregent for a time. During his reign, Egypt returned to religious orthodoxy and Akhetaten was abandoned. After a nine-year reign, Tutankhamun died and was interred in KV62 in the Valley of the Kings, famously discovered nearly intact by Howard Carter and his team in 1922.

Ay: Short-lived king who followed Tutankhamun. He was probably part of the extended royal family, perhaps Nefertiti's father. Before becoming king, he served Akhenaten at Akhetaten using the title "God's Father," and had a tomb prepared here (South Tomb 25). He was also an influential figure during the reign of the young king Tutankhamun. He was buried in WV23 at Thebes.

Horemheb: A military officer, likely from Memphis (near Cairo), who assumed the throne after the death of Ay and probably ruled for over 20 years. He was also an important official during the reign of Tutankhamun. Prior to becoming king, he had a grand tomb carved at Saqqara, but as ruler he was buried in KV57 in the Valley of the Kings. He began the process of dismantling the temples and palaces of Akhetaten.

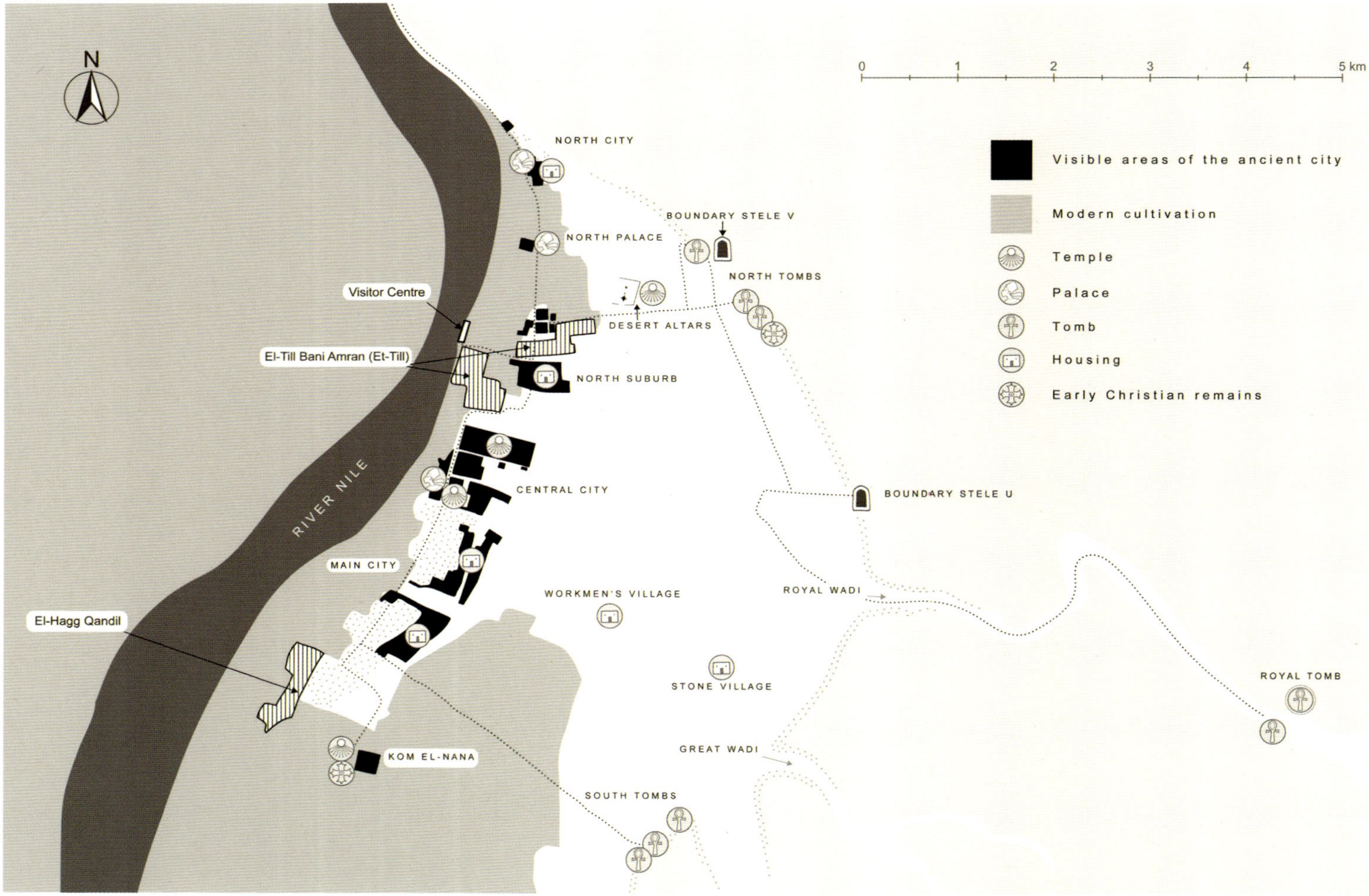

Figure 2. Map of Amarna. The names now used to refer to the ancient city at Tell al-Amarna (Central City, Main City, etc.) are mostly modern designations, although some original names are known from ancient sources. Illustration by Mary Shepperson.

CHRONOLOGY

Predynastic Period	4800–3100 BC
Dynasty 0	3100–3000 BC
Early Dynastic Period	
Dynasty 1	3000–2800 BC
Dynasty 2	2800–2675 BC
Old Kingdom	
Dynasty 3	2675–2625 BC
Dynasty 4	2625–2500 BC
Dynasty 5	2500–2350 BC
Dynasty 6	2350–2170 BC
Dynasties 7–8	2170–2130 BC
First Intermediate Period	2130–1980 BC
Middle Kingdom	
Dynasty 11 (after reunification)	1980–1938 BC
Dynasty 12	1938–1759 BC
Dynasties 13–14	1759–1630 BC
Second Intermediate Period	1630–1539 BC
New Kingdom	
Dynasty 18	
Ahmose	1539–1514 BC
Amenhotep I	1514–1493 BC

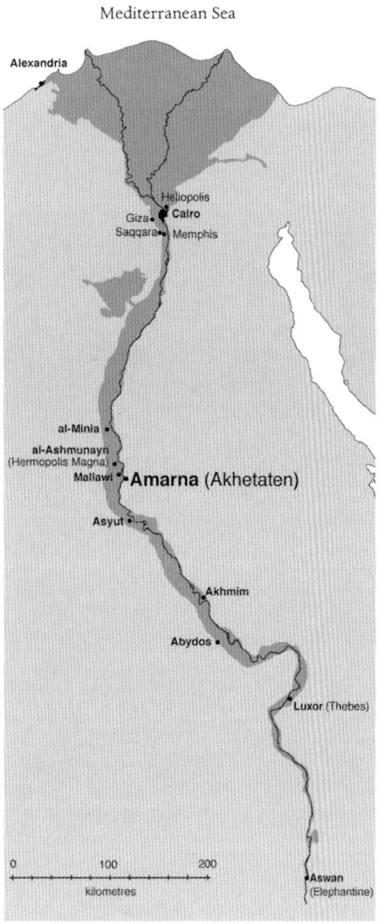

Figure 3. Map of Egypt.

Thutmose I, II	1493–1479 BC
Hatshepsut	1478–1458 BC
Thutmose III	1479–1425 BC
Amenhotep II	1426–1400 BC
Thutmose IV	1400–1390 BC
Amenhotep III	1390–1353 BC
Akhenaten	1353–1336 BC
Neferneferuaten and Smenkhkare	1336–1332 BC
Tutankhamun	1332–1322 BC
Ay	1322–1319 BC
Horemheb	1319–1292 BC
Dynasty 19	1292–1190 BC
Dynasty 20	1190–1075 BC
Third Intermediate Period	1075–656 BC
Late Period	664–332 BC
Ptolemaic and Roman periods	332 BC–AD 642

(After Freed et al., *Pharaohs of the Sun: Akhenaten, Nefertiti, Tutankhamen*, p. 13.) Note that Egyptian chronology is not perfectly fixed and the start and end dates of kings' reigns should be considered somewhat flexible.

SETTING THE SCENE

Amenhotep III and Akhenaten's Early Years

Akhenaten likely spent much of his childhood at Memphis (near Cairo) and Thebes (modern Luxor), surrounded by the opulence of his father Amenhotep III's court. At birth, he was named Amenhotep, meaning "(the god) Amun is satisfied." It was a common name, and reflected the popularity of Amun, the patron god of Thebes. There is little information about Akhenaten's early years, although we know he had an older brother named Thutmose, who died young, leaving Akhenaten as successor to the throne.

Akhenaten's father, Amenhotep III, was one of the most influential rulers of the New Kingdom. He reigned for 38 years at a time of stability and prosperity in Egypt. He managed Egypt's vast empire with few recorded conflicts and was a prolific builder. Ramesses II ("the Great") would mimic, and partly usurp, Amenhotep III's building program several decades later. Amenhotep III's grand architectural visions—which were entwined with celebrations of divine kingship and the solar cult—formed the backdrop to Akhenaten's childhood.

Among Amenhotep III's most enduring monuments are those he built for his Jubilee Festivals, the celebration of kingship, first held after 30 years on the throne. In Nubia, the gold-rich land to Egypt's south, he constructed twin temples at Soleb and Sedeinga. There, he and his wife Tiye were worshiped as divinities, Tiye as the goddess Hathor and Amenhotep III in his own divine form. For his jubilee celebrations in western Thebes, he constructed a huge ceremonial complex on an expanse of desert south of the royal mortuary temples. Now known as Malqata, it contained palaces, temples, workshops, and an enormous T-shaped ceremonial lake, the Birkat Habu, measuring some 2km long and 1km wide. It is easy to imagine that this grand, ritualized annexation of the landscape may have inspired Akhenaten. The solar cult, too, was prominent in Amenhotep III's reign.

Rise of the Solar Cult

Before and after the Amarna period, the ancient Egyptians engaged with a vast range of divinities to help them explain, understand, and navigate the world. There were gods of creation, kingship, afterlife, occupation, domestic well-being, and many others. Some divinities were associated with natural features and phenomena, like the sky, sun, earth, or river flood. Ancient Egyptian religion was practiced for some 3,000 years and to many is defined by its great stability. But this longevity was due partly to its inherent flexibility. The popularity of individual gods waxed and waned over the centuries, and aspects of deities could merge together to create new hybrid gods. Foreign gods could be integrated into the Egyptian pantheon and there was fluidity across the boundary between the mortal and the divine. Kings exploited this fluidity to promote their own divinity. The Egyptians were also flexible in how they perceived time and creation. There were multiple versions, for example, of creation myths explaining the beginning of the Egyptian world. The Egyptians were comfortable with religious contradictions that would be unacceptable in modern-day religious philosophies.

The most significant deities were those associated with kingship or creation, including the god Amun. Amun, "the Hidden One," was the patron god of the royal household and emerged only in the Middle Kingdom. By the time of Akhenaten's reign, the cult of Amun had grown to be the most powerful in the land, centered upon Thebes.

The greatest of the solar gods was Re. His cult center was in the north of Egypt at On (later called Heliopolis, now a suburb of Cairo). Excavations at Heliopolis have revealed the footprint of a vast temple complex that must have rivaled Karnak in scale. The solar cult was connected with creation. Each night, the god died and passed through the netherworld, domain of Osiris, to be reborn again at dawn. As the sun god rose in the morning in the east, it created the world anew. The solar cult was also intimately connected with royal power: each king was the Son of Re.

Solar worship emerged in the Old Kingdom, the age of the pyramids, and rose to prominence again in the New Kingdom. In the reigns preceding Akhenaten's, new hymns to the sun were written and solar themes became ever more visible. Increasingly, the dead were thought to join the sun god on his journey through the afterlife, taking part in his eternal cycle of life and death. Deities were assimilated into the solar cult, a practice that increased in the reign of Amenhotep III, Akhenaten's father. For example, Osiris, lord of the underworld and judge of the deceased, became the nocturnal manifestation of the sun god. Amenhotep III also began to align himself with this new form of the solar cult to underline his own divinity. At his Soleb Temple in Nubia, Amenhotep III was worshiped as the solar form of his own deified self. Under this king, the disc of the sun, known as the Aten, also began to be seen as a divinity in its own right. When he celebrated his Jubilee Festival at Malqata, Amenhotep III was towed on a barge on the Birkat Habu, the great sacred lake, celebrated as the divine manifestation of the "Dazzling Aten." Akhenaten's reign may have been defined by his devotion to the sun god, but these beliefs certainly did not emerge in a vacuum.

Akhenaten as King: Change on the Horizon

Like many Egyptian pharaohs, Akhenaten was young—perhaps in his early teens—when he came to the throne. The death of Amenhotep III probably prompted his ascension, although some scholars believe the two kings shared a period of co-rule.

He spent his first four years, as Amenhotep IV, overseeing building projects. In Nubia, he completed his father's temples at Soleb and Sedeinga. He further consolidated Egyptian presence in this important region by completely rebuilding the Egyptian colonial town at Sesebi, a gold-mining hub. He also finished his father's decoration of the third pylon at the Temple of Amun at Karnak. These projects were part of the traditional undertakings of a new king with resources to hand. Yet Akhenaten's affinity with the solar cult—and commitment to doing things differently—was soon apparent.

Early in his reign, he took the extraordinary step of celebrating a Jubilee Festival instead of waiting for the traditional 30-year anniversary of his ascension to the throne. Other jubilees may have followed. At Karnak, he constructed at least four ritual buildings partly connected to these celebrations. Their remains have been partially uncovered through excavation.

Akhenaten's early temple decoration embraced a range of gods, executed in traditional style. At Sesebi, he decorated the temple crypt with scenes of gods including Amun, the deified Amenhotep III, and Atum. But it was the Aten who would soon dominate his building program. Initially, the god was shown as a falcon-headed man, identified as the composite figure Re-Horakhty-Aten (more fully: "Re-Horakhty Who

Rejoices in the Horizon in His Name of Shu Who Is [in] the Solar Disc [the Aten]"). But the iconography of the Aten was soon changed to that of the disc of the sun, with solar rays that end in hands. A series of name changes were to clarify the god's character further until—toward the end of Akhenaten's reign—all references to other deities had been removed. Early in his reign, the king changed his own name from Amenhotep to Akhenaten, "One Who Is Effective for the Aten."

The excavated remains of Akhenaten's jubilee buildings at Karnak all show the Aten in this new form, and this god only. Traditional Jubilee Festivals embraced the cults of all of Egypt's gods, but Akhenaten's Jubilee celebrated only the Aten. One of the Karnak buildings, called the Gem-pa-aten, or "The Sun Disc Is Found," included a huge court lined with colossal statues of the king with extraordinary exaggerated and androgynous features, setting him apart from the mortal world (fig. 4). A second building, called the Hut-benben, "Mansion of the Benben-Stone," depicted the Aten not in the company of the king, but with his queen Nefertiti and the royal daughters, showing the important position royal women held in the Aten cult. The royal family was to play a central role in state religion in Akhenaten's reign.

Akhenaten's Karnak monuments are striking not just in their decoration, but in the small building blocks from which they are constructed. Called talatat, they measured c. 53 x 21 x 24cm and weighed about 70kg.

Figure 4. Colossal statues of Akhenaten emerge from the ground during excavations of the Gem-pa-aten at Karnak in 1927. Image © CNRS-CFEETK 52452/H. Chevrier.

They were to become a signature of Akhenaten's reign. Their small size permitted speedy construction, suggesting a sense of urgency in his building activities.

Denouncing the Gods

At the Temple of Karnak, Akhenaten erected a stela announcing that all deities other than the Aten had ceased to exist. He began redirecting revenue from Egypt's temples to the cult of the Aten. Then, from around the fifth year of his reign, he began to send teams of workers to destroy the names and images of traditional gods from the walls of Egypt's monuments. Amun, Mut, and Khonsu, the patron gods of Thebes, were especially targeted. The work was often sloppy and incomplete, but it was a shocking move nonetheless. Egyptian art, like any art, was informed by societal attitudes and beliefs. Showing a god receiving offerings meant that the god would receive those offerings forever: to remove such an image made the god's cult inactive. There must have been shockwaves on multiple fronts for Egypt's religious institutions, priests, and the people.

IN FOCUS: AKHENATEN AND THE ATEN: WHY WERE AKHENATEN'S REFORMS SO DRAMATIC?

Akhenaten's Atenism evolved out of the familiar, but came to be something markedly different from what Egyptians had known before. At its heart, Atenism stressed the uniqueness of the Aten and of Akhenaten's relationship with him. All Egyptian kings were gods on earth, but the elevation of the Aten elevated Akhenaten, too. There was only one god, and only one person who now knew the god. This established a ritual framework whereby access to the god was gained through worship of the king.

The essential elements of the Aten—which was both unique and at one with the king—were inherent in how the god was presented. In Amarna-period art, the rays of the disc shine upon Akhenaten and the queen, communicating their special relationship to the Aten (fig. 5). Early in his fourth year, Akhenaten had the name of the Aten written in cartouches, giving it the privileges of kingship, an unprecedented move. The components of the god's name were refined, in several stages, removing the names of the deities Re-Horakhty and Shu. By the end of his reign, the name no longer contained references to any other deity.

The cult afforded a special place to royal women, especially Nefertiti, whose name was also shown in a cartouche, linking the king, the queen, and the Aten in a divine triad. The three were assimilated with the deities in one of Egypt's most important creation myths: the birthing of the twins Shu and Tefnut from the androgynous creator god Atum, the first separation of one god into many. In this way, royal women helped to legitimize the Aten cult. They stood in for goddesses in contexts where female divine power was needed, and so became semi-divine themselves. On Akhenaten's sarcophagus, for example, found in pieces in the Amarna Royal Tomb, Nefertiti stands on the corners in the positions usually occupied by the goddesses Isis, Nephthys, Selkis, and Neith. Nefertiti, the royal princesses, and the king's mother, Queen Tiye, were often assimilated especially with Hathor, a fertility goddess with close links to the solar cult, and can sometimes be seen with insignia of this goddess such as sistra (sacred rattles) and plumed crowns with sun discs.

The nature of the sun god is explained in the Hymns to the Aten, which are carved in the tombs of Akhenaten's officials at Amarna. The texts are similar to poems, written as though spoken by Akhenaten himself, and celebrate the creative powers of the sun god. They are among the most striking pieces of religious writing preserved from the ancient world. The most complete version can be seen on the walls of the Tomb of Ay (South Tomb 25). They draw upon an existing tradition of solar hymns, although here the focus is only on the one solar god, the Aten. The Aten is presented as the creative power of light that comes through the disc of the sun. The Hymns stress that the Aten is the only god and works alone. The Aten is concerned with beauty and love and is often presented as the creator of the world. Much has been said about Akhenaten's tolerance of aspects of other gods and whether he can rightly be called a monotheist, but pursuing a rigid definition of this term is largely a modern preoccupation. Uniqueness and singularity were the essential elements of the Aten as presented in the ancient texts.

The Great Hymn to the Aten

Beautifully you appear from the horizon of heaven, O living Aten who initiates life—

For you are risen from the eastern horizon and have filled every land with your beauty;

For you are fair, great, dazzling and high over every land,

And your rays enclose the lands to the limit of all you have made;

For you are Re, having reached their limit and subdued them <for> your beloved son;

For although you are far away, your rays are upon the earth and you are perceived.

When your movements vanish and you set in the western horizon,

The land is in darkness, in the manner of death.

(People), they lie in bedchambers, heads covered up, and one eye does not see its fellow.

All their property is robbed, although it is under their heads, and they do not realize it.

Every lion is out of its den, all creeping things bite.

Darkness gathers, the land is silent.

The one who made them is set in his horizon.

(But) the land grows bright when you are risen from the horizon,

Shining in the orb (=Aten) in the daytime, you push back the darkness and give forth your rays.

The Two Lands are in a festival of light—

Awake and standing on legs, for you have lifted them up:

Their limbs are cleansed and wearing clothes,

Their arms are in adoration at your appearing.

The whole land, they do their work:

All flocks are content with their pasturage,

Trees and grasses flourish,

Birds are flown from their nests, their wings adoring your Ka;

All small cattle prance upon their legs.

All that fly up and alight, they live when you rise for them.

Ships go downstream, and upstream as well, every road being open at your appearance.

Fish upon the river leap up in front of you, and your rays are within the Great Green (sea).

(O you) who brings into being fetuses in women,

Who makes fluid into people,

Who gives life to the son in his mother's womb, and calms him by stopping his tears;

Nurse in the womb, who gives breath to animate all he makes

When it descends from the womb to breathe on the day it is born—

You open his mouth completely and make what he needs.

When the chick is in the egg, speaking in the shell,

You give him breath within it to cause him to live;

And when you have made his appointed time for him, so that he may break himself out of the egg,

He comes out of the egg to speak at his appointed time and goes on his two legs when he comes out of it.

How manifold it is, what you have made, although mysterious in the face (of humanity),

O sole god, without another beside him!

You create the earth according to your wish, being alone—

People, all large and small animals,

All things which are on earth, which go on legs, which rise up and fly by means of their wings,

The foreign countries of Kharu and Kush, (and) the land of Egypt.

You set every man in his place, you make their requirements, each one having his food and the reckoning of his lifetime. Their tongues differ in speech, their natures likewise. Their skins are distinct, for you have made foreigners to be distinct.

You bring the inundation from the underworld,

And you bring it to (the place) you wish in order to cause the subjects to live,

Inasmuch as you made them for yourself, their lord entirely, who is wearied with them,

The lord of every land, who rises for them,

The orb (=Aten) of the daytime, whose awesomeness is great!

(As for) all distant countries, you make their life:

You have granted an inundation in heaven, that it might come down for them

And make torrents upon the mountains, like the Great Green, to soak their fields in their locale(s).

How functional are your plans, O lord of continuity!

An inundation in heaven, which is for the foreigners (and) for all foreign flocks which go on legs;

(And) an inundation when it comes from the underworld for the Tilled Land (=Egypt),

While your rays nurse every field:

When you rise, they live and flourish for you.

You make the seasons in order to develop all you make:

The growing season to cool them, and heat so that they might feel you.

You made heaven far away just to rise in it, to see all you make,

Being unique and risen in your aspects of being as "living Aten"—manifest, shining, far (yet) near.

You make millions of developments from yourself, (you who are) a oneness: cities, towns, fields, the path of the river.

Every eye observes you in relation to them, for you are Aten of the daytime above the earth (?).

You have traveled just so that everybody might exist.

You create their faces so that you might not see [your]self [as] the only (thing) which you made.

You are in my heart, and there is none who knows you except your son, NEFERKHEPRURE-WAENRE,

For you make him aware of your plans and your strength.

The land develops through your action, just as you made them (= people):

When you have risen they live, (but) when you set they die. You are lifetime in your (very) limbs, and one lives by means of you.

Until you set, (all) eyes are upon your beauty (but) all work is put aside when you set on the western side.

(You) who rise and make [all creation] grow for the king, (as for) everyone who hurries about on foot since you founded the land,

You raise them up for your son, who issued from your limbs, the King of Upper and Lower Egypt, who lives on Maat,

The Lord of the Two Lands, NEFERKHEPRURE-[WAENRE],

Son of Re, who lives on Maat, Lord of Crowns, AKHENATEN, long in his lifetime;

(And) the King's Chief Wife, his beloved, the Lady of the Two Lands, NEFERNEFERUATEN-NEFERTITI—may she live and be young forever continually.

(Translation and notes by W. Murnane, *Texts from the Amarna Period in Egypt*, pp. 113–16.) —AS

IN FOCUS: THE ART OF ATENISM

Akhenaten's reign is renowned not only for Aten worship, but for the remarkable way in which the royal family was represented: with fluid and exaggerated forms (fig. 6), and in intimate postures—even kissing and embracing, something unparalleled in pharaonic art.

Figure 5. Akhenaten, Nefertiti, and their three eldest daughters venerate the Aten in a scene from the Tomb of Ipy at Amarna (South Tomb 10). After N. de G. Davies, *The Rock Tombs of El Amarna*, Part 4: *Tombs of Penthu, Mahu, and Others*, pl. XXXI. Image courtesy of the Egypt Exploration Society.

Egyptian art was an important part of the ritual framework that upheld Egyptian world order. It was formulaic and stylized, often blatantly so. Amenhotep III, by the end of his long reign, was sometimes represented with distinctly youthful features, while the female pharaoh Hatshepsut gradually began to show herself as male in statues to conform to the appearance of the typical male king. The revolutionary nature of Amarna art was intimately linked to the Aten cult and was an essential part of Akhenaten's religious program. It may have sought to prompt sense-based reactions more strongly than Egyptian art had before. Interpretations of Amarna art as portraiture—including the suggestion that the king's distorted proportions reflect a physiological disorder—misunderstand Egyptian art, which rarely sought to represent an individual's real-life appearance.

The earliest representations of Akhenaten are in a traditional style. Images in his Karnak buildings, however, are a striking departure from this, the king's body now elongated and androgynized. Most remarkable are the giant colossi with their drawn-out faces, broad hips, and distended bellies (fig. 4). Egyptologist Dimiti Laboury has stressed the importance of perspective in viewing these images. The colossi look particularly odd when photographed front on, but somewhat less so when viewed from their intended vantage point below. These colossi are the most extreme examples of Amarna art, created early in Akhenaten's reign, around the time when the image of the Aten was also altered to that of the sun disc. The exaggeration of the king's form set him apart from the mortal world, his androgyny linked to his role as divine provider of fertility and prosperity, like his father the Aten. For inspiration, Akhenaten drew from the iconography of a god of fertility called Hapi, who is shown with a similarly shapely and androgynous form. A softer version of the new style is generally found after the first years of Akhenaten's reign, although there is still much to learn about how Amarna art developed and the ways in which it was used.

Figure 6. Akhenaten's image, with its drawn-out features, carved on a slab of stone that was probably used by an ancient sculptor as a "trial piece." MMA 66.99.40. Photo courtesy of the Metropolitan Museum of Art.

Egyptian art used grids to guide and precisely align elements of the human body. In the Amarna period, the new appearance of the human body was achieved by deliberately changing the underlying grid system. In two-dimensional representations, the traditional 18-square grid was changed to 20 squares, with extra space inserted at the chest, between the armpits and the navel, and also at the neck, elongating these areas. Traces of the original grids used by the artists of Akhetaten are still visible in some of the Amarna tombs (especially that of Ahmes, North Tomb 3). Grids could also be used for statues. As Egyptologist Rolf Krauss pointed out, the proportions of the famous painted bust of Nefertiti seem to have been determined in this way. Although the bust is often hailed as naturalistic, in fact, there is almost nothing "natural" in its execution or appearance.

Elements of the new art style fed into private representations, too, as seen on a stela excavated at one of the non-elite cemeteries at Amarna (fig. 7). The stela shows a non-royal couple with rounded bellies and broad hips sitting side by side, embracing. The stela was probably made in one of the suburban workshops of Akhetaten, where images of the royal family were also being produced. It suggests that elements of the aesthetic of the new royal image (or simply of elite culture) were appealing to at least some members of the public. The exaggerated style of Amarna art was gradually phased out from the reign of Tutankhamun, but something of its sensuousness and organic nature lived on in later art. —AS

Figure 7. A limestone funerary stela showing a man and woman seated, and receiving offerings. They are shown in a languid and intimate style that recalls representations of the Amarna royal family. Photo courtesy of the Amarna Project.

Amarna: Building a Vision

With his Karnak monuments, Akhenaten had stated to his people and to the gods his devotion to the Aten cult. In the fifth year of his reign, he then announced his plan to create a new cult arena entirely for the Aten, at the place now known as Amarna. He named it Akhetaten, "Horizon of the Aten." Shortly after, between his sixth and ninth years, he shifted the entire royal court to Akhetaten. We cannot know Akhenaten's reasons for this relocation, but regardless of whether he was driven by religious fervor or by political agenda—perhaps wanting to escape the disgruntled priesthood of Amun—it was a remarkable step: a great push against the status quo.

Something of the king's first steps at Amarna can be traced through inscriptions he carved on a series of boundary stelae, set into the cliffs around the perimeter of the site (fig. 8). In these inscriptions, he states why he chose Amarna: the Aten had guided him to it, and the land had not been claimed for the cult of any prior god. Perhaps its location, about halfway between the great cities of Thebes (modern Luxor) and Memphis (near Cairo), was convenient, or its isolation appealed. Egyptologist Cyril Aldred suggested that Akhenaten chose the Amarna bay because one of the wadis (valleys) in the eastern cliffs, probably the one known today as the Great Wadi, has a broad, regular shape that is a close match to the hieroglyphic sign for "horizon," a pictorial rendering of the sun emerging from a wadi.

Akhenaten's claim that Amarna was an unoccupied site has been supported by archaeological excavation, although there was certainly life in its vicinity when the king and his court arrived. Just over the river, near modern Mallawi, lay the great city of Hermopolis Magna (modern al-Ashmunayn), cult home of the god Thoth. Giant baboon-form statues of Thoth erected by Amenhotep III are among the ruins still visible there today. Small farming villages would also have been scattered around the hinterland of Hermopolis.

On the east bank of the river, however, the Amarna bay offered a vast blank slate, ready to be transformed into a ritual stage for the sun god. On the Boundary Stelae, Akhenaten listed the institutions he intended to build here: temples to the Aten, cult buildings for the royal women, a new royal burial ground, a tomb for the Mnevis bull (the sacred bull of Heliopolis, associated with the sun god), and more. He began by placing key buildings into the landscape, spread out from north to south: the North Riverside Palace, the North Palace, the Central City's temples and palaces, and a southern temple at Kom al-Nana. Initially these would have been simple plots, perhaps with little more than a few wooden structures or tents, with sacred gardens at the temples. They were linked together by a long north–south road, called the Royal Road by archaeologists, which created the spine for what was to become a narrow sprawling city, running parallel to the riverbank. Work on the Royal Tomb probably also started early on.

These first steps in laying out Akhetaten must have been driven in part by practicality. Spreading buildings out across the plain helped to claim the land for the god, and secure key positions and borders. Building close to the riverbank was sensible in terms of access to water and mud for making bricks. But there was probably a symbolic element to the way Akhetaten was laid out, too. Notice on the map of the city (fig. 2) how the temples and palaces in the Central City lie opposite the valley containing the royal tombs. This is unlikely to be coincidence and may indicate a symbolic connection between the tomb and temples. The Small Aten Temple, especially, lines up with the Royal Wadi (fig. 9).

The Royal Road was also probably envisaged as an avenue of royal display, drawing on the long-held tradition of formal processional routes (like the avenues of sphinxes at Thebes). Scenes of Akhenaten and the royal family in their chariots are a feature of Amarna tomb scenes, as though people glimpsed Akhenaten—the god on earth—as he sped past. The city plan probably had a kind of axial symbolism. The sun moved east–west overhead, passing over the open-air temples and setting in the western horizon. Akhenaten, as the Aten's representative on earth, correspondingly traversed the human world north–south to undertake rituals at the rising and setting of the sun. Was there more to the city plan than this? Some believe so, seeing the city's key buildings carefully located using distance ratios drawn from the surrounding landscape and the position of the Royal Tomb, or a city plain laid out with distinct sacred and secular zones.

Figure 8. Boundary Stela U, one of the huge tablets carved into the cliffs around the perimeter of Akhetaten on which Akhenaten claimed territory for the sun god. Photo courtesy of the Amarna Project.

Figure 9. The sun rises in the Royal Wadi behind the Small Aten Temple. Photo courtesy of the Amarna Project.

Once the basic layout of Akhetaten was established, it grew rapidly upward and outward. Its temples and palaces were transformed into vast mud-brick and stone buildings. Archaeology shows that the temples of Akhetaten went through several iterations. During the short period it was occupied, as Akhenaten's vision took shape, Akhetaten was probably an ever-changing place. Not all of the monuments listed on the Boundary Stelae, however, can be matched with places uncovered in the archaeological record. Most famously, the Tomb of the Mnevis Bull has never been identified at Amarna. Does it remain for future archaeologists to find, or did Akhenaten never construct it? It is probably incorrect to think of Akhetaten as the product of a rigid plan. Akhenaten's initial vision for Akhetaten, as stated on the Boundary Stelae, was evidently flexible enough to accommodate the king's changing understanding of the god and its needs. This is well in keeping with ancient Egyptian attitudes toward cult spaces, which often mixed formality and organic development: consider the monumental, yet somewhat piecemeal, nature of the great temple of Karnak.

A City of People

Then the people flooded in: officials, priests, laborers, servants, and families with children. Many must have come from Thebes and Memphis, although people may have arrived from all over Egypt, if not also beyond its borders. Like all major cities in Egypt at this time, the population of Akhetaten would have had diverse origins and many of its occupants would have been immigrants to Egypt, directly or by ancestry.

Some Theban officials, who had already started their tombs in the Theban mountains, relocated to Akhetaten and began new tombs here. Also relocated, it seems, was the famous tomb builders' community of Deir al-Medina, likely shifted to a new workers' village on the eastern desert edge of Akhetaten. Evidently, not all officials moved to Akhetaten, however. The elite necropolis at Memphis seems to have stayed in use in the Amarna period and not all Theban officials known from Akhenaten's reign have tombs at Amarna. A strong administrative network was still needed across the country and many of the country's officials were left in their posts. One of the two viziers, Nakhtpaaten (owner of South Tomb 12), served from Akhetaten, but the second probably remained in place at Memphis, to serve the king in the country's north.

Figure 10. A small stone stela from the time of Akhenaten showing a soldier of Syrian origin named Terura drinking wine from an elaborate straw and strainer, perhaps during a festival. He is accompanied by his wife Arbura and a servant. Terura's ethnicity is potentially conveyed through features such as his patterned kilt, headband, and beard, while his dagger and lance mark his occupation. © Ägyptisches Museum und Papyrussammlung, Staatliche Museen zu Berlin, ÄM 14122. Photo: Sandra Steiß.

Did the people of Akhetaten have a choice whether to come? Any emerging population center brings with it opportunities for trade and employment, and some people may have come to Akhetaten in search of new beginnings. Yet Egyptian society operated through long-established chains of dependence. Officials were under obligation to the king, and the rest of the population reliant in turn upon them for their livelihoods. Moving the royal court meant that many would have had little choice but to uproot their lives. Servants and indentured laborers would have had no choice at all, their lives defined by complete reliance on others. The relocation of the royal court to Akhetaten must have been an enormous social upheaval. For many Egyptians—soldiers, peasants called up for seasonal labor, or officials sent on posts around the country—a transient lifestyle would not have been unfamiliar. This, however, was an uprooting of whole families and communities on a scale that had never been seen before in Egypt.

Arriving at Akhetaten, the people began filling the empty desert with their houses. Residential areas at Akhetaten were not planned out according to a grid or formally imposed system, and tended to spread gradually and organically, although their development was undoubtedly based on long-held ideas of how residential space should function. The arrangement of the ancient houses can look haphazard to us today, but would have been logical to their inhabitants.

Large houses of officials were plotted first. Around these estates grew little village-like neighborhoods, probably for people who were economically tied to each official. Many families likely built their own homes, using river mud and desert sand. Some of the holes they dug were then turned into wells. Often, one long wall would be built first and several houses then constructed against it. Potsherds with drawings of house plans suggest that people were working to guides of how a house could

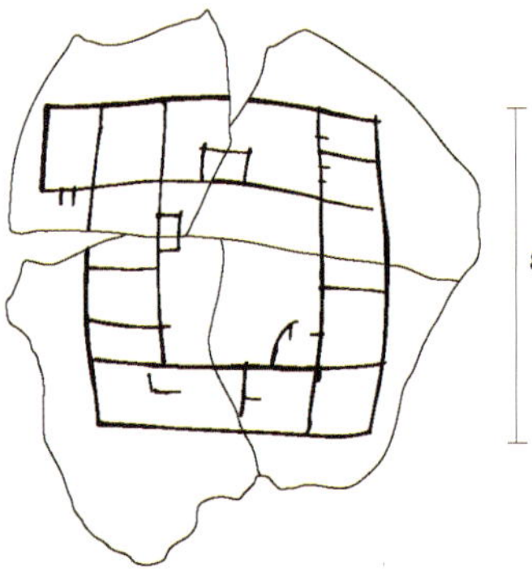

Figure 11. The floor plan of an Amarna house (with a typical large central room) sketched on a potsherd by a resident of the ancient city. It was perhaps a guide for how a particular house was to be configured. After Egypt Exploration Society object card 35/468. Redrawn by Mafdy Mansour.

be laid out (fig. 11). Yet houses were rarely built to a standard plan. They were of different shapes and sizes, and often improvised to fit into available space. In part, people might also have been remodeling social and living patterns they were familiar with before moving to Akhetaten. Streets and alleys developed in the gaps left between houses, creating winding access routes through local neighborhoods.

Akhetaten

Soon, Akhetaten was up and running. Its hub was the Central City (figs. 2, 13)—dominated by great palaces and temples fronting on to the Royal Road, and, behind them, a kind of administrative zone spreading eastward into the desert. Extending north and south from the Central City were large residential areas, now known as the Main City (fig. 12) and North Suburb, and, at the far north end of the bay, two palaces with more housing at the North City. Had the city been occupied longer, the North Suburb and North City would perhaps eventually have spread and joined up.

The desert toward the cliffs was left largely free of settlement apart from two small villages, the Workmen's Village and Stone Village, which housed specialized laborers and their families, including those who worked on the Royal Tomb. Something of a ritual zone developed in the desert to the southeast of the city, where Akhenaten built sun temples dedicated to the royal women. Another temple complex, now known as the Desert Altars, was founded on the desert plain to the northeast of the city.

In the eastern cliffs, the king created a new royal burial ground, deep in a winding valley, and his officials cut and decorated tombs for themselves and their families in the cliff face overlooking the city (the North Tombs and the South Tombs). Most of the rest of the population used pit-grave cemeteries located nearby to bury their dead. The cliffs were also the location of huge quarries where talatat blocks were removed to build the king's city. The quarries extended some 10km north of the Amarna bay, as

Figure 12. The ruins of ancient houses spread across the Amarna plain. Photo courtesy of the Amarna Project.

Figure 13. A view across the Central City taken by the Royal Egyptian Airforce in 1932. Photo from B. Kemp, *The City of Akhenaten and Nefertiti: Amarna and Its People*, p. 36, fig. 1.8.

good-quality rock was sought out. Small encampments for quarry workers and other laborers were perhaps scattered through the desert wadis, although none now survive.

Akhetaten also encompassed a vast area of farmland on the west bank of the Nile, within the territory marked out by the Boundary Stelae: "hills, uplands, marshes, new lands, basin lands, fresh lands, fields, waters, towns, banks, people, herds, groves and everything that the Aten, my father, causes to come into existence continually forever" (Murnane, *Texts from the Amarna Period*, 84). The produce of the west-bank villages was diverted to support the new city.

Akhetaten was perhaps never envisaged by the king as a "city" as such, but that is what it became, as people arrived and sought to re-establish their lives and livelihoods. It is difficult to know how large the population grew to be. Over 1,000 mud-brick houses have been excavated, but they represent perhaps only half of the original habitations, and we lack reliable accounts of how many people would have lived in each house. There is also the question of how many people lived in less formal shelters that do not survive at all in the archaeological record. The cemeteries of Amarna contain well over 10,000 people, suggesting a substantial population for the city. An estimate of 20,000–50,000 people is often suggested, and something toward the upper limits of this range, if not beyond it, certainly seems feasible. Today, around half of the ancient city survives, making it by far the best-preserved of any ancient Egyptian settlement.

IN FOCUS: AMARNA'S WORKERS' VILLAGES

Not everyone at Akhetaten lived in the riverside city proper. On the desert plain, between the city and the cliff face, there were two small workers' villages. The larger of the two, today called the Workmen's Village, housed tomb workers and their families (fig. 14). They were probably the same community who lived at the famous village of Deir al-Medina at Thebes, to which they likely returned after Akhenaten's reign ended. Their main role was to cut, and perhaps decorate, the royal tombs at Amarna.

The Workmen's Village contained 72 small houses, each with the same basic layout, and one larger house that probably belonged to an overseer. The houses were contained within a compound enclosed by a thick mud-brick wall. Structures connected with the transport and distribution of supplies to the village, such as stone emplacements to support huge water jars, are found on the route leading into the site. In the ground outside the village, the residents built animal pens, garden beds, and mud-brick chapels in memory of their ancestors, some of whom were buried nearby. The chapels were once brightly decorated with colorful wall paintings showing scenes of commemoration and celebration (fig. 15). These painted chapels appear to be unique at Amarna, and probably occur here a result of the special artistic skill within this community.

Although the village was isolated, the tomb workers seem to have been far from the most impoverished residents of Akhetaten. Their work on the Royal Tomb provided them with a level of state support that was above their basic needs. Their water supplies were adequate to keep pigs and farm small gardens (fig. 16). Some of their tombs contained furniture and meat offerings, more than most people took to the grave. Records left by the Deir al-Medina tomb workers' community several hundred years later saw them striking in protest against unpaid wages, a reminder that tomb workers were not always well supported.

The Stone Village is a much smaller and simpler site. Built mostly from unworked boulders mortared with desert clay, it had a less regular layout than the Workmen's Village and no chapels or gardens. It looks to be a far more modest site, as though the people employed here were less skilled or less important to the king's vision. Part of the Stone Village has the appearance of a large open-air kitchen. The role of the village is difficult to pinpoint. In part, it might have supplied desert-based workers with bread, stone tools, and other goods, but might also have housed laborers who assisted with the huge task of quarrying stone out of the cliff face to create the royal tombs.

Both the Workmen's Village and Stone Village are now largely covered by sand and there is little to see at these fragile and difficult-to-access sites. —AS

Figure 14. The Workmen's Village when first excavated by the Egypt Exploration Society in the 1920s. EES Amarna Archive Negative 1922.32. Photo courtesy of the Egypt Exploration Society.

Figure 15. A painted scene (partly reconstructed) from a chapel at the Workmen's Village showing two figures who are probably deceased members of the village community. They are dressed in finery and wear tall wax "perfume cones" on their heads. Reconstruction by Fran Weatherhead. Photo courtesy of the Amarna Project.

What Kind of City?

All cities and towns, ancient or modern, have their own character. Akhetaten was the home of the royal court and an arena for solar worship: the religious capital of the country. It was Egypt's administrative capital of sorts, although it probably never entirely replaced Memphis as such. And it must also have been, for the time it was occupied, a city that was still finding its feet. None of these aspects was necessarily unique, but each brought its own rhythm and characteristics that, combined with the backdrop of everyday life, shaped Akhetaten as a living city.

Figure 16. An ancient pig pen at the Workmen's Village, uncovered during excavations in the 1980s. Photo courtesy of the Amarna Project.

Figure 17. Meryre II is rewarded for his service to the king with golden collars, handed out by the royal family themselves at an elaborate Window of Appearance. Scene in the Tomb of Meryre II (North Tomb 2). After Davies, *The Rock Tombs of El Amarna, Part 2: The Tombs of Panehesy and Meryre II*, pl. XXXIII. Image courtesy of the Egypt Exploration Society.

The city's palaces formed the hub of court business, where the highest-level decision-making took place. An administrative zone occupied the eastern fringe of the Central City, where teams of scribes set court orders into action (fig. 18). To run the city, the king relied on a loyal

Figure 18. The Small Aten Temple (the large rectangular building) and the sprawling zone of administrative buildings nearby, photographed in 1993. Photo courtesy of Gwil Owen/ The Amarna Project.

core of officials, whose villas, scattered all over Akhetaten, also became centers for business and bureaucracy. Akhenaten continued the tradition of rewarding these officials with such gifts as the Gold of Honor collar (fig. 17), handed out during ceremonies at the Window of Appearance. Allocation of space for a rock-tomb in the eastern cliffs would also have been a form of royal reward.

The Aten Cult

Akhetaten was a huge ritual arena for the sun god, whose cult contributed much to the rhythms of city life, both spiritual and practical. Although we know relatively little about how the Aten cult was performed, the two traditional cornerstones of temple cult likely continued at Akhetaten: the daily maintenance of the god (although no longer focused on a cult image) and special festivals on the god's behalf. The presentation of luxury offerings, especially food, was crucial, and is something that Akhenaten seems to have taken to an extreme. Akhenaten's Boundary Stelae present one list of appropriate offerings to the Aten: "bread, beer, long- and short-horned cattle, (assorted) animals, fowl, wine, fruit, incense, and all sorts of good plants" (Murnane, *Texts from the Amarna Period*, p. 83). Inside the temples, the main daily offering to the god was made by the king at dawn, against a backdrop of music, singing, and dancing. If tomb scenes are to be believed, huge spreads of offerings for the Aten were also laid out on open-air offering tables in the temples, at least on occasion.

Figure 19. Cattle being hand-fed to fatten them up (Tomb of Meryre, North Tomb 4) and led into an Aten temple to be slaughtered as offerings to the sun god (Tomb of Tutu, South Tomb 8). After Davies, *The Rock Tombs of El Amarna*, Part 1, *The Tomb of Meryre*, pl. XXIX; Part 6, *The Tombs of Parennefer, Tutu, and Ay*, pl. XVIII. Image courtesy of the Egypt Exploration Society.

This focus on temple offerings gave the cult a pragmatic edge, creating a great industry around the continuous preparation of offerings. The official in charge of this undertaking was a man named Panehesy, the owner of North Tomb 6. He was granted a house immediately beside the Great Aten Temple, close to bakeries, a stone-lined court where cattle were kept, and the slaughterhouse inside the temple itself, where cattle were sacrificed beneath the Aten's rays (fig. 19). A great many of the city's citizens would have been in Panehesy's employ, the Aten cult providing their means of economic survival.

The cult supported the population in other ways, too. According to Egyptian tradition, offerings dedicated in temples would be given back to the people who worked in them for consumption. This system, we assume, remained in place at Akhetaten, although how widely offerings were dispersed is unknown. Signs of malnutrition on some skeletons of the non-elite individuals excavated from the cemeteries of Amarna might suggest they were not regular recipients of food from the temples, but it is very difficult to be sure.

How far the Aten cult impacted the ritual lives of the people of Akhetaten is also hard to measure. Akhenaten's officials donated goods to the cult, and were the benefactors of mortuary offerings in some of the city's temples. They also maintained their own small shrines to the royal family and Aten in the gardens of their villas. Private worship of the royal family was not just an elite prerogative, however, and some people who lived in smaller houses also owned small statues of the royal family. Might the rising and setting of the sun have prompted rituals at domestic shrines, as in the Aten temples? In tomb scenes, people bow as the king drives by. Little performances and gestures of this kind may have contributed much to the character of Akhetaten as a city. The huge open courts of the Great Aten Temple also prompt the question: did people gather here en masse to celebrate the Aten cult during festivals?

Supplying the City

Few cities are entirely self-sufficient and Akhetaten was no exception. To keep the ritual machine of the Aten cult running, and support the growing population, imports of food and other supplies were needed. Organizing a constant flow of goods into the city would have been a major undertaking. Most imports were first centralized before being redistributed. They included foodstuffs such as wine, granite from Aswan, and sandstone from quarries south of Thebes. Vast quantities of gypsum were brought in to make cement to secure talatat blocks in place. Even rough lumps of quartzite were imported to be shaped into grinding stones for people to make their own flour. Exotic goods were also secured from outside Egypt. Precious commodities, including oils and perhaps opium, were brought in from Mycenaean Greece and Cyprus in small pottery jars with distinctive shapes and decoration (fig. 20). A large dump of broken Mycenaean vessels was found in the Central City in the late 19th century, perhaps marking a place where they were originally stockpiled. Pieces of these vessels are also found across the city, however, suggesting their contents (or perhaps just the empty, exotic-looking containers) were then widely redistributed. From the southern Levant came incense, transported in large amphorae. Much of it was consumed in the city's temples, but it, too, found its way across the city, where it was burned in houses in small pottery bowls.

Procuring exotic goods required complicated foreign trade networks, forged variously through domination or diplomacy across the eastern Mediterranean and into North Africa. The Egyptian taste for exotica is evident in tomb scenes showing a grand ceremony in the 12th year of Akhenaten's reign, where all manner of luxury items are presented to the king, including gold, animal skins, and elaborate metal vessels. Pitched as tribute to Akhenaten, much of it in reality represents diplomatic gift exchange between the Egyptian king and his foreign counterparts in order to maintain good will and access to trade.

Figure 20. A group of well-traveled sherds. Above, distinctively decorated pieces of pottery from Cyprus and Mycenaean Greece, and, below, part of an amphora that was probably used to import oil from the Levant. The amphora sherd has two inked inscriptions: "boat of the captain (chief of the archery) Any" and the probable place name "Perunefer," Egypt's chief northern port. The inscriptions were likely added when the vessel arrived at Perunefer to log its contents. The vessel was then transported upriver to Akhetaten and emptied of its contents. It eventually ended up at the Stone Village where it had probably been used to bring water to this desert-based community. Photo courtesy of the Amarna Project.

Securing Akhetaten

Security also shaped everyday life at Akhetaten. Enemies, whether real or imagined, were always thought to lie beyond the safety of the Nile Valley. Egyptian kings no doubt had reason to be paranoid for their personal safety, too, at a time when regicide was not unheard of. Whether Akhenaten felt this more acutely than others can only be speculated. Soldiers are often depicted in the Amarna tombs (fig. 21), frequently accompanying the king, but whether as a show of strength or sign of real threat is impossible to know. In the Boundary Stelae inscriptions, Akhenaten vows to repair the stelae should they ever be damaged, but there are otherwise no records of overt threats to Akhetaten or to the king himself. A military presence was probably just a familiar part of the backdrop of everyday life, as it would have been in any royal city.

The most remarkable attestation of Akhetaten's security system is a network of "roadways" that crisscrossed the low desert east of the city (fig. 22). The roads were formed by clearing the desert of large stones and piling these in ridges along the edges. Some of the roads can still be seen today near the North Tombs. They are fragile, enigmatic remains. Many were probably chariot routes, used by officials to inspect progress on construction of their tombs, but the military also likely employed them to patrol the city's borders. Some roads cross land so steep that they

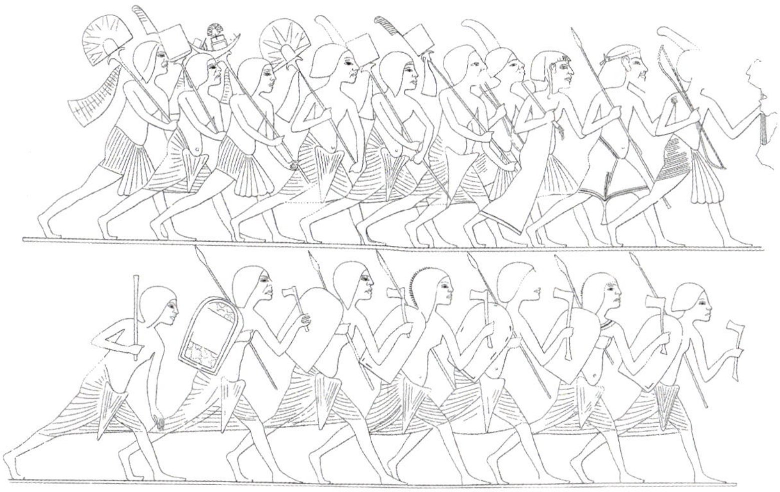

Figure 21. A military escort, which includes Nubian, Syrian, and Libyan soldiers, tasked with guarding the royal family in a scene in the Tomb of Meryre (North Tomb 4). They clutch weapons typical of the time, such as batons, hatchets, spears, and shields. After Davies, *The Rock Tombs of El Amarna*, Part 4, pl. XV. Image courtesy of the Egypt Exploration Society.

Figure 22. An ancient Amarna roadway stretches into the distance. Photo courtesy of the Amarna Project.

would have been impossible to travel on by chariot and seem instead to be boundary markers—the ancient equivalent of "keep off" signs. The prominence of the military almost certainly brought with it a level of scrutiny for the people of Akhetaten, especially when traversing or living on the city's fringes. The two workers' villages on the eastern desert plain (the Workmen's Village and Stone Village) are encircled by roadways that seem designed both to contain the activities of the villagers and to define patrol routes so that guards could keep a watch on their activities (see fig. 23 for a military standard from the Workmen's Village).

Figure 23. A wooden standard (its handle now lost) that was once carried by a member of the military at Akhetaten. It shows a soldier venerating a jackal deity, probably Wepwawet, god of warfare. Photo courtesy of the Amarna Project.

IN FOCUS: CHARIOTS IN ANCIENT EGYPT

Chariots, the racing cars of the ancient world, were introduced into Egypt late in the Second Intermediate Period, but became a common feature during the New Kingdom, peaking in the Eighteenth and Nineteenth Dynasties. Several actual chariots have survived from ancient Egypt, notably six from the tomb of Tutankhamun, while depictions are another important source of information. Chariots feature prominently in the tombs at Amarna, drawn by a pair of horses and driven by the royal family, elites, and the police as they traverse the city. On a daily basis, the king would drive in his chariot—said to have been made of gold—accompanied by Nefertiti, from his palace at the north of the city to the Central City temples and back. Only in the Amarna period are women shown driving chariots, although there are texts that suggest they drove chariots before this time, too. In some Amarna scenes, the royal daughters drive in processions, accompanied by attendants in their own chariots (fig. 24). Several pieces of chariots—elaborately decorated leather straps, bowcases, quivers, yoke saddle pads, and stone finials—have also been found during excavations at the city, while the desert road network is an indirect survival of their importance. They were a marker of elite and military privilege at Akhetaten.

Shortly after the chariot was introduced to Egypt, the Egyptians improved the design, turning it into the perfect war machine—its prime function—as well as a comfortable means of transportation, including on hunting expeditions. Common chariots, in contrast to those used by the court, consisted of a light, open frame of wooden rods that were lashed together with rawhide strips. The solid pole was attached to an axletree with big wheels positioned far back, combining strength with maneuverability and high speed. The body was partially or entirely covered with bright red and green decorated leather, with quivers and bowcases hung at one or both sides. Holes below the top railing provided grips for holding on for dear life while speeding through the desert. —AV

Figure 24. Two princesses drive along in a chariot as their female attendants are driven separately behind, in a scene in the Tomb of Meryre (North Tomb 4). Photo courtesy of Gwil Owen/The Amarna Project.

An Emerging City

Another of the defining characteristics of Akhetaten must have been its status as an emerging city. It was under constant construction for much of the time it was occupied. How did this affect the experiences of those living at Amarna? Although Akhetaten was initially more spacious than cities with longer occupation histories, parts of it were already becoming densely occupied. As bioarchaeologist Jerome Rose has pointed out, it is also important to consider the impact of the new site on public health. Did the move give people a fresh start in a clean new environment, with less buildup of rubbish and waste? Or might it have instead been detrimental to health, upsetting natural routines of disease as the population was relocated to Middle Egypt?

IN FOCUS: EPIDEMIC AT AKHETATEN?

A tantalizing question shadows ancient Akhetaten: did epidemic disease sweep through the ancient city? And might this illness be the cause of the apparent rapid deaths in the royal family at the end of the Amarna period? The suggestion is not without basis. The Amarna period coincides with one of the most famous ancient references to an outbreak of disease, recorded in texts from the land of the Hittites in Anatolia, modern-day Turkey. The texts describe the Hittite capital as having been ravaged by disease for almost 20 years late in the 14th century BC. Captured Egyptian prisoners are blamed for spreading the disease.

Outbreaks of epidemic disease are notoriously difficult to confirm in the distant past. Ancient historical sources tend to be very vague. The Hittite texts, for example, offer few clues on the identity of the disease, and we cannot be sure that Egyptian prisoners were really its source. Whether the disease was a true epidemic as defined today is also uncertain, although it was evidently an impactful event for the Hittites.

Amarna preserves huge cemeteries containing thousands of skeletons of the people of Akhetaten. They show that Akhetaten was, for many people, a difficult place to live. But do they provide evidence of an epidemic?

Most of the diseases common to epidemic outbreaks leave no markers on the skeleton itself. When infected with these diseases, which are generally viral, people either die or recover before the skeleton is modified. Cholera, influenza, smallpox, bubonic plague, polio, typhus, and yellow fever all fit this mold. One disease common to epidemic outbreaks that does leave skeletal traces, in the form of lesions, is malaria. Malaria seems to have been fairly common at ancient Akhetaten, although the skeletons usually show signs of long-term infection, as though the individual lived with the disease for a considerable time. Malaria is much more likely to have been an endemic disease (constantly present) than an epidemic disease (a shorter-term widespread strike) at Akhetaten.

The age structure of a cemetery population can also provide information on the potential for epidemic disease. Typically in ancient cemeteries there are high proportions of young people, aged less than four or five years old, as well as of older adults. Generally, not too many people die between older childhood and young adulthood, when females and males enter into workforces and females begin to bear children. If many people die during these age periods, an epidemic is one possible explanation.

One extensive cemetery at Amarna, near the North Tombs, does have a large number of deaths in the normally stable period from 7 to 25 years old. But here, the age profile is so restricted—and is coupled with signs of hard work from an early age—that the cemetery seems most likely to have served a specialist population, probably laborers. There are so few individuals outside the 7-to-25-year age range, including infants and young children, that it is unlikely to be a general-use cemetery for a population under attack by epidemic or a burial ground solely for victims of a such an outbreak. Another very large cemetery near the South Tombs, which probably served the population of the Main City, has an entirely typical demographic curve for a population of this antiquity.

All in all, while the cemeteries of Amarna have revealed some very high frequencies of disease, they do not fit the profile of epidemic cemeteries. They are much more likely to reflect endemic disease—which could also have struck down members of the royal family—and other high levels of stress, such as heavy workloads and nutritional deficiency. This is not to say that a disease like malaria might not have spread out of Egypt and brought devastation to areas where it was less common. But, for the moment, there is little evidence that the population of Akhetaten itself was subject to a concentrated short-term strike by any one disease. —GD

Great human effort—physical as much as bureaucratic—must have been required to get Akhetaten up and running. From agricultural toil to produce food for a rapidly growing population to the extraction of limestone for the king's monuments, mass physical labor was one of the characteristics of life at Akhetaten. Gypsum, wood, and stone fittings all had to be procured and processed to build Akhenaten's temples and palaces. Huge quantities of mud bricks were required.

The Egyptian state was perpetually engaged in grand building schemes, harvests, and mining expeditions, achieved through mass human labor.

Figure 25. Captives, probably from the Kingdom of Kush (in Nubia), are presented to Akhenaten in the scene of foreign tribute in the Tomb of Meryre II (North Tomb 2). They include children, some of whom are carried in baskets. After Davies, *The Rock Tombs of El Amarna*, Part 2, pl. XXXVIII. Image courtesy of the Egypt Exploration Society.

The army, when not called up in battle, formed one standing workforce for the king, as did peasant farmers—the bulk of the Egyptian population. The situation at Akhetaten would have been no different. Foreign slaves and prisoners of war were also absorbed into the Egyptian labor system and it can be noted that captives from the Kingdom of Kush (in Nubia) and Syria–Palestine, including women and children, are among the "gifts" presented to Akhenaten in the foreign tribute ceremony in his 12th year of rule (fig. 25). The destination of these groups at Akhetaten, assuming the tomb scenes reflect reality, is not stated, but some perhaps ended up in temple workshops and others in menial labor forces engaged in agriculture, quarrying, and construction work (figs. 26, 27).

In addition to outdoor labor, there was the task of decorating the king's monuments with reliefs, paintings, inlays, and statues. Many of the city's residents were artists and craftspersons, of various skill levels, engaged in work of this kind. Craft and industry—the working of materials—seems to have been particularly prevalent in the Main City, which contained a number of workshops of varying degrees of formality. Another possible hub of artistic output was the Workmen's Village on the eastern desert fringe of the city, the inhabitants of which perhaps decorated the Royal Tomb.

In many ways, Akhetaten can probably be understood as a vast factory in the service of the king. Study of skeletons excavated at the Amarna cemeteries suggests this took a serious toll on much of the population, with widespread signs of heavy workloads. Was this typical of non-elite populations at the time, or was it exacerbated at Akhetaten because of the pressure to build the king's new city? One remarkable cemetery near the North Tombs contains almost exclusively adolescents and young adults,

Figure 26. A scene of workers cutting talatat blocks out of the cliffs. The image is carved on an actual talatat that once formed part of a building at Akhetaten. It is now on display in the Mallawi Museum. Photo courtesy of the Amarna Project.

Figure 27. One of the ancient limestone quarries cut into the cliffs north of Amarna, where vast quantities of stone were extracted to build Akhenaten's temples and palaces. Photo courtesy of Kristin Thompson.

numbering several thousand in total. Their skeletons show signs of hard labor as though they were part of the work force: recruited when young, then worked so hard they became susceptible to diseases and died in large numbers. Perhaps, had Akhetaten continued to be occupied, the toll extracted from the population might have subsided. But it is probably no exaggeration to say that the people of Akhetaten were effectively the city's infrastructure, building and maintaining the city of the sun god.

At the same time, Akhetaten was a place shaped by the rhythms of everyday concerns and individual lives. Jewelry and cosmetic containers found in houses and burials speak to care in personal appearance, and to magical and spiritual beliefs (fig. 28). Figurines were thought to offer protection against animals, illness, or nightmares, and to help with the conception of children and safeguarding of families. For some, there were opportunities to participate in banquets, an occasion to dress up in finery and celebrate with food, wine, dancing, and music. Two young adults excavated at Amarna's cemeteries were buried wearing wax cones on their heads—the first examples ever found in Egypt—perhaps symbols of beauty or fertility. We might see humor in the little monkey figurines found at the site (fig. 29); certainly they demonstrate a keen observation of the natural world. The late Eighteenth Dynasty was also a time of artistic creativity and innovation, and glass and faience were used extensively. All over the city, people created for themselves little pendants and beads in these colorful materials. Birth, death, love, family, joy, and celebration all continued amid upheaval (fig. 30), and while the experiences of the people of Akhetaten would have varied widely, it was not a place devoid of humanity.

Figure 28. Pieces of jewelry once worn by the people of Akhetaten. The top row shows mostly earrings, although the metal loop at the right is a rare example of an ancient Egyptian toe ring. The middle row contains amuletic beads and two finger rings (on the right). Pendants of blue faience and carnelian occupy the lower row, including a large image of the domestic deity Bes. The Bes pendant, and the *wedjat*-eye ring, above it, are in a shade of blue that was particularly common at Amarna. The scale is in mm. Photo courtesy of the Amarna Project.

Figure 29. Few objects from Amarna display more character than these little monkey figurines. Figurines such as these can show animals with their young, eating food, playing musical instruments, and even driving chariots. Many were probably carved in sculptors' workshops from leftover pieces of stone. Look closely and you can see the fur and eye of the larger monkey painted in black. Photo courtesy of the Amarna Project.

IN FOCUS: FEEDING A CITY

The production and procurement of food was a central part of daily life at Akhetaten (fig. 31). Installations for food production and storage, along with charred and desiccated plant and food remains, including animal bones, are important sources of information. Most are found in ancient rubbish dumps, but occasionally storage containers within houses still contain goods such as cereals. Food remains may be present in pottery vessels deposited in graves as gifts for the afterlife. Tomb art can also provide evidence for the different stages of food procurement, from growing cereals to the production of bread, beer, and other foodstuffs. It is highly unlikely that Akhetaten was self-sufficient, and almost certain that the local food supply was augmented by imports, some of which can be considered to be luxury produce, from both the surrounding area and further afield.

Cereals and other crops would have been grown in the thin green belt at the edge of the Nile (fig. 32). Cereals such as emmer wheat and barley were sown after the annual Nile flood subsided by around October. The extent of crop cultivation was closely dependent on the flood: the higher the water level, the greater the area of land that could be cultivated. Once the floodwaters receded, the deposit of fertile silt left behind was plowed, and cereal seeds broadcast sown (scattered). Emmer and barley were harvested in April or May, and then processed by threshing and winnowing. The emmer was kept as spikelets (the part of the ear containing the grain) to protect the grain against insect and fungal attack, and the barley stored within its husk.

Emmer spikelets were pounded to release the grain, which was ground to produce flour, and then made into bread. Sometimes the grain was used instead to make beer. There is abundant archaeological evidence for cereal processing and bread making at Akhetaten, where most houses had their own room to grind the grain and circular pottery ovens for baking bread. The barley would have been malted and then fermented to make beer. The grain was also fed to livestock. Ancient bread and beer residues have been found at the site, and experimental archaeology has been used to reconstruct the processes that went into making bread, from pounding and grinding the grain, to baking.

Other plant foods included a range of fruits: dates, figs, pomegranates, watermelons, cucumber/melon, olives, grapes (eaten and used for wine), and almonds. Pulses such as peas, lentils, and white lupin were consumed, as well as onions and garlic. There is evidence for carrots, spinach, and lettuce. Herbs and spices such as basil, dill, coriander, celery, fenugreek, and black cumin added flavor to food. Tubers of a sedge called chufa/tiger nut would have been either roasted and eaten whole or made into a drink.

Oil crops such as safflower (which also produces a dye and a spice similar to saffron) and castor beans were also grown. Safflower oil was used for cooking, and castor oil for lighting. Flax was grown for both its fiber to make linen and its seeds to produce linseed oil. Most of these plant foods would have been grown in gardens, such as those at the Workmen's Village, rather than in fields. They would have required a constant water supply. Wild foods would also have been gathered to supplement the diet, such as sidder and doum palm. Other wild plants, and some of the herbs and spices, may have been used for their medicinal properties.

Figure 30. A stela from Amarna showing a group of men and women dressed in finery, the men being served drinks in small bowls. They are probably taking part in a festival or feast. Museum of Man, San Diego 14881. Photo courtesy of the San Diego Museum of Man.

Although the main diet for most Egyptians probably consisted of plant foods, meat and fish were consumed by at least some of the population. The remains of animal bones are widespread at Amarna, although never present in large numbers. Whether this is due to a real lack of meat at the city or issues of preservation is uncertain. Sheep and goats, cattle, and pigs would have been kept in pens and fed cereal crop-processing waste, barley grains, and other household refuse. They may also have been fed clover (*bersim*: still the main fodder in Egypt today), especially the cattle, which were mainly kept for temple offerings. Sheep and goats may have been grazed under the watchful eye of a shepherd, and pigs were perhaps allowed to wander the streets, eating food remains dropped by the inhabitants. It is likely that wild game such as gazelle—and even hyena—was hunted to supplement the diet.

The meat would have been eaten fresh and also preserved by drying or salting, and perhaps stored in jars. The River Nile was a source of fish such as Nile perch, Nile catfish, and tilapia, caught by techniques including nets, hooks, spears, and fish traps. Some of the fish may have been eaten fresh, but, because of the high temperatures, it would spoil quickly, and most was probably also dried and salted. The river also provided wildfowl, such as ducks and geese. These birds, and also pigeons, would have provided both meat and eggs. Honey would have been used to add sweetness. Wine and beer would have been drunk along with water.

Most food was centrally distributed from agricultural land owned by the state, and a monthly allowance of cereals given, from which bread and beer would have been made. Individual households would have stored their state-supplied rations in either sacks or pots. Elite members of the city had their own large grain stores. Other foods may have been grown in individual garden plots, such as those at the Workmen's Village. Meat supply would have perhaps come from the temples, especially for the elite, who also kept their own livestock. Others would have supplemented their meager meat ration by raising poultry or keeping a few goats and sheep. Cooking took place on a hearth or oven situated in the kitchen.

Although the plant and animal remains suggest that the diet at Amarna was rich and varied, it is not certain if all citizens had access to the same range of foods. There is evidence from Amarna's cemeteries that many people buried there were malnourished, perhaps having a poorer diet than those with greater civic responsibilities. —AC

Figure 31. Fish, bread, water jars, flowers, sacks of grain, and other supplies make their way around Akhetaten, with stops at a possible market place (lower right) and depot (left/upper left), as scribes keep a tally of accounts. From the Tomb of Mahu (South Tomb 9). After Davies, *The Rock Tombs of El Amarna*, Part 4: *Tombs of Penthu, Mahu, and Others,* XXIV. Image courtesy of the Egypt Exploration Society.

Figure 32. A rare scene of agricultural life along the water's edge in the Tomb of Huya (North Tomb 1). After Davies, *The Rock Tombs of El Amarna*, Part 3: *Tombs of Huya and Ahmes*, pl. VIII. Image courtesy of the Egypt Exploration Society.

IN FOCUS: RELIGION OF THE PEOPLE

Akhenaten may have pursued his beliefs in a single god, but traditional religion was not entirely wiped from people's lives at Akhetaten. The absence of festivals for deities other than the Aten at the new city may have left a gap in people's celebratory lives. Yet everyday religion in ancient Egypt often focused on the home and family, and practical rituals to protect these domains. There is abundant evidence that activities of this kind continued at Akhetaten, engaging, for instance, the dwarf god Bes or the composite hippopotamus–lioness–crocodile goddess Taweret (fig. 33). Jewelry decorated with images of Bes seems even to have been included in the Royal Tomb. Pottery figurines of females were probably used in rituals connected with fertility, and also perhaps against illness (fig. 34). Little statuettes of cobras may have been used to magically protect household grain supplies from vermin, and to guard against visitations from harmful beings in bad dreams. The commemoration of deceased ancestors also continued as an important component of domestic cult.

It is not just household gods that are represented in the archaeological record at Amarna. In the Main City, one group of people built a small shrine in which they placed a stela for Khnum, Satis, and Anukis, the patron gods of Elephantine, perhaps to remember local gods they had left behind. At the Workmen's Village, there is evidence that the villagers worshiped Amun and Isis in chapels they built also to venerate deceased family members. At the pit-grave cemeteries, some individuals were buried in coffins decorated with traditional funerary gods. While it is possible that objects and images showing traditional gods circulated at the city only after Akhenaten's death, this need not be the case. Nor should it be assumed that images of traditional gods were kept hidden. Coffins, for example, would have been difficult to hide—paraded through the streets and out across the open desert to reach the cemeteries.

Public response to the cult of the Aten and the royal family is difficult to gauge. The Great Hymn to the Aten speaks of people filled with adoration at the sight of the Aten rising, conjuring images of a city full of sun worshipers. There is no way to really test this idea, although the Great Aten Temple is certainly large enough to have accommodated crowds, and a few private donation items have been found here. Some city officials seem also to have received mortuary offerings inside the Aten temples. Death was probably one catalyst for people to engage with the cult, as they approached the uncertainty of what lay ahead. Akhenaten's officials, for example, erected shrines decorated with images of the royal family and Aten in the gardens of their homes. These may have served as places to worship the king, queen, and sun god, but also to remember ancestors and secure for them a place in the company of the Aten after death. Engagement with the cult was not entirely an elite prerogative, though. Little statuettes of the royal family have been found in smaller houses at the site, and some people buried in the pit-grave cemeteries used coffins that no longer depicted traditional gods. Others erected little pyramids and pointed stelae at their graves, both symbols of the solar cult.

All in all, there is little evidence to support the idea that the people of Akhetaten followed Akhenaten to Middle Egypt as some prophet-like figure. Nor were they forced to worship the sun god once there, although those close to the court must have been under considerable obligation to show loyalty to the cult. It is likely that most people were left largely to their own devices to navigate their changing spiritual surroundings. It is uncertain, in fact, to what extent individuals sought out close personal relationships with gods in this period of ancient Egyptian history. At Akhetaten, familiar rituals probably continued to a considerable degree, oriented toward household and family well-being and acquiring an afterlife. The people of Akhetaten engaged traditional gods and rituals where they could, and also took on some elements of the Aten cult. Perhaps, had occupation of Akhetaten continued, people would have adopted the Aten as a real local patron. —AS

Figure 33. Hippopotamus amulets from the burial of a woman and child. The hippopotamus images invoke goddesses such as Taweret, who is also shown on the underside of the largest amulet. The other two amulets show Bes and the goddess Mut. These divinities were all connected with the protection of women and children. Notice how the glaze is worn, suggesting the amulets had a role not just in the burial, but were also used during life. Photo courtesy of the Amarna Project.

Akhenaten's Amarna Years

Akhenaten was to live out the rest of his life at Akhetaten, although we can assume he spent time in other parts of the country, too. On the Boundary Stelae, he gave orders that he was to be buried at Akhetaten should he die elsewhere. There are few records that document the mid-to-later part of Akhenaten's reign, although those that do survive, and

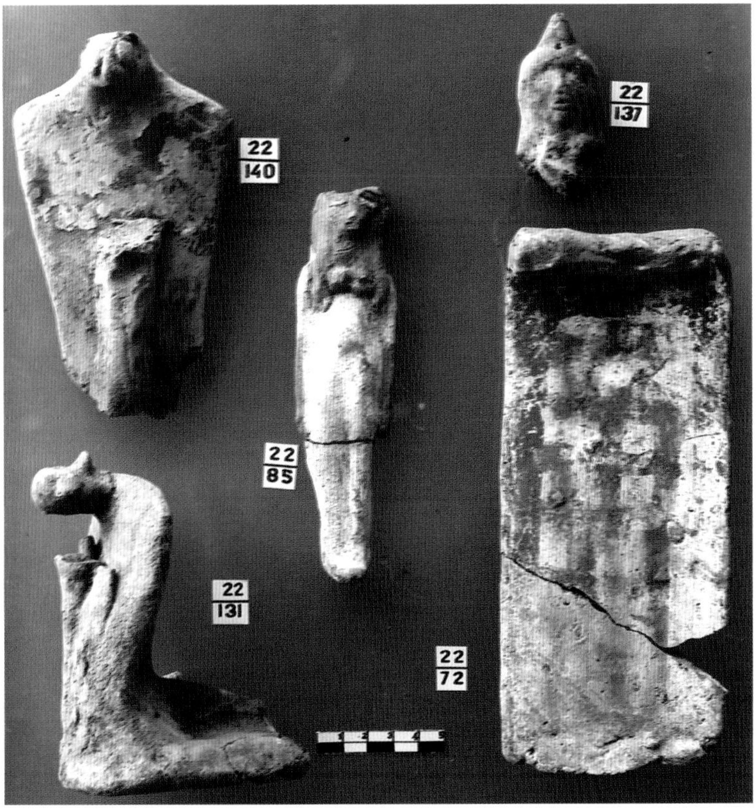

Figure 34. Little pottery statuettes of snakes and female figures are often found in houses at Amarna. They were probably used in rituals to help protect the household. EES Amarna Archive Negative 1922.28. Photo courtesy of the Egypt Exploration Society.

the physical footprint of Akhetaten itself, give the impression of a king whose main focus was the Aten cult. With the establishment of ritual and bureaucratic infrastructure for the cult, including texts that legitimized his conception of Atenism, it is possible that the king's backlash against other gods may have lessened.

It is often claimed that Akhenaten was lax in maintaining the Egyptian empire and there may be some truth to this. Most of the Amarna Letters, a great cache of diplomatic correspondence found in the Central City at Amarna, document actions not of Akhenaten himself, but undertaken in the reign of his father Amenhotep III. This may be a matter of preservation, but there are also hints in the content of the letters that Akhenaten was a somewhat distant figure. When the ruler of Byblos was threatened by a rebellious tribe and appealed to his patron, the Egyptian king (probably Akhenaten), for help, his requests went unanswered. Akhenaten seems less inclined toward diplomacy and direct intervention in external affairs than Amenhotep III had been. He did, however, subdue a rebellion against Egypt's colonial occupation in Kush (Nubia) in the 12th year of his reign, an important counterargument to the idea that he was a pacifist. Tomb scenes of the Reception of Foreign Tribute also held in his 12th year of rule show, similarly, that he was not entirely shut off from the outside world.

A Collapsing Dynasty

Then, after less than 20 years, the experiment with Atenism came to a rapid end. After 17 years on the throne, Akhenaten died, aged probably in his 30s. The cause of his death is unknown. He was buried at Akhetaten, in a tomb cut deep in the eastern cliffs, in which his daughter Meketaten, and perhaps his mother Tiye, had already been interred. The end of the Amarna period was marked by a quick succession of reigns, and possibly more deaths in the royal family. The details of this time have caused much discussion among Egyptologists and some may never be fully clarified.

Toward the end of his reign, Akhenaten seems to have shared the throne with one or more family members. The first was a male king called Smenkhkare, who was apparently married to Akhenaten's daughter Meritaten. Smenkhkare was part of the royal line, perhaps the son or brother of Akhenaten. He appears only briefly in the historical record—including a scene in the tomb of the official Meryre (II) at Amarna (North Tomb 2)—and then disappears, presumably having died. It is not clear if he was interred at Akhetaten, although the Royal Wadi contains several unfinished tombs, one of which was perhaps intended for his burial.

Nefertiti also seems to have taken the throne for a short period, using the name Neferneferuaten. Details of her rule are, again, frustratingly scarce. She may have reigned briefly with Akhenaten just before his death, or served as coregent in the early years of Tutankhamun's reign. Some believe she held the throne in her own name. In any case, her time as king also lasted just a few years. The last known record of King Neferneferuaten is a graffito in a Theban tomb, dating to the third year of her rule. She may have died or, if caretaker ruler for Tutankhamun, simply passed the throne on to her young successor. The Royal Tomb at Amarna contains a prominent, but unfinished, side chamber that was probably intended for her, although it was never used.

A young Tutankhaten (later Tutankhamun) next assumed the throne. He was probably Akhenaten's son from a secondary wife, and already at a young age had married Akhenaten's daughter Ankhesenpaaten (later Ankhesenamun). He spent the first part of his reign at Akhetaten, but within a few years had closed down the city and relocated the royal court to Memphis, the traditional seat of government. He issued an official decree, carved on stelae erected at temples around the country, announcing the restoration of the cults of Amun and the other gods. The future kings

Ay and Horemheb were both influential members of Tutankhamun's court. Tutankhamun's reign was noticeably more militant than that of Akhenaten. Egypt's northern empire had come under threat from the rising power of the Hittites in Anatolia, who had by this time overrun the Mitannians, Egypt's former ally in the region. The Egyptian army was engaged in skirmishes both here and in Nubia. Akhenaten's apparent distance from international matters may have contributed to this state of affairs.

Tutankhamun's early death, without leaving an heir, seems to have prompted the widowed Ankhesenamun to undertake the extraordinary step of appealing to the Hittite king for a prince to marry. The tale is documented in several letters from the ancient capital of the Hittites, Hattusa (modern Bogazköy in Turkey), in which an Egyptian queen asks the Hittite king Suppiluliuma to send her a son to marry and make king of Egypt. The queen is unnamed, but Ankhesenamun seems the most likely candidate. The Hittite king responded by sending his son Zananzash to Egypt, but the prince was seemingly assassinated en route. His murder prompted several years of conflict with the Hittites.

Egypt's next king was instead Ay, who had already paved an influential career as an official under both Akhenaten and Tutankhamun. He was probably a member of the extended royal family, perhaps Nefertiti's father. He may have married the young widowed queen, Ankhesenamun. Ay ruled for only a few years and was buried in the Western Valley of the royal cemetery at Thebes (Tomb WV23). His chosen successor was an army commander called Nakhtmin, but another army man, Horemheb, a prominent general from Memphis, assumed the throne. This brought the line of kings from Thebes to an end.

Sometime in the aftermath of Akhenaten's reign, probably during the rule of Tutankhamun, some contents of the Amarna Royal Tomb were relocated to the Valley of the Kings at Thebes. At least one royal individual from Akhetaten seems to have ended up in the tomb now numbered KV55. When excavated in 1907, this tomb contained many pieces of Amarna-period burial equipment, including a reused coffin with its mask and inscriptions partly defaced. The adult male inside the coffin is often suggested to be either Akhenaten—although the mummy may be too young to be this king—or Smenkhkare. Other Amarna-period royal mummies and pieces of burial equipment have been recovered from the Tomb of Amenhotep II (KV35) as part of a cache of royal burial material collected together by priests in the Third Intermediate Period, to protect them from tomb robbery. It is not clear where these Amarna-period mummies and burial items had come from.

While the possible relocation of his mummy to Thebes seems to imply a degree of respect toward Akhenaten, there was quickly a shift in attitude. Tutankhamun's restoration inscriptions record the country in turmoil during the Amarna period. A good part of this must be rhetoric, but it became a matter of official record. When later kings documented the great line of rulers from which they had descended, Akhenaten's name was left out. So, too, were those of Smenkhkare and Neferneferuaten. Even Tutankhamun and Ay were not listed, despite their roles in restoring the country to orthodoxy. The official, lasting narrative of Akhenaten's reign was that of a dangerous heretic.

A City Abandoned

Just as people had flocked to Akhetaten initially, so, too, most of them left with the royal court, although a small settlement seems to have remained, its ruins now under the village of al-Hagg Qandil. The stone temples and palaces of Akhetaten provided a handy source of construction materials, already in small transportable blocks. Beginning in the reign of Horemheb, the stonework of Akhetaten was dismantled. Many talatat blocks were taken over the river to Hermopolis Magna (modern al-Ashmunayn) where they were used in the foundations of new temple buildings. In 1939, around 1,500 of these talatat blocks were discovered at al-Ashmunayn, providing an unparalleled resource for studying the decoration of Akhenaten's buildings at Akhetaten.

As the centuries passed, Akhetaten lay open and exposed. The roofs of the houses eventually collapsed, followed by the walls, and, as sand slowly accumulated and the mud bricks decayed, Akhetaten began to look less like a city and more like the archaeological site we see today. In the Third Intermediate Period/Late Period, many centuries after Akhenaten's reign, the South Tombs may have been used as shelters for army regiments on the move through Middle Egypt, leaving masses of pottery behind. A few centuries later, graffiti were written on the walls of the North Tombs, which had become a source of curiosity for early "tourists." One Greek visitor, perhaps a soldier from Thrace, wrote of "marveling at the art of the holy quarriers" at the Tomb of Ahmes (North Tomb 3). A few centuries later, parts of the ancient city were resettled, new structures built over the city's ruins, and graves dug down into the ancient buildings. During the late Roman period, especially, parts of the North Suburb were resettled in this way. Amarna is also one of a number of sites in Middle Egypt with important remains of early Christian activity. A monastery was built on the site of Nefertiti's Sun Temple at Kom al-Nana, while the

North Tombs provided ready-made accommodation for a community that used the tombs as houses and a church.

Like all archaeological sites in Egypt, the ruins of Akhetaten have also become a source of mud brick for use as fertilizer, and of salable antiquities. Disturbance to the site probably began soon after the city was abandoned; even as the houses still stood, people seem to have dug through their floors looking for buried goods. A concerted period of disturbance also took place centuries later, during the Late Period. Hundreds of pottery sherds of this date have been found scattered across Amarna, their edges smoothed as though they were used as shovels to dig through the collapsed mud brick. The city's cemeteries have also suffered terribly over the centuries from robbery, badly damaging the burials and skeletons of the people of Akhetaten. Much ancient looting at the site probably focused on metal objects, which could be melted down and reshaped. Later looters looked for anything salable, driven by the growth of the market for Egyptian antiquities starting in the 1800s. In the 20th century, the looting of Amarna continued, in part prompted by antiquities dealers and the buyers who backed their activities. Legislation making the sale of antiquities illegal was passed in 1983, but a thriving black market remains. This activity may have brought profit to a small few, but has caused terrible damage to the history and heritage of Amarna.

IN FOCUS: THE REST OF EGYPT

Akhenaten's reign is known mostly through evidence from Amarna and Luxor, but what was happening in the rest of the country? The surviving Restoration Stela of Tutankhamun speaks of the country in disarray: "the temples and the cities of the gods and goddesses, starting from Elephantine [as far] as the Delta marshes ..., were fallen into decay and their shrines were fallen into ruin, having become mere mounds overgrown with grass. Their sanctuaries were like something that had not come into being and their buildings were a footpath—for the land was in rack and ruin" (Murnane, *Texts from the Amarna Period*, 213). While a strong element of propaganda must exist in such texts, there is little reason to doubt that the country's major temples were indeed shut down. A private graffito written on the wall of a Theban tomb in the reign of Neferneferuaten (probably Nefertiti as king) is perhaps a more spontaneous record of events; it, too, contains a plea for the god Amun to return. There are, however, hints that some smaller shrines may have continued in use, and gods such as Anubis, Atum, and Ptah appear on Amarna-period stelae from sites including Saqqara and Heliopolis.

We know that Akhenaten built temples for the Aten elsewhere, including in the north at Heliopolis, great city of the sun god Re, and at Memphis. Other Aten temples undoubtedly remain to be discovered. There are scenes of Theban officials shown worshiping the Aten in rooftop shrines in their houses (fig. 35), suggesting the cult was also actively upheld at Thebes. More work on the impact of Akhenaten's reign outside Akhetaten is much needed, and will likely provide an important step forward in Amarna-period studies in the future. We might expect, perhaps, that the impact of Atenism was most acute at sites where Akhenaten was active. In any case, a single consistent response to Akhenaten's reforms—which is not even detectable at Amarna itself—seems unlikely. —AS

Figure 35. A priest's house with a rooftop shrine to the Aten is shown in a relief from Karnak—a hint that the Aten cult was sometimes maintained beyond Akhetaten itself. Reproduced from K. Spence (2004), "The Three-dimensional Form of the Amarna House," *Journal of Egyptian Archaeology* 90, fig. 11 (after C. Traunecker (1988), "Les maisons du domaine d'Aton à Karnak," *Cahiers de Recherches de l'Institut de Papyrologie et d'Egyptologie de Lille* 10, figs. 1–2).

IN FOCUS: AMARNA TODAY

Today, Amarna is more than an archeological site; it is home to many thousands of people. The three largest towns on the site are Tell Bani Amran (al-Till), al-Hagg Qandil, and East Amiriya. Although they appear on maps since the end of the 18th century AD, little is known of their origins. The area was named Tell al-Amarna after the Bani Amran tribe, one of many Arab tribes that settled in the region in recent centuries. They seem to have been present in the area before 1737, when the district was already associated with the name Bani Amran or Amarna. The tribe split into several groups that make up the villages of the area today. The Arabic word *tell* means "hill" or "elevated place" and refers to the position of the villages in one line between the cliffs of the high desert and the Nile River, the lifeline of the area.

Many of the people living at Amarna today work in agriculture. Despite the scarcity of agricultural lands in the area, a variety of crops, such as *bersim* (clover used as animal fodder), *qamah* (wheat), *dura* (corn), and *fuul sudani* (peanuts), are cultivated and sold. Families also grow vegetables and fruit for local consumption, such as *tamatim* (tomatoes), *basal* (onions), and *betingan* (eggplants). Most homes also have livestock, such as goats, cows, water buffaloes that provide them with milk, cheese, and meat. The river is also a source of profit, where fishermen use nets for catching fish. Some families also raise rabbits and pigeons on rooftops, particularly in al-Till. Recently, chicken breeding has developed and long white buildings have been constructed on the outskirts of the towns to house the birds. Although sugarcane cultivation is widespread in Middle Egypt, it has not been widely grown in Amarna. Instead, limestone has formed an important source of income for the area, and the local quarrying industry used to employ many people, although it has now moved north to the city of Minya.

Family represents the social cornerstone of life in Amarna today. Although the towns are large, they are made up of a small number of extended families that are like one big family. The close bonds between families strengthen the ties between different people in society. People help each other when in need and come together for various occasions. While local concerns are often a focus of people's lives in these towns, community members also occupy advanced positions in education on a regional level. They uphold their identity in their dress and style, such as in their wearing of their distinct version of the traditional Egyptian garb, the *gallabiya*, indicating their attachment to heritage. We can see the connection and affection between people in the welcome and affection that visitors experience, especially from the young children who greet visitors in the streets.

When we speak of the magnificence of pharaonic civilization in the area of Amarna, we cannot ignore the religious civilization in this region. In addition to the historical and archeological nature of the area, Amarna also provides an excellent example of harmony and coherence between religious communities. Amarna and its population receive visitors from all over the world to marvel at the grandeur of their pharaonic forefathers. Similarly, they welcome visitors to witness their religious festivities that take place every year. But words cannot describe what you need to see with your own eyes!

—Written by the excavation team from al-Hagg Qandil and al-Till

Figure 36. Some of the members of the excavation team from al-Hagg Qandil and al-Till who help investigate Amarna today. Back row (left to right): Ahmed Said Nasser, Ahmed Mokhtar Mahmoud, Mohamed Mahmoud Derwish. Middle row (left to right): Mohamed Rabia Fathi Senousi, Bilal Nassar Omar, Abdel Malak Mohamed, Salah Osman Mehani, Abu Zeyd Azzil-Din, Waleed Mohamed Omar, Yahya Sabit. Front row (left to right): Bakr Amin, Hafiz Abdel Aziz Ibrahim, Mohamed Rafaat Rabia, Nasr Mohamed Sayed Ali, Mohamed Hosni Osman. Photo courtesy of the Amarna Project.

IN FOCUS: ARCHAEOLOGICAL CONNECTIONS

A number of the families living in Amarna have long connections with archaeological work and the protection of the site. Jobs range from excavation and guard duties to managing the Dig House, driving, and running errands for the archaeological team. Skills are often passed from father to son down the generations. This continuity leads to close relationships between the visiting archaeological teams and local families. Many of the archaeologists have spent decades working at Amarna, and have watched the small boys and girls who used to play around them grow up, get married, and have families of their own.

Mohamed Omar is the *ghaffir* (guard) of the current Dig House. Mohamed's father also worked with the British archaeological team from the Egypt Exploration Society in the early 1900s. At this time, the team used a mud-brick house at the north of the site, and another at the south, which was originally constructed for the German archaeological team from the Deutsche Orient-Gesellschaft. The house was built on top of an ancient Amarna house and followed its basic layout. The (now) Ministry of Tourism and Antiquities took over the building when the British left in 1937. Mohamed's father was made *ghaffir* of the house, and, some years later, Mohamed was born there. When Barry Kemp was given a concession to start work at Amarna for the Egypt Exploration Society in the 1970s, Mohamed's father began working with him. By this time, the house was beginning to fall apart, the windy desert conditions gradually destroying the wood and mud brick. Three craftsmen were brought in from the local towns to repair the house. By this time, Mohamed was old enough to take charge. He was given the key and became *ghaffir*, overseeing the completion of the renovation work. It was a busy time; every day someone would have to go across the river to buy materials for the house or the excavation, as it was not possible to source everything on the east bank. Abdu, one of Mohamed's sons, started working with him at the Dig House in the 1990s, when he was still a boy. At first, he was an assistant to the cook, Mohamed Abdel Badia. Today, he is the main cook and keeps the team happy and healthy with excellent meals. The family connection doesn't stop with the Dig House, as another of Mohamed's sons works on the excavations and one is a guard at the Amarna Visitor Centre.

When asked by the archaeological team, Mohamed recounts how life has changed in Amarna since he was a boy. "The villages used to be very quiet and the weather was less hot. All the houses were made of mud brick with palm roofs, and there were no electric machines for cooking. There were lots of craftspeople making baskets and only a few people lived in each house—now some have 30 people living there! Prices are higher now. People build with fired bricks or limestone, and the houses are three and four stories high, not just one or two. The land is more exhausted as the Nile does not flood and we even grow a different variety of corn these days. Now the children get a better education. Before, there was just one school with three classes and only 50 pupils. Today, there are numerous primary and secondary schools with so many pupils that you can't see the ground for the children!" —GT

Rediscovering Amarna

In many senses, Akhetaten was never a "lost city," as generations had been living on and around its ruins, below the painted tombs in the cliffs above. What had been lost, though, was an understanding of the origins of the sprawling mud-brick ruins and of the identity of its founder king, who had been erased from Egyptian history.

Scientific interest in Amarna began from the turn of the 19th century, when French scholars, in Egypt as part of Bonaparte's military and exploratory campaign of 1798–99, produced the first partial map of the site, published in the famous *Description de l'Égypte*. Further mapping of Amarna followed in the early 1800s. Using simple survey techniques, such as pacing out measurements, English Egyptologist John Gardner Wilkinson (1824, 1826), followed by the German K. Richard Lepsius (1840s), produced improved plans of the site (fig. 37). These early maps remain important today, in part for what they show of the changing appearance of Amarna over recent centuries. During the 1800s, attention turned also to recording the cliff tombs, and a first series of copies and translations of their decoration and texts was produced.

The period around the turn of the 20th century saw a number of advances in understanding Amarna and the reign of Akhenaten. In the 1880s and 1890s, French and Italian Egyptologists investigated the site; Urbain Bouriant and his team undertook an initial record of the officials' tombs and Alessandro Barsanti partially cleared the Royal Tomb, by this time already robbed. In around 1887 came the discovery of the Amarna Letters in the Central City by local villagers, an event that would transform understanding of the Bronze Age Mediterranean.

In the early 1890s, British archaeologist Flinders Petrie turned his interest to Amarna as part of his great campaign to explore ancient Egypt not only through art and texts, but also archaeology. His approach was to target the center of a site to extract as much information as possible in a short period of time. In a single season at Amarna, he uncovered parts of the Great Palace (including its famous painted pavements, now in Cairo), nearby industrial areas and dumps, and a few large houses. He also produced a new survey of the site that included the desert hinterland and ancient roadways, and discovered most of the Boundary Stelae. Among those who assisted him was a young Howard Carter, who would later go on to excavate the tomb of Tutankhamun.

The first translation of Akhenaten's Great Hymn to the Aten was made in 1895 by James Henry Breasted. From 1901 to 1906, Norman de Garis Davies produced the most comprehensive copy of the Boundary Stelae and the rock-cut tombs, including the first English translations of

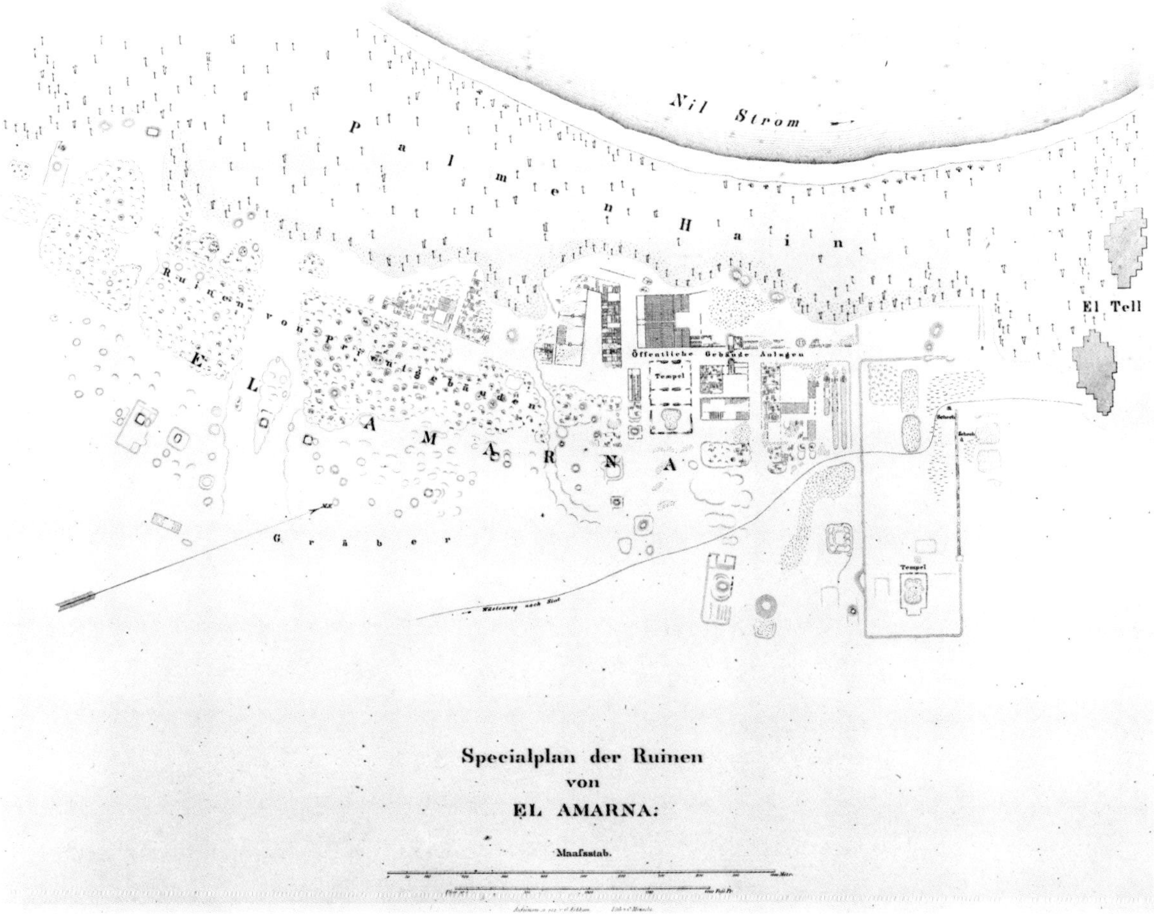

Figure 37. One of the earliest maps of Amarna, produced by K. Richard Lepsius in the 1840s. After K.R. Lepsius (1849–59), *Denkmaeler aus Aegypten und Aethiopien* (Berlin: Nicolaische Buchhandlung, Abth. I), 64.

the Great Hymn, in a six-volume monograph set that remains the principal publication of the tombs, still indispensible to researchers.

As records of the ruins of Amarna began to take shape, evidence for Akhenaten's reign was also being uncovered elsewhere in Egypt, especially in and around Luxor, one focus of the king's early building work. As early as the 1840s, dismantled and reused stonework from Akhenaten's Karnak temples began to appear, followed by the discovery in the 1890s of thousands of his talatat temple blocks which had been reused as fill, many of them inside the great pylon gateways of Karnak (pylons 2, 9, and 10). A further breakthrough came in 1925, when Georges Legrain found the in situ foundations of one of Akhenaten's Karnak temples, its walls lined with strange-looking colossi of the king. More blocks were recovered from the 1960s and a major project to reconstruct the decorative schemes of Akhenaten's Karnak temples was launched (the Akhenaten

Temple Project). Two other groundbreaking discoveries took place in the Valley of the Kings, with the discovery in 1907 of a cache of Amarna-period burial materials in KV55, including a mummy likely to be either Akhenaten or Smenkhkare, and then, in 1922, the unveiling of the largely intact tomb of Tutankhamun.

Akhenaten had been rediscovered, and Egyptologists began to piece together the complicated story of the king, his reign, and its aftermath, a story that continues to be refined today.

Discovering City Life

Early research on Amarna and Karnak focused on Akhenaten and his reign, but, from the early 1900s, archaeologists also began to expand their sights, recognizing the remarkable preservation of housing areas at Amarna and the opportunity this presented to study urban life in the past. Most cities and towns are occupied for long periods of time, during which buildings fall down and are rebuilt, often for centuries or even millennia. This creates a complicated archaeological record and it becomes difficult to isolate contemporary parts of a single city. Most of ancient Egypt's towns and cities are now lost or difficult to access, buried beneath modern settlements or under field systems along the riverbanks. Amarna is different, lying open and easily accessible on the desert plain. It offers us a kind of time capsule of a single generation of people who lived some 3,000 years ago. Very few archaeological sites anywhere in the world provide such a complete view of an ancient city, with large expanses of temples, houses, cemeteries, and the original landscape intact.

From 1911 to 1914, a German team from the Deutsche Orient-Gesellschaft worked at Amarna. Today, their work is best known for the discovery of the painted bust of Nefertiti in a workshop south of the Central City, but their focus was really on recording ancient housing, and they cleared large tracts of the Main City. Between 1921 and 1936, the London-based Egypt Exploration Society excavated widely across Amarna, including in the housing suburbs, the Workmen's Village, at the North Palace and North Riverside Palace, the outlying temples, and within the Central City (figs. 38, 39). A vivid account of work at the site in the 1930s is provided by Mary Chubb, secretary to the EES, in her book *Nefertiti Lived Here*. Her book stresses how much the early excavators relied on a large team of support staff, including men, women, and children from the local communities of al-Till and al-Hagg Qandil, who were employed as excavators, cooks, and assistants during the field seasons. Specialist workmen, initially trained in excavation methods by Flinders Petrie, were also brought in from the village of Qift near Luxor.

Figure 38. Hilary Waddington, who worked as an architect at Amarna for the Egypt Exploration Society in the 1930s, sets up a camera high on the cliff face. Waddington, and dig director John Pendlebury, produced several short films documenting life on the dig, which were intended to fundraise and help keep the excavation running. EES negative TA.WAD.01.PICT.10. Photo courtesy of the Egypt Exploration Society.

Figure 39. An archive photograph from the 1930s showing the frantic pace of work of the time, here in a housing area in the North Suburb. EES Amarna Archive Negative 1930/31.A.36. Photo courtesy of the Egypt Exploration Society.

These early excavations at Amarna focused largely on clearing buildings and mapping their remains. The work progressed rapidly, with huge areas uncovered very quickly, in keeping with excavation standards of the time. Unfortunately, such was the speed of the work that much important information was lost. Only a very small percentage of artifacts was recovered from the sand and rubble, and there was no interest in environmental materials, such as animal bone or plant remains, now considered invaluable for shedding light on the past. Nor was there much effort to understand the stratigraphy of the site—the layers of buildings and deposits, and what they might indicate of different patterns of activity across the ancient city.

The records that were kept, especially site plans, were often of a high standard, and the early excavations produced an important set of building plans, particularly of houses, that now serve as an atlas of ancient Egyptian housing (fig. 40). In excess of 1,000 buildings were cleared. Some of the areas they worked at have since been lost under agriculture or settlement, making these records an invaluable source of information of what was once present. Nonetheless, the work omits much that is considered essential to archaeology as we know it today, and its legacy is certainly a mixed one. The colonial context of the work, too, did much to establish hierarchical systems of fieldwork that are still in evidence today.

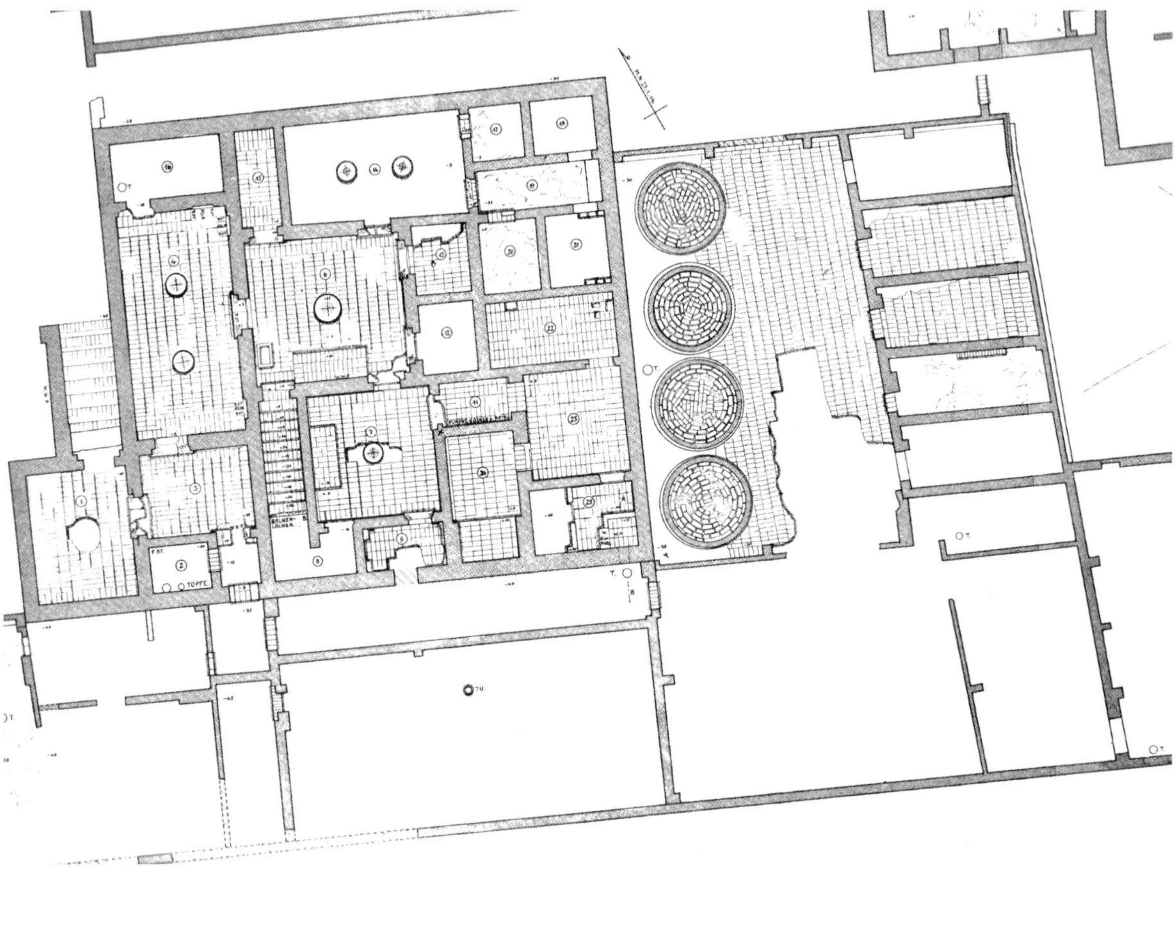

Figure 40. One of the very detailed house plans (of building number P47.17) produced by the Deutsche Orient-Gesellschaft team in the early 20th century. After L. Borchardt and H. Ricke (1980), *Die Wohnhäuser in Tell El-Amarna* (Berlin: Deutsche Orient-Gesellschaft/Deutsches Archäologisches Institut, Abt. Kairo), Plan 31. Image courtesy of the Deutsche Orient-Gesellschaft and Deutsches Archäologisches Institut.

From the 1960s, archaeology around the world began to change and better fieldwork methodologies were sought out. Archaeologists began to abandon rapid large-scale clearance and instead focused on applying careful methods of excavation, recovering as much ancient material as possible, no matter how "mundane." In Egypt, Amarna became one of the flagship sites for this kind of approach, through the renewed work of the Egypt Exploration Society, and now the Amarna Project, from the 1970s.

Modern fieldwork at Amarna has often focused on houses and suburban workshops, although state institutions such as the Small Aten Temple, North Palace, Kom al-Nana temple complex, and Great Aten Temple have also seen extended excavations. The Egyptian Ministry of Tourism and Antiquities has also investigated both housing areas and Kom al-Nana in recent decades. Excavation today is combined with a detailed study of artifacts and environmental materials, including animal bones and plant remains, and also with survey work to continue mapping the site, including its desert perimeter. A new dimension was added to our understanding of the ancient city with the discovery of the non-elite cemeteries of Amarna in the early 2000s, launching a multidisciplinary initiative to study the physical remains and burial materials of the people of Akhetaten. Amarna has become a case site for a kind of data-driven social archaeology that seeks to reconstruct the way cities appeared, functioned, and were experienced by their inhabitants.

Community members from al-Hagg Qandil and al-Till continue to make an invaluable contribution to the work, from excavating, to sieving to look for the smallest remnants of human activity in the past, or helping to consolidate ancient monuments with new bricks and stone. Their intimate knowledge of the local environment is particularly important. Local members of the team also help with the logistics of running the Dig House, helping the research run smoothly.

Figure 41. John Pendlebury, excavation director for the Egypt Exploration Society in the 1930s, examines a cast of a sculpted head of Nefertiti found at the site in 1933 (the original is in Cairo). The cast appears as part of an exhibition of finds that was a fundraising event for supporters of the Amarna dig. Photo courtesy of the Egypt Exploration Society.

IN FOCUS: EGYPTOLOGY IN THE EARLY TWENTIETH CENTURY: JOHN DEVITT STRINGFELLOW PENDLEBURY

By the early twentieth century, when excavation at Amarna began in earnest, professional Egyptology had been around for about 100 years. Unlike in the 19th century, debates on how to read hieroglyphic texts had been largely settled, European institutions were long invested in Egyptology, and new centers for its study were appearing in Egypt. During this period, museum collections around the world continued to grow, and approaches to fieldwork continued to develop. Outside of academia, Egyptology became incredibly popular, thanks in part to the discovery of Tutankhamun's tomb in 1922. Egyptian motifs and themes were worked into everything from stories to cigarette containers to buildings.

Just as had been the case in the 19th century, Egyptology and the people who practiced it were directly connected to the debates and events of the 20th century. John Devitt Stringfellow Pendlebury, Amarna's excavation director on behalf of the Egypt Exploration Society from 1930 to 1936, is a good, albeit tragic, case in point (fig. 41). Born in London, Pendlebury studied Classics (Greek and Roman language, literature, and civilization) as a young man. Rejecting a sedentary, scholarly life, Pendlebury focused himself on fieldwork. At only 26 years of age, he became both director of the excavations at Amarna and curator of the site of Knossos in Crete. This dual appointment meant that he could excavate in Crete in the summer and Egypt in the winter.

All archaeological work is a product of its time, and Pendlebury's excavations at Amarna were no different. Unlike his 19th-century predecessors, Pendlebury did not fixate on a need to find texts or statuary. His interests, in keeping with the German mission that came before him at Amarna, focused on rather unglamorous buildings and important cult structures that were at the heart of ancient life at the site. Like many of his 19th-century predecessors, though, Pendlebury pushed for a quick pace to his excavations as he worked large areas of Amarna. Over the course of six seasons, he excavated houses in the northern part of the site, uncovered the Desert Altars, and cleared much of the Central City. His penchant for rapid clearance and recording stands in contrast to other work done at the site, such as T. Eric Peet and Leonard Woolley's excavation of the Workmen's Village in the 1920s. The slow, steady, methodical pace of work that we now associate with archaeology would only become more widely accepted as that century progressed. Like those Egyptologists who came before him, and those of today, Pendlebury also believed in the need to share his findings with the broader public. His book, *Tell el-Amarna*, published in 1935, is a lively and accessible account of the site and his work.

And like all of the scholars before and after him, Pendlebury was enmeshed in the world around him. He anticipated the Second World War and the strategic importance that Crete would play. As a result of his career in, and love for, archaeology, Pendlebury had spent years living and working in Crete. He had an intimate knowledge of, and affection for, the land and its people and spoke fluent Greek. He placed this knowledge at the service of British intelligence, and fought against the German invasion of the island in 1941. He was ultimately shot, wounded, and later dragged from his sickbed to be executed. —AB

IN FOCUS: AMARNA AROUND THE WORLD: AN ARCHAEOLOGICAL SITE DISPERSED

Before 1980, excavated artifacts were allowed legally to leave Egypt through partage, a system used in Egypt (and also in Iraq, Turkey, and Afghanistan) to divide ownership of artifacts between foreign-led excavation teams and local government. The system allowed excavators, often hard pressed for funding, to find sponsors, whether museums or private backers, who covered fieldwork costs in return for a share of excavated artifacts. It saw the widespread dispersal of materials to museums and private collections around the world, and impacted what was collected, putting pressure on excavators to find museum-worthy objects. It leaves a complicated legacy, of which Amarna provides a classic example.

From the 1891–92 season, Flinders Petrie and his team were the first to systematically excavate at Amarna after years of periodic looting of the site, focusing on the Central City. Despite the looting, Petrie found a rich domestic and religious material culture. The finds were shared between the Egyptian Antiquities Service, Petrie's donors, and foreign museums. Objects from Petrie's excavations can now be seen in museum displays around the world, including in Cairo, Copenhagen, London, and Oxford.

Objects from Amarna continued to make their way across the globe. From 1911 to 1914, a German team from the Deutsche Orient-Gesellschaft, led by Ludwig Borchardt, excavated large areas of housing in the Main City. Famously, in 1912, this team discovered the workshop of the sculptor Thutmose and the bust of Nefertiti, which, along with a large selection of other objects from these excavations, was transferred to the Egyptian Museum (now the Egyptian Museum and Papyrus Collection) in Berlin. Other objects were taken to the Egyptian Museum in Cairo. The Egypt Exploration Society, working at the site from 1921 to 1936 (fig. 42), had a particularly widespread group of backers worldwide, who also received finds from these excavations. Objects from Amarna made their way as far as New Zealand, Brussels, the USA, and Canada, while many were also retained at the Egyptian Museum, Cairo. Objects purchased from the EES excavations at Amarna by Sir Henry Wellcome were also presented to UK museum collections after his death, including to Liverpool, Swansea, and Birmingham.

These early excavations were important initiatives of the time. The methods they employed, however, and the practice of dispersing finds, impacts how objects from Amarna can now be displayed, studied, and appreciated, and who has access to them. Finer details of the archaeological context of objects were usually not recorded, meaning that the specific provenance of museum objects is often subsequently vague. Objects recovered during these excavations were generally larger and more colorful

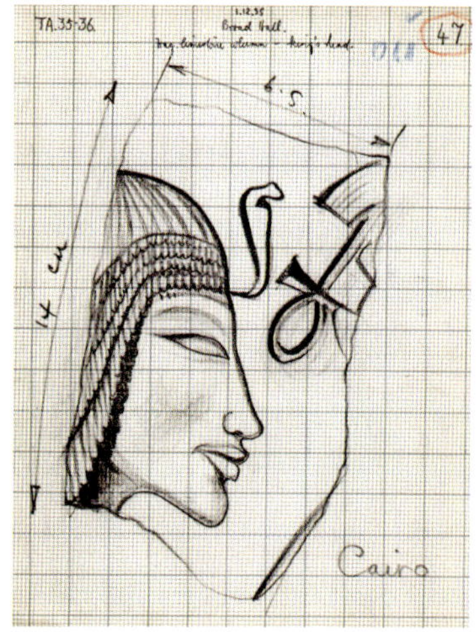

Figure 42. One of the "object cards" used to record artifacts found during the early Egypt Exploration Society excavations. This one shows a fragment of a column carved with a royal figure. Egypt Exploration Society Amarna Archive AT.OC.35-36.047. Image courtesy of the Egypt Exploration Society.

pieces, meaning that museum displays are not representative of the full diversity of material culture from Amarna. Many "minor" finds remain in museum stores, unpublished and unknown. Object assemblages were also broken up, and contextual information relating to their discovery has sometimes since been lost, meaning that displays of objects from Amarna often do not (and cannot) tell the full story of their discovery.

The presence of objects from Amarna in museums across the world continues to inspire generations of visitors to become fascinated with the Amarna period and its enigmatic royal family. But the legacy of partage for researchers, who often rely on studying groups of objects that were excavated together, is not straightforward. Access to these collections is also now restricted to those able to travel internationally. Modern heritage management prioritizes the retention of excavated artifacts in their country of origin, so that they can be curated as pieces of local and national heritage, identity, and scientific value. —AG

How Can We Recover the Past?

Vast expanses of time, space, and culture separate us from the ancient Egyptians, and recovering their world is a challenging task. Attempting to do so requires a combination of technical skill—of knowing how to extract evidence from the ground, to draw pottery vessels, or to read hieroglyphic texts—and of considering the biases both in the material under study and in our own experiences and backgrounds.

In broad terms, researchers have two kinds of sources at hand in reconstructing the human past. Formal evidence might comprise a temple, or a royal or elite relief or text. Sources of this kind were often created purposefully in the past to tell or reinforce a narrative, and because of this they are of great value when we try to reconstruct something of the mindset of the ancient Egyptians—of how they saw their world. So rich is formal material in Egypt, with its great temples, tombs, and papyri, that it is the foundation on which our understanding of the Egyptian past is largely built. At the same time, formal material can be used to present an ideal, deliberately curated by people in the past, which need not fully present the reality of a situation. Texts, images, and architecture can be carefully chosen to present the world in an idealized way. Unsavory aspects may be ignored, or considered unsuitable for a particular context. This idealizing tendency of texts and images is particularly acute for ancient Egypt, due to belief in the power of the image, and of the written and spoken word. If something was shown or spoken, it was believed to exist, and to occur in perpetuity. In this milieu, idealism naturally arose.

Informal source material is more incidental in nature—the kind of ordinary by-products of ancient lives. It might be the refuse from industry, or the skeletons of the ancient Egyptians themselves. There are also, of course, texts and images that have a degree of informality, such as graffiti, although informal sources often take the form of material or biological evidence, which are central to the field of archaeology. This material, of course, can be just as misleading. Imagine if archaeologists in the future excavated your home as you left it this morning—how might they misinterpret you and your experiences? Naturally, source material can have elements of both formality and informality, and the best interpretive approach is to consider as many, and as diverse a range, of pieces of evidence as possible.

Archaeology is a kind of anthropology of the past, a research endeavor—not treasure hunting—that seeks to understand ancient people through what they left behind (figs. 43–45). Ultimately, it seeks to contribute perspectives on our place in the world today and into the future. Most of the real work of archaeology involves building up slow pictures of life in the past from often modest materials, something that is particularly apparent when archaeologists work at ancient cities. Context, for the archaeologist, is everything, and this is why looted finds lose their value as sources of information. A looted figurine, stripped of its find context, tells us little, but a figurine recorded by archaeologists from a grave, with information on whom it was buried with, when, and what else was in the grave, can tell us an enormous amount, not only about the figurine, but of the life of someone who lived in the past.

At Amarna, the decades-long study of the pottery used by the people of Akhetaten involves the cataloging of hundreds of thousands of sherds of broken vessels, recording their size, shape, and the kind of clay they are made from, and then plotting this data across the site to study distribution patterns. The pioneering study of the city's textile industry saw the cataloging of close to 4,000 pieces of textile, along with hundreds of pieces of spindles and spinning bowls, and the experimental reconstruction of an ancient loom. More than a week's work can go into recording a single burial from Amarna's cemeteries, of which more than 700 have been studied. Excavations that, in the early days of archaeology, might have been published in a single page now take books to cover. And the range of specialists involved is extensive, including excavators, surveyors, conservators, bioarchaeologists, material-culture specialists, illustrators, photographers, and support staff.

Figure 43. Excavation underway at one of the Amarna cemeteries. Gretchen Dabbs, Waleed Mohamed Omar, and Ahmed Said Nasser remove and sieve the desert sand to make sure all ancient materials are recovered. Photo courtesy of the Amarna Project.

Figure 44. Experimental archaeology helps researchers understand ancient technology and processes. Here, bread is baked in a replica Amarna oven, as Delwen Samuel and Paul Nicholson monitor the temperature inside. Photo courtesy of the Amarna Project.

Archaeological stories are slow-building ones, involving years of painstaking work. Their importance is, to a large degree, in contributing alternative perspectives on ancient Egypt to the "top down" tendency of history, which is often based on sources created by the elite. Archaeology broadens our perspectives and sheds light on the lives of the people whose stories are not told on tomb and temple walls.

Figure 45. Care for excavated materials is a priority of modern archaeology. Conservators Lucy Skinner and Julie Dawson clean the surface of a fragile wooden coffin and apply a consolidant to it before the coffin is lifted out of the ground. Photo courtesy of the Amarna Project.

IN FOCUS: POTTERY AT AMARNA

Visitors to Amarna today will be struck by the vast numbers of ancient potsherds scattered across the surface of the city. These give a sense of the scale of human activity that once took place here, but, in fact, they represent only a small part of the pottery in ancient use. Excavation produces hundreds of thousands more fragments, although only very rarely complete vessels: the fine, usually decorated pots seen in museums are very much the exception rather than the rule. Potsherds form by far the most common artifact from Amarna and are a key source of information about the life of the ancient population.

Analysis of the pottery covers everything from its manufacture and technology to how it was used, and how it reflects social issues. Kiln and workshop excavations have shown that much of the pottery at Akhetaten was manufactured locally, using clay from the Nile. Scientific analysis of clays shows that other vessels, particularly those for transporting commodities, were brought to Akhetaten from other parts of Egypt, including the western desert oases, and from further afield. Particularly common at Amarna are transport vessels from the Levantine coast, fragments of which are found throughout the city. Once their original contents were removed, the vessels were often reused to hold other commodities, such as water or foodstuffs. A distinctive trail of broken jars runs from a well in the city out to the remote Workmen's Village in the desert beyond, showing the route taken by those bringing water to the village.

The most common role of pottery in archaeology is to help provide a date for the site or archaeological layer under study, a role that is largely redundant for such a short-lived site as Amarna. Instead, our work focuses on distribution analyses, comparing the types of pottery found in different parts of the site, to help identify how these areas of the ancient city were used. The identification of vessel function plays an important role in this. Pots for cooking, consumption, storage, and transport can all be identified, and their distribution gives an idea of how spaces functioned. For example, the large scatters of broken molds used in bread production seen in the Central City enabled the identification of bakeries providing bread for temple rituals. There are other vessels that have specialized functions, such as bowls used in the production of thread, and oddly complicated vessels that seem to have supported cooking pots over the fire.

Patterns of distribution also suggest social differences. In the 1890s, Flinders Petrie found a concentration of Mycenaean potsherds, imports from the Aegean Mediterranean, in dumps in the Central City. These sherds are far more common here than elsewhere at Amarna and suggest that the Central City, with its palaces, temples, and official buildings, had greater access to such exotic products than the residents of other areas. Elsewhere, it seems that vessels from other parts of Egypt, made from desert-based clays, are indicators of status. By contrast, pottery with blue-painted decoration, once assumed to signify high status and described as "palace ware," is found throughout the city and was clearly widely available.

Pottery was also used at the Amarna cemeteries, although for the ordinary population only a small number of vessels, usually to hold offerings, were included with the burial (fig. 46). These include vessels rarely found in the city—often miniature forms in desert clay—and suggests choices were made specifically related to the burial. The vessels show almost no evidence of use and were probably obtained especially for inclusion in the grave.—PR

Viewing Akhetaten from Afar

Amarna is an archaeological site that elicits great fascination for a wide range of people. Archaeologists, historians, artists, tourists, and followers of Atenist-inspired religions today all find something to be intrigued by. Many are fascinated by Akhenaten as an individual and the question of what kind of person he was: visionary, despot, or something in between. Modern visions of Akhetaten are almost as diverse, from shantytown to urban utopia.

The esoteric and idealistic elements of the Amarna tale are undeniably appealing. With time, though, and the development of archaeological approaches, the story of Amarna has become less about one king and

Figure 46. Pottery vessels placed in an Amarna grave to accompany the deceased. The bowl at the top contains the remains of figs, grapes, persea-fruit, dates, and tiger nuts; beer residue was found in the jar. Photo courtesy of the Amarna Project.

has begun to encompass wider human experience. Amarna is just as important as a place where we can learn about how people really lived in the past and coped with the kind of upheavals that Akhenaten's reign imposed upon them. How do people respond to reform? What drives social change and how does this play out in real life? The significance of Amarna runs much deeper than the life of one individual. Akhetaten was undoubtedly many things at once to many different people, and few would have stood back and considered it as a whole as we attempt to do today. Nonetheless, many of the stories from Amarna are difficult ones, involving huge divides between rich and poor and mass hardship in order to implement the vision of one individual. History becomes less neat and far more human at a place like Amarna.

Archaeological heritage has great potential to bring people together, through work collaboration or by opening our minds to the experiences of others, past and present, and to our own place in the world. Few sites encompass this potential as acutely as Amarna. The challenge ahead is to bring people together in a shared commitment to protect this uniquely significant but desperately fragile heritage site.

IN FOCUS: WHY IS AMARNA IMPORTANT?

The site of Tell al-Amarna is considered to be one of the most significant historical places in Middle Egypt in terms of the excavations and discoveries that have been made here, as well as for foreign tourism. It represents a very important historical era and has a close relationship with the New Kingdom heritage preserved at Luxor.

The Antiquities Inspectorate of Southern Minya, based in Mallawi, is working hard to create public awareness for local communities in Tell Bani Amran and al-Hagg Qandil to teach and educate the residents. We hope that they, and coming generations, look to the archaeological area as an important historical heritage that has been left to us by our ancient ancestors, something that it is owned by mankind and not bought and sold as treasure. Our history is not only artifacts found in museums, but also all the surviving monuments found in the timeless city of Amarna. This is the only place where you can see an example of a residential city that contains the places where the king, the government officials, the farmers and peasants, and others all lived, worked, and were buried. Many tourists also view the archaeological area as a sacred place, reflecting the glory of our ancient ancestors, and are attracted to the unique visions of the royal individuals who lived at the site.

We call upon the local communities now residing at Amarna to visit the ancient tombs, which contain unique and realistic views of the everyday lives of our ancient ancestors and represent our history. Come and see the tombs of Meryre (North Tomb 4) and Huya (North Tomb 1) for their beautiful and lively images of the royal family on tour, food, musicians, the people of the city, and livestock. Visit the Tomb of Mahu (South Tomb 9), the police chief, and the Tomb of Tutu (South Tomb 8), responsible for foreign correspondence. They contain special scenes, unique to Amarna, that made the era of King Akhenaten and his city an integral part of the history of the Eighteenth Dynasty, connected to his father, Amenhotep III, and Akhenaten's probable son Tutankhamun, and their tombs in the Valley of the Kings in Luxor.

The archaeological site of Tell al-Amarna is thus a very important destination for tourists and an economic resource. It is also part of the identity of Minya Governorate, which has taken as its symbol the Head of Nefertiti, an icon that is of course connected to Amarna and was discovered at the site in 1912. It is important that we try to link generations to each other through the past and the present, and work to protect history and the heritage of our ancestors, because these belong to all future generations.

—FA, HK

VISITING AMARNA

A one-day visit to Amarna will allow you to take in most or all of the following highlights (but make sure to arrive early):

North Palace: One of the best-preserved palaces from ancient Egypt. The lower parts of the walls have been partly rebuilt to help protect the monument and make it understandable to visitors.
Small Aten Temple: Glimpse the vastness of Akhenaten's monuments for the Aten at this partially reconstructed temple.
North Tombs: The elaborately decorated tombs of Akhenaten's officials are a highlight of any Amarna visit.
Boundary Stela U: Akhenaten's vision inscribed in stone on this striking rock-cut tablet.
Royal Tomb: Wind your way through the stark Royal Wadi to visit the original resting place of Akhenaten, hidden deep in the eastern cliffs.
Visitor Centre: See models of famous Amarna artifacts and walk through a full-scale replica of a house of one of Akhenaten's officials.

A two-day trip will give you more time at the monuments above and allow time to visit the remaining sites listed in this guide (e.g., South Tombs, Kom al-Nana).

Getting There and Around

Amarna is located on the east bank of the Nile River, opposite the town of Deir Muwas. Most visitors arrive by car or chartered bus from the Eastern Desert Highway. Take the turnoff to Mallawi. As you drive westward toward the Nile, the entrance to Amarna is on the left, just before crossing the bridge over the river. You will then enter Amarna via the ancient North City. If arriving from the south, you will enter the site near the South Tombs. If coming from the west bank, Amarna is reached either by the bridge over the Nile between Deir Muwas and Mallawi, turning right just over the bridge, or by ferry crossing.

It is possible to visit Amarna by train or public bus, although this is less straightforward. The arrival station is Mallawi or Deir Muwas, where it is necessary to hire a local car to bring you to Amarna. Retain the car all day—the site is too large to walk around. Amarna is also a stop on some Nile cruises.

Accommodation

There are no hotels at Amarna itself. Small hotels can be found in the city of Mallawi on the west bank of the river, around 20 minutes away, and there is a guest house at Deir Abu Hinnis on the east bank some 10km north of Amarna. Most visitors, though, stay in the regional capital, Minya, about 1.5 hours north of Amarna, where a wide range of hotels is available. Visitors coming from the south may choose to stay in Asyut, which is also around 1.5 hours' drive away.

Ticket Office and Opening Hours

The site is open to visitors every day from 8:00am to 4:00pm. Tickets for the main monuments must be purchased from the ticket office situated on the road to the North Tombs.

Amarna Visitor Centre

The Amarna Visitor Centre is located on the banks of the Nile in the town of al-Till. It is open every day between 8:00am and 4:00pm. Panels in English and Arabic introduce Amarna and the reign of Akhenaten. There is a series of models of famous Amarna artifacts and the centerpiece is a full-size replica of the house of an Amarna official, which visitors can walk through.

Food, Drinks, Toilets, and Shopping

Amarna has modest tourist infrastructure. There is a visitor Rest House opposite the ticket office which sells drinks. There are also a number of small shops, especially on the drive through the town of al-Till, selling drinks, fruit, and snacks. Buying these locally, rather than bringing them in to Amarna, is a great way to support the local economy. Many hotels in the region will provide lunch boxes for day trips upon request. Toilets are available at the Rest House opposite the ticket office and at the Visitor Centre. The Rest House has a small selection of souvenirs for sale.

Accessibility

Visitors with impaired mobility will find Amarna difficult to visit. The surface of the site is largely unpaved desert. There are few handrails, and limited shade and seating. The North Tombs and Boundary Stela U are accessible only by high staircases. The South Tombs are not located high in the cliff face, but are quite spread out, and the first tomb (no. 7) is reached by a short, but fairly steep, incline. The Royal Tomb involves a descent down a staircase and ramp (both with handrails). The Royal Tomb has a modern wooden floor in its main burial chamber, but the original stone floors inside the rock-cut tombs are often uneven. There is wheelchair access at the Visitor Centre, although not through the reconstructed house.

Tips for Visiting

Amarna can be a challenging place for the uninformed visitor. Preservation of its monuments varies widely from remarkably intact tombs to areas of falling-down houses. Little survives vertically of its temples and palaces. But what is still accessible at Amarna is a sense of the scale, materiality, monumentality, and landscape of an ancient city. In a way, Amarna challenges visitors to meet it halfway—to use your experiences of the site today to imagine the city in the past. Try to pick out the ancient ruins from the landscape. Almost all the gray-brown mud brick you see is part of the ancient city. Look down on the ground for pieces of pottery discarded by the ancient inhabitants. Take in the vastness of the site and the contrasts in the natural landscape, from the fertile river's edge to the starkness of the desert and cliffs. Imagine the rays of the sun penetrating down from above, embracing the Aten temples, as the king raced by in his chariot. Consider the effort it took to build this great city, and then to dismantle it. Imagine the place alive with people.

Don't forget to bring good shoes and a hat. A flashlight can also be useful to see details inside the tombs. And please take care of the fragile ruins by not walking or climbing on the remains. Note that it is illegal to remove any ancient materials (including pottery sherds) from archaeological sites in Egypt.

IN FOCUS: THE AMARNA VISITOR CENTRE

Construction of the Amarna Visitor Centre began in 2001, on 1,000 square meters of land allocated to the Supreme Council of Antiquities on the riverbank in al-Till. The Visitor Centre was built to provide information about Amarna, including its temples, tombs, and royal palaces. It is also an education center, meant to increase awareness of archaeology, as well as an important regional tourist attraction that showcases the history and civilization of ancient Egypt. Visitors can first learn about the history of Amarna and then visit the historical areas of the site itself.

The Centre contains a selection of impressive archaeological models, including of the Royal Tomb, North Palace, Great Aten Temple, and the entire city of Akhetaten itself. It also contains images that show how the city was planned and its borders. The centerpiece is a full-scale replica of the house of an official named Ranefer (fig. 47), which helps visitors understand housing in the Amarna period. In addition, there is a selection of replica statues of the royal family. Information panels are located throughout the Centre to explain the monuments and history of Amarna.

The Centre has a lecture hall where history and archaeology professors are invited to give lectures to increase awareness of archaeology. It has the latest technology, from surveillance cameras and fire-extinguishing equipment to central air conditioning, an x-ray security scanner, and electronic gates. It also has many talented Ministry of Tourism and Antiquities inspectors who accompany student and tourist groups during their visit to explain the contents of the Centre and increase awareness and appreciation of archaeology (fig. 48).

The Visitor Centre began accepting guests on March 20, 2016, on the national day of Minya. We reach out to surrounding schools, education departments, and university students to invite them to visit the Centre and a Facebook page has also been created (under the name "Amarna Visitor Centre") to attract guests. We look forward to welcoming you to the Amarna Visitor Centre soon! —HH

Figure 47. The reconstructed house of the chariotry officer Ranefer in the Amarna Visitor Centre. Photo courtesy of the Amarna Project.

Figure 48. Ministry of Tourism and Antiquities Inspector Ahmed Mostafa guides a school group around the Amarna Visitor Centre. Photo courtesy of the Amarna Project.

Figure 49. A scene of activity along the riverbank in the Tomb of May (South Tomb 14). After Davies, *The Rock Tombs of El Amarna*, Part 5: *Smaller Tombs and Boundary Stelae*, pl. V. Image courtesy of the Egypt Exploration Society.

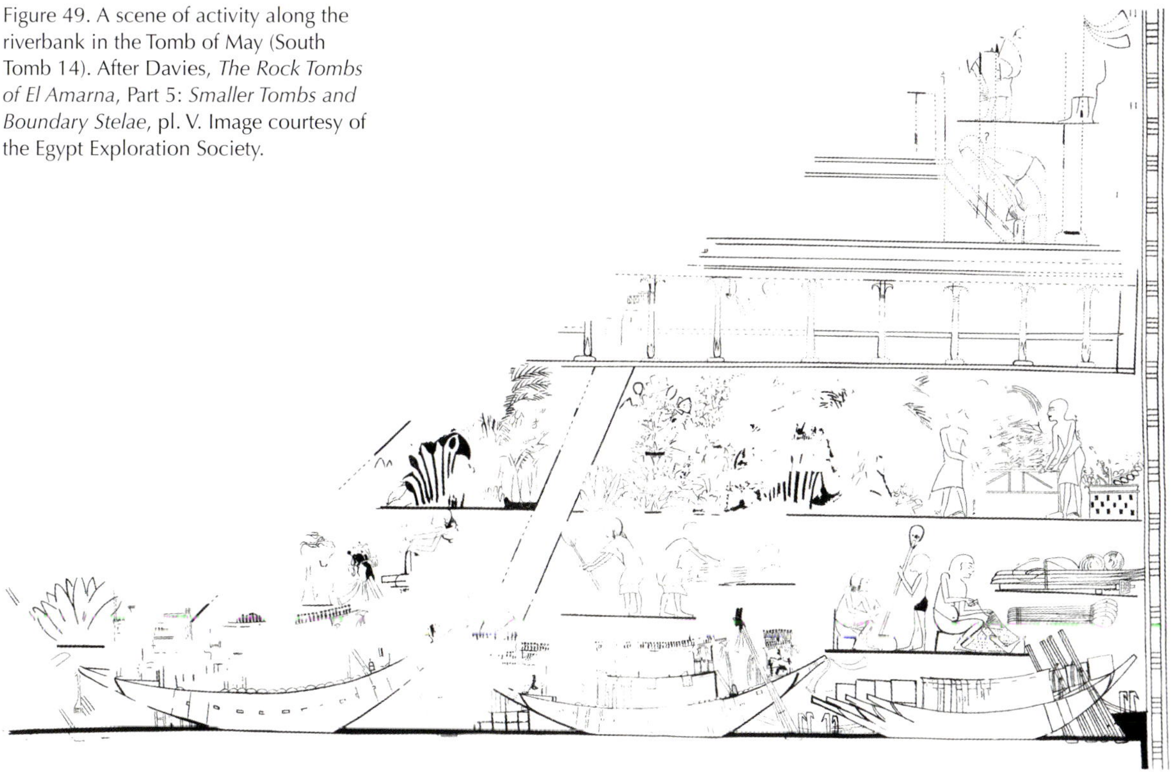

IN FOCUS: THE ANCIENT LANDSCAPE

The city of Akhetaten was built on a flat desert plain bordered to the north, south, and east by limestone cliffs, reaching up to 100m, and the River Nile to the west. The cliffs form the edge of a high desert plateau. The Amarna bay stretches some 10km north–south and at its widest point reaches 5km across. The limestone cliffs and the desert plain are cut by dry valleys (wadis) which were formed by floodwaters from desert storms in the distant past. These wadis are still active today, each flood cutting into the deposits laid down by previous floods. Closer to the Nile, the dry stony desert gives way to a thin band of vegetation. The width of this green belt varied from year to year depending on the height of the annual Nile flood. It is here that cultivation of food crops would have taken place.

What would Amarna have looked like before Akhetaten was built? The desert plain itself likely had very few plants growing on it. Drought-resistant trees and shrubs such as acacia and tamarisk must have been present in the wadis, where their deep roots reached the very low water table. After intermittent rains and floods, the desert would have been transformed into a temporary green oasis as seeds that had lain dormant in the sand since the last rains germinated, grew, and flowered in the short time that the floodwaters remained, before evaporating in the hot sun. Then the cycle was repeated with later rains and floods.

The green belt by the Nile would have appeared lush in comparison to the desert (fig. 49). Reeds and other water plants grew by the riverbank, along with trees such as willows, Nile acacia, and date and doum palms in shady groves here and there. After the annual flood receded, the sparse local population, most likely living in small scattered villages on the west bank, would have been able to grow their crops of cereals such as emmer wheat and barley, along with legumes such as lentils and peas. Dates, pomegranates, figs, and grapes would also have been grown.

A first-time visitor may have thought Amarna, with its hot, dusty, sterile, waterless desert, was the last place for a new city to be built, and for people to thrive. —AC

NORTH CITY AND PALACES

Arriving by road from the north, you will first notice a series of Old Kingdom tombs cut high in the cliff face many centuries before Akhetaten was built. The ruins of Akhetaten itself are then quickly upon you as you round the bend into the Amarna bay. Watch for the mud-brick walls on the left of the road—your first glimpse of Akhenaten's city.

The Amarna-period ruins at the far north of the bay are known today as the North City (figs, 50, 51). This was an important locale, home to one of Akhetaten's four palaces (the North Riverside Palace) and hundreds of houses, many of them probably for palace workers. A huge mud-brick complex at the very north end of the bay was perhaps a depot for supplies imported into the city.

A strict check must have been kept on this northern border. Notice how the cliffs form a natural boundary as they curve around to meet the river. Guards were probably posted around the cliff face to monitor people coming into the bay. Huge quantities of limestone were extracted from the cliffs to build Akhenaten's temples and palaces, and quarry workers may have lived in simple encampments nearby. The ancient quarries continue for up to 10km to the north. The Minya region is still an important source of limestone for Egypt today.

Abandoned Dig House

One of the most prominent ruins in the North City is the house used by a team of British archaeologists who excavated Amarna for the Egypt Exploration Society (London) in the 1920s and 1930s (fig. 52). The house was built over the ruins of a large ancient villa that belonged to

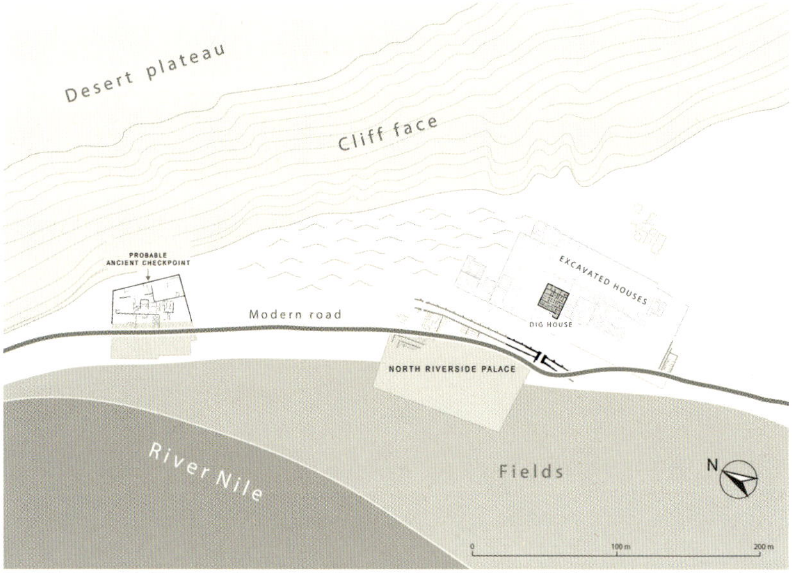

Figure 50. The North City. Illustration by Mary Shepperson.

Figure 51. A view across the low desert mounds that mark the ancient North City, taken from the cliffs at the north end of the Amarna bay. Photo courtesy of the Amarna Project.

one of Akhenaten's officials. His name is no longer known, but he must have been an important figure in the ancient city, since his house stood directly opposite the North Riverside Palace.

The Dig House provided workspace, accommodation, and even a darkroom for processing photographs. Specialist workmen from the village of Qift (near Luxor) were employed to help during the excavations (fig. 53), and lived in accommodations nearby. They were joined by local workers from the villages of al-Till and al-Hagg Qandil.

Figure 52. Life of the North Dig House: the ruins of the original Amarna villa on which the house was built (left); the first stage of building the Dig House itself in the 1920s (center); and the house during use in the 1930s (right). EES Amarna Archive Negatives 1923.54, 1923.59A, 1933–4.A.31. Photos courtesy of the Egypt Exploration Society.

Figure 53. The team of workmen from Qift, in Egypt's south, who joined the Egypt Exploration Society and local community members to investigate the ruins of Amarna in 1921. EES Amarna Archive Negative 1921.74. Photo courtesy of the Egypt Exploration Society.

The house is the setting for the book *Nefertiti Lived Here*, a vivid account of dig life at Amarna by Mary Chubb, first published in 1954.

If you're wandering through the house, please be careful of the fragile mud-brick walls.

North Riverside Palace

A huge mud-brick gateway marks the entrance to the North Riverside Palace, one of four palaces at Akhetaten, and by far the least explored (figs. 54, 55). The palace once extended down to the riverbank, now marked by the distant line of palm trees. It was richly decorated with colorful wall paintings. For centuries, it has been mostly buried beneath fields.

Many believe that Akhenaten himself lived at the North Riverside Palace, which was probably one of the first buildings founded at Akhetaten. The distant location of the palace, away from the bustle of the Central City, perhaps saw it function mainly as a place of residence, rather than a hub of court business.

It was also one end point of the city's main processional route, the Royal Road, along which Akhenaten traveled every day in his golden chariot to worship in the city's temples. As the Aten moved overhead in the sky above, the daily procession of the king along the Royal Road gave the public a glimpse of the Aten's representative on earth.

Note that the Royal Road originally passed along the front of the gateway, between it and the cliffs, not along the line of the modern road. And, although it is tempting, please don't climb on the ancient gateway!

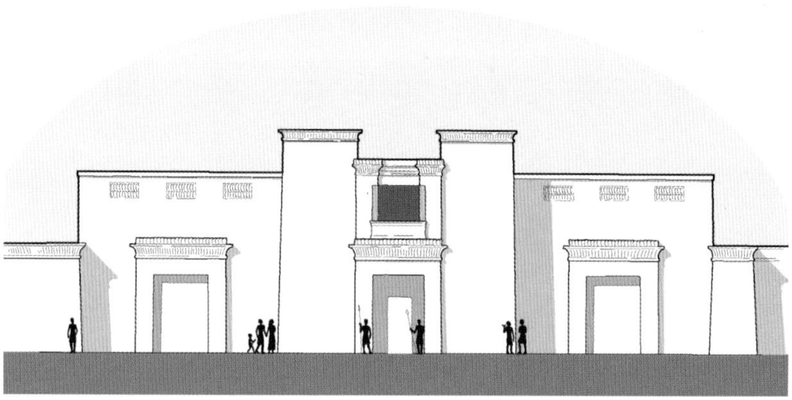

Figure 54. Reconstruction of the gateway of the North Riverside Palace. Not to scale. Some features, like the window above the entrance, are hypothetical. Illustration by Mary Shepperson (based on a reconstruction drawing made by Ralph Lavers in the 1930s).

Figure 55. A view across the interior of the gateway of the North Riverside Palace after it was cleared in the 1930s. The view is roughly to the northeast. EES Amarna Archive Negative 1930–1.A.203. Photo courtesy of the Egypt Exploration Society.

IN FOCUS: AMARNA'S PAINTED PALACES AND THE WINDOW OF APPEARANCE

At least four major palaces have been identified at Amarna, two at the north end of the city (known today as the North Palace and North Riverside Palace) and two in the center (the Great Palace and the King's House). Palaces housed the king and members of his family: their living quarters were designed primarily with comfort and luxury in mind, and service areas were built to house staff and domestic activities. However, palaces also served ritual and ceremonial purposes and some had huge courtyards, gardens, stone features, and statuary designed to impress visitors. Textual records from elsewhere in Egypt make it clear that palaces were also the center of administration and state decision-making, although locating these various activities within the known palaces is difficult: a number of representations of palaces have been found in the tombs at Amarna, but these are very hard to relate to specific buildings on the ground.

Like houses, most Egyptian palaces were constructed of sun-dried mud brick, but with important elements such as doorways and columns made of stone. Ceremonial parts of palaces were designed to be particularly large and imposing, as seen in the central courtyards and rooms of the Great Palace at Amarna: these were built largely of stone and decorated with colossal statuary, but there is a much smaller brick-built private wing hidden behind the courtyard walls. Stone walls and columns were usually carved and painted with texts, patterns, and images; mud-brick walls and floors were plastered and often richly painted.

One of the most prominent features of palaces represented in tomb scenes is the "Window of Appearance." This was a richly decorated raised balcony from which Akhenaten and Nefertiti handed out luxury items such as gold necklaces as rewards to loyal officials. The frequency with which the "window" is represented in elite tombs, both as part of representations of the ceremony and also closed when not in use, highlights the importance of this feature to Amarna's inhabitants. The decoration of the "window" focuses on traditional elements of royal iconography and serves to frame the king and his family, and to separate them from their audience.

A number of themes can be seen in palace decoration at Amarna. Traditional royal motifs such as the "palace façade" design, heraldic plants, cobras, cartouches, and other protective signs adorn the walls; bound captives and bows (representing enemies) mark pathways for the king across decorated floors, crushing enemies beneath his feet as he walked. The natural world features prominently (fig. 56): vines, flowering plants, pools full of fish, thickets with birds and calves, and tables piled with food and flowers. The king and his family also feature heavily in the decoration:

scenes of the royal family relaxing are known from the King's House; a royal chariot scene is thought to have adorned a room above the entrance to the North Riverside Palace; while the bridge linking the Great Palace and King's House seems to have featured Akhenaten and Nefertiti handing out rewards from a window. —KS

Figure 56. A view across the garden court in the North Palace, including the basin that once held a sunken garden. The central chamber in the background is the so-called Green Room, which was once painted with a continuous scene of riverside life. A facsimile painting of part of the scene is shown below. It was copied from the original by Norman and Nina de Garis Davies in 1926. Photo courtesy of the Amarna Project; painting (MMA 30.4.136) courtesy of the Metropolitan Museum of Art.

North Palace

A little further down the road is one of the best-preserved palaces from ancient Egypt (figs. 56, 57). The North Palace may originally have been the residence of Kiya, a secondary wife of Akhenaten, although it was later occupied by Meritaten, the king's eldest daughter.

The palace ruins, now partly reconstructed, speak of a busy complex that supported the religious, ceremonial, and private lives of the royal family. It was built around two open courts and a possible "Window of Appearance," a kind of ceremonial balcony from which the royal family rewarded their loyal officials. Much of the palace would originally have been built to at least a second story.

Look for the throne room, the bathroom, and the large basin that once contained a garden. An underground limestone conduit channeled water into the garden from a central well and sunken garden, the location of which is marked today by a group of palm trees in the center of the complex. Another side court was used to keep animals, its walls lined with feeding bins showing painted reliefs of ibexes, antelopes, and cattle (fig. 58). When excavated in the 1920s, tethering stones still remained in place beside each bin.

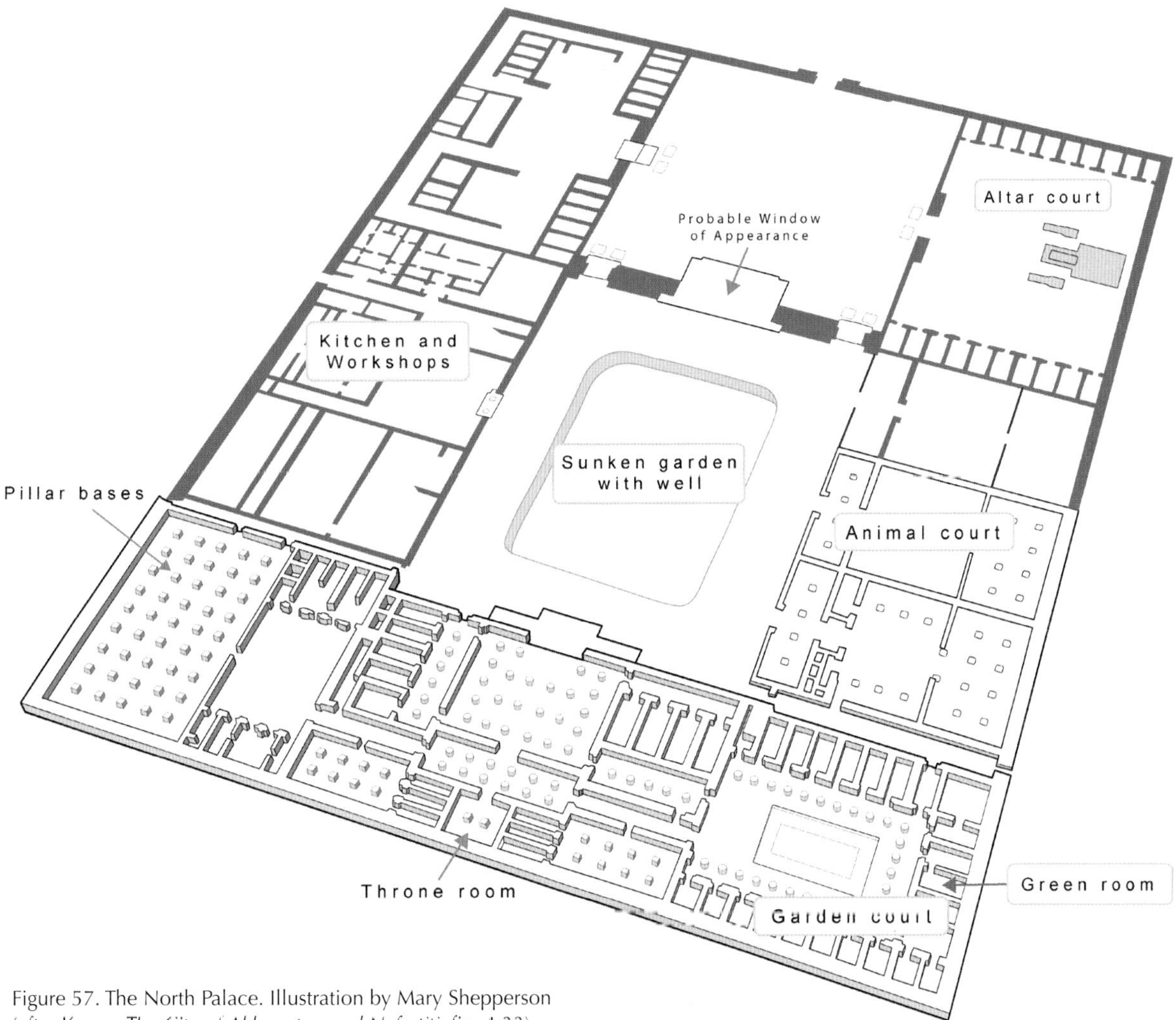

Figure 57. The North Palace. Illustration by Mary Shepperson (after Kemp, *The City of Akhenaten and Nefertiti*, fig. 4.22).

Paintings were also added to the palace walls in vivid colors (figs. 56, 59). Many of the best preserved were from the so-called "Green Room," one of the side chambers in the garden court, which bore a continuous scene of marsh life around its walls. The plant and animal life in the palace invoked the life-giving themes of the Aten cult. Wall paintings and decorated fittings from the North Palace were largely removed at the time of excavation (fig. 60) and can now be seen in museum collections worldwide.

Figure 58: Some of the feeding troughs and tethering stones that lined the "animal court" in the North Palace. Look closely to see the lower parts of cattle carved in the stone. EES Amarna Archive Negative 1923.141. Photo courtesy of the Egypt Exploration Society.

Figure 59. Part of the famous "Green Room" frieze at the North Palace when it was first uncovered in the 1920s, showing a bird diving for prey. EES Amarna Archive Negative 1926–7.131. Photo courtesy of the Egypt Exploration Society.

Figure 60. The EES Amarna Archive records the process of removing the wall paintings from the North Palace in the 1920s, and the important role of the local community in achieving this. Top: "Shaking to dissolve the celluloid." Center: "Pasting on the cloth" (left), "Fastening on the boards" (center), and "Breaking away the wall" (right). Below: "Putting of plaster in mud." EES Amarna Archive Negatives 1926–7.43, 44, 45, 46, 48. Photos courtesy of the Egypt Exploration Society.

EASTERN CLIFFS AND DESERT

Driving south, the turnoff to the ticket office, which will also take you to the North Tombs, Boundary Stela U, and the Royal Tomb, lies just before the town of al-Till. Site guards will be deployed to unlock the North Tombs and Royal Tomb for your visit (a tip is always welcome).

Desert Altars

On your left, just past the ticket office, lie the Desert Altars, set back from the road on the open desert plain (fig. 61). The Desert Altars are one of several huge temple complexes that Akhenaten had built around the outskirts of Akhetaten, and the only one known in the northern part of the city. Three large open-air mud-brick shrines survive. Each has a unique layout, something that is particularly evident when they are seen from the air (fig. 62).

The purpose of the Desert Altars is poorly understood, although they seem most likely to have been funerary shrines for the high-ranking officials buried at the nearby North Tombs: a place where they could join the sun god after death. This idea is supported by the presence of an informal roadway leading out from the altars across to the tombs. If this function is correct, it demonstrates the high status of these men, upon whose loyalty the king depended.

An alternative explanation is that the altars were built for the famous Reception of Foreign Tribute held in the 12th year of Akhenaten's reign. A scene in the Tomb of Huya (North Tomb 1) shows Akhenaten receiving exotic gifts during the ceremony, as offerings were made to the Aten at a set of distinctly shaped open-air altars. The image of the altars is no

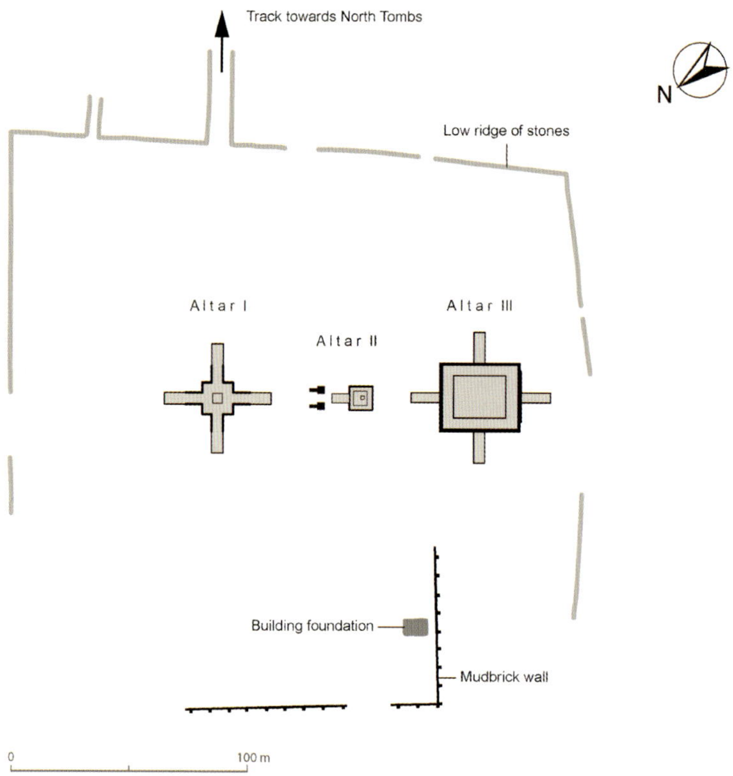

Figure 61. The Desert Altars. Illustration by Mary Shepperson (after B. Kemp, "Outlying Temples at Amarna," in *Amarna Reports* 6, fig. 15.25).

Figure 62. When seen from the air, the unique layout of each of the Desert Altars becomes clear. Photo courtesy of Gwil Owen/The Amarna Project.

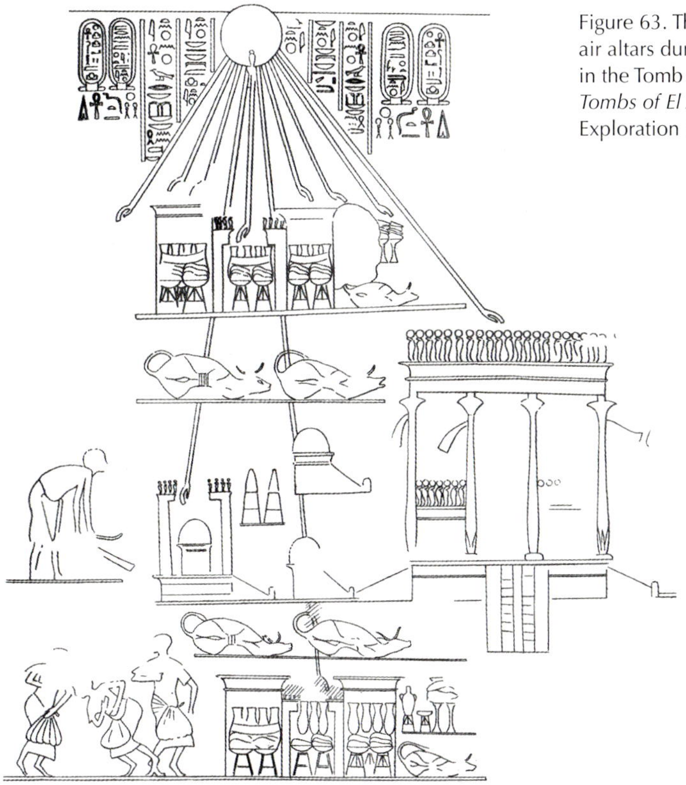

Figure 63. The rays of the Aten reach down to a set of open-air altars during the Reception of Foreign Tribute ceremony in the Tomb of Huya (North Tomb 1). After Davies, *The Rock Tombs of El Amarna*, Part 3, pl. XIV. Image courtesy of the Egypt Exploration Society.

longer preserved, but it was recorded in the early 20th century (see fig. 63). Perhaps these were the Desert Altars—although the Central City might be argued to offer a more suitable location for this important event.

The North Tombs

The North Tombs—elaborately decorated tombs belonging to some of the highest officials in Akhenaten's court—are a highlight of any trip to Amarna. Here you can see firsthand the written and visual evidence on which so much of our understanding of the Amarna period is based: images of the royal family worshiping the Aten, Hymns to the Sun God, and vivid scenes of temple and palace life. The Tomb of Meryre, High Priest of the Aten (North Tomb 4), is the most often visited, but all of the tombs contain much of interest.

Notice the prominent position of the North Tombs in the landscape, a reflection of the high status of their owners, although, in the end, most of these men and perhaps their families were buried elsewhere when the city was abandoned. Nearby lie several important pit-grave cemeteries for the non-elite population of Akhetaten, which offer very different perspectives on life in the ancient city.

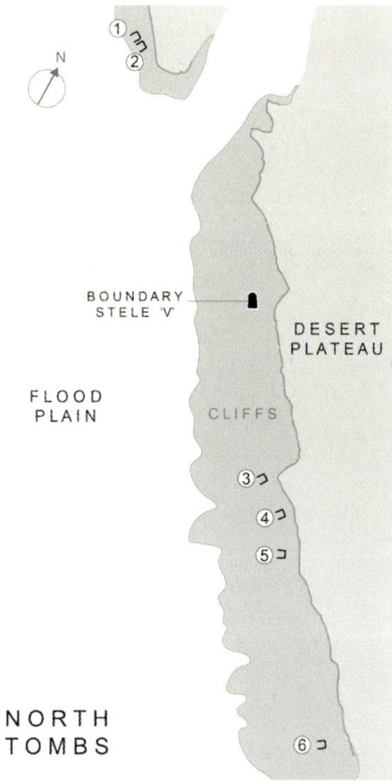

Figure 64. The North Tombs. Image by Mary Shepperson (after Davies, *The Rock Tombs of El Amarna,* Part 2, pl. I).

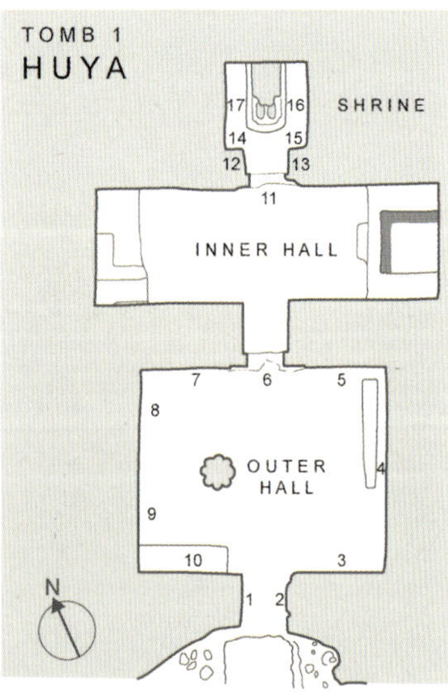

Figure 65. North Tomb 1: Huya. Illustration by Mary Shepperson (after Davies, *The Rock Tombs of El Amarna,* Part 3, pl. I).

From the top of the cliffs outside the tombs there is a wonderful view across to the Nile.

Tomb 1. Huya, "Overseer of the Royal Harim and of the Treasuries, and Steward of the Great Royal Wife, Tiye"

Huya was an important official in the household of Akhenaten's mother, Queen Tiye. His tomb (fig. 65) contains many interesting scenes, including several showing Tiye herself. It also depicts a grand "foreign tribute" ceremony in year 12 of Akhenaten's reign, where exotic goods including ivory, metal vessels, and animal skins are presented to the king. In the shrine, beside a large statue of Huya, is a scene of his funeral and burial equipment, rare subject matter within the Amarna tombs (see fig. 71).

Watch your head as you enter the tomb!

Entrance to the outer hall **(1, 2)**. On the sides of the entrance are figures of Huya in prayer, wearing elaborately pleated garments and a "perfume cone" on his head. The texts are Hymns to the Aten.

Outer hall. One of two original columns survives in the outer hall, taking the form of a bundle of papyrus stems. The ceiling was once decorated with paint, patches of which are preserved.

Following the scenes counterclockwise from the doorway:

(3): A royal banquet (fig. 66). Akhenaten and Nefertiti sit on the left and Queen Tiye on the right, wearing a crown of double plumes and horned disc. Akhenaten eats meat and Nefertiti consumes a bird. Two of the princesses sit beneath Nefertiti while Queen Tiye's daughter (Akhenaten's sister), Princess Baketaten, sits beneath her. Of the two servants in the middle, one is Huya himself. In a narrower scene below, servants apparently taste the food, while two groups of musicians play: girls with lutes and a hand-held lyre (a harp-like instrument) at the top left and foreign men on the lower right, with a huge standing lyre. At the foot of this and other walls is a badly damaged strip depicting life in the country at harvest time (see fig. 32).

(4): Queen Tiye visits her Sunshade Temple (see fig. 145). Akhenaten and Tiye stand in the center, hand in hand beneath the rays of the Aten. Behind them is a group of servants and, at the front of the lower row, Queen Tiye's daughter Baketaten. Huya is one of two bowing figures in front of the king. The temple they visit is one of several "sunshade" temples built at Akhetaten for royal women. Sunshades connected the king to the regenerative

Figure 66. Akhenaten, Nefertiti, and Queen Tiye, Akhenaten's mother, enjoy a ritual banquet under the rays of the Aten, feasting on meat as musicians play. Tomb of Huya (North Tomb 1). After Davies, *The Rock Tombs of El Amarna*, Part 3, pls. IV–V. Image courtesy of the Egypt Exploration Society.

powers of the sun god. This one was built for Tiye herself. They featured open-air altars, shown here reached by a flight of steps and heaped with and surrounded by offerings. The temple courtyard is surrounded by a colonnade with statues of the royal family. A second temple is shown to the left, also decorated with statues. Most of the statues in these scenes are of Amenhotep III and Tiye, although those of other royal figures also occur, including Akhenaten and Nefertiti.

Below the main scene (see fig. 145) are three rows of attendants. In the lowest, largely destroyed, they are subdivided into named groups, and Huya stands in front of each one. The narrow strip portraying country life continues at the base of the wall, with life by the river, including bird-trapping (left) and fishing (right).

(5): Huya is rewarded by Akhenaten and Nefertiti at a Window of Appearance. To the right of the Window, in the upper register, there were once figures of princesses Meritaten and Meketaten. In the space under the Window, below a line of bowing attendants, is a damaged scene of palace craftsmen at work. They are supervised by Huya, the larger figure in a pleated kilt and "perfume cone" in the upper register. Jewelry, metal vessels, and chests are being made and a palm-leaf column is being decorated. Note, in the top right-hand corner, the miniature scene of a sculptor's studio (see fig. 122). The chief sculptor is named Iuti, and is shown at work on a statue of Princess Baketaten, daughter of Queen Tiye.

(6): The inscriptions on the frame around the door are of great interest in that they name Amenhotep III and Queen Tiye, as well as Akhenaten and Nefertiti. On the lintel both royal families are depicted (fig. 67). On the left: Akhenaten and Nefertiti are seated, four daughters waiting on them (right to left Meritaten, Meketaten, Ankhesenpaaten, Neferneferuaten the Younger). On the right, Amenhotep III and Tiye sit facing each other, with their daughter Princess Baketaten in front of Tiye. The scene reflects Huya's devotion to his royal patrons and need not imply that Amenhotep III was still alive when it was carved.

(7): A second scene of reward at the Window of Appearance. In this case, the texts explain that the occasion is the appointment of Huya to his principal offices. Below, Huya stands in a courtyard surrounded by storerooms shaded by a portico. He seems to be supervising the weighing out and registration of valuables, including a gold collar.

(8, 9): The Reception of Foreign Tribute. The west wall is occupied by the record of an event dated to year 12 of Akhenaten's reign, described as the reception of tribute from Syria–Palestine, the Kingdom of Kush (in Nubia, to Egypt's south), the West, and the East. It begins at the left end (9) with Akhenaten and Nefertiti leaving the King's House, shown in the top left. The king and queen travel in elaborate carrying-chairs decorated with figures of lions and sphinxes, borne by groups of men. The princesses and their nurses follow behind, and bowing attendants walk below. Many of the attendants are desert warriors with curved sticks and feathers in their hair. In the middle is Huya himself.

Figure 67. A scene of two royal couples on a door lintel inside Huya's tomb: Akhenaten and Nefertiti (left), and Amenhotep III and Tiye (right), all encompassed by the rays of the sun god. After Davies, *The Rock Tombs of El Amarna,* Part 3, pl. XVIII. Image courtesy of the Egypt Exploration Society.

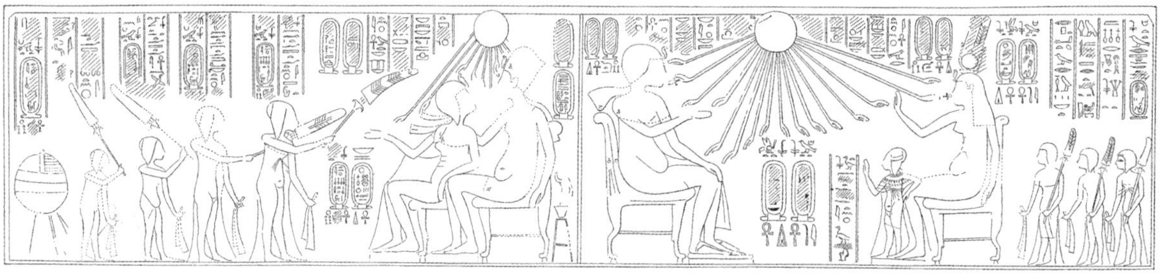

More desert warriors walk in front of the royal family, toward the reception area (8). One of them acts as a priest, burning incense. Three others, in the fourth register down, perform a dance. The front part of the procession also includes three empty chariots, and representative gifts from the foreign lands.

The tribute of the North (Syria–Palestine) is at the top: two chariots, pillow-shaped ingots of metal, and elaborate gold vessels. At the upper right-hand edge of the wall, the list continues: more metal vessels in stands and, below this, eight rows of prisoners or hostages of "Syrian" appearance. Similar scenes in tombs at Thebes identify such people as children of the princes of the city-states of Syria–Palestine. The remaining registers to the left of the Syrians depict the tribute from the Kingdom of Kush (in Nubia), consisting of a line of slaves wearing wooden manacles on their wrists. Below them is a line of men carrying two yokes hung with skins and gold rings, and two elaborate golden bowls with molded foliage. They are followed by men with a panther, monkeys, and elephant tusks. In a third register come more bearers of ivory and of chairs (of ebony?), with stands bearing rings and bags of gold, and perhaps a heap of incense between them. Behind them come women leading children by the hand and carrying others in baskets fastened around their foreheads, and finally a group of antelope.

Below all is a badly damaged scene that once showed Huya being congratulated at home. Only parts of a group of female musicians survive. The center of the right-hand part of the scene (8) was once occupied by a picture of an open pavilion, reached by flights of steps on each side, where the king and queen would sit to review the tribute. To its left was a group of three altars, the largest surrounded by a wall and containing an offering table (see fig. 63). Might these be the Desert Altars? Above and below were simplified pictures of storerooms containing offerings.

Running below the entire scene (8–9) is a continuation of the narrow and much damaged strip recording country life. Note the hoopoe bird in the tree (left), plowing, and (right) the sail of a boat.

(10): The last scene in the outer hall returns us to Queen Tiye's visit, and to a drinking party. On the right sit Akhenaten and Nefertiti with two princesses: Ankhesenpaaten is standing on the cushion, the other is possibly Meketaten. On the left sits Tiye with her daughter Baketaten. In the center, Huya supervises the serving. Below are groups of fan-bearers and musicians very similar to those on the companion wall (3).

The agricultural strip at the bottom of the wall has perished entirely.

Inner hall. This is unfinished and undecorated. At the eastern end, behind a rock parapet, is the shaft, some 10.2m deep, leading to the burial chamber.

Shrine. Huya's tomb is one of only two of the North Tombs where the shrine was decorated (the other is Tomb 6 for Panehesy). Its focus is a statue of Huya carved in the rock face, now badly damaged.

The doorframe **(11)** has blue-painted hieroglyphs on a wine-colored background, probably to imitate red granite. The texts are simple prayers to Akhenaten, Nefertiti, Tiye, and the Aten. The carved and painted details at the top are derived from a long-standing traditional design for important doorways, although the rows of cobras bearing sun discs are an innovation. Above the doorway itself is a carved representation of a rolled-up strip of matting.

The sides of the doorway **(12, 13)** show large figures of Huya facing toward the shrine, accompanied by prayers for offerings. On the insides of the doorway **(14, 15)** are figures of his sister Wen-her (left) and his wife Tuy (right). Piles of bread offerings appear above. On the east wall **(16)** is a scene of the funeral (see fig. 71). The focus of attention is the mummified body of Huya, placed upright (and now largely chiseled out). Four women mourn behind, the top two probably his wife and sister. In front of the body is a heap of offerings, then a priest and rows of male mourners. Sacrificial oxen and more mourners occupy the lowest part. Mourners and the funeral procession appear on the west wall **(17)**. Some in the procession carry chests suspended on yokes. More of the burial furniture is carved on the wall spaces around the statue. It includes a chariot, chests, and canopic jars (left); a bed, two chairs with pairs of sandals hung on poles, two chests or shrines on sledges, and two folding stools.

IN FOCUS: SCENES OF THE CITY

The Amarna tombs are renowned for containing pictures of buildings in far more detail than is common for Egyptian art. In style, they follow the old convention of combining ground plans with elevations. They are a remarkable source of information on the vertical appearance and activities conducted in the buildings of Akhetaten, although interpreting these scenes is rife with challenges.

The buildings are drawn from the artist's mind and are unlikely to have been verified with direct observations at the buildings themselves. The artists also chose to give greater or lesser degrees of priority to individual buildings or to parts of them, according to a scale of values of their own. This is most obvious in the treatment of the palaces. The largest building at Amarna, and the building using the most stonework and containing the most statuary, was the Great Palace in the Central City. Yet the tomb pictures show nothing that resembles this building as we know it from its excavated ground plan and details. What is shown several times is a building that is small in comparison to pictures of the main temple, is not identified by a name, yet includes a king's bedroom and the Window of Appearance from which the king would reward his officials. Logically, this should be the Great Palace, and we have to explain the discrepancy in appearance by saying that the artist has reduced the details to what is, in effect, an elaborate hieroglyph of a palace. The visual details, which included a huge courtyard surrounded by colossal statues of the king, were less important than the elements that identified it as a place where the king spent some time and performed duties.

We must also allow for the fact that building projects took several years to complete, and some buildings saw considerable modifications, remaining, perhaps, unfinished at the time when the city was abandoned. Usually, we cannot be sure at exactly what moment in time an artist has drawn a particular building, which might have still been a building site. This especially applies to the Great Aten Temple. The tombs of Meryre (North Tomb 4) and Panehesy (North Tomb 6), both of whom held senior positions in the cult and administration of the Great Aten Temple, contain very detailed pictures of this complex. In Meryre's tomb it is shown twice, once with the main axis vertical (fig. 68) and once horizontal. When we compare these pictures with the excavated ground plans, we can immediately identify features common to both. Yet there are also many differences. The first court, for example, is shown surrounded by many small individual chapels, centered on a large offering platform reached by a staircase. There are no signs of these chapels in the recovered archaeological plan, while the large offering platform was located between the pylons.

Meryre's tomb also includes an attempt at showing the urban surroundings of the Great Aten Temple. Buildings which are densely subdivided into rooms and corridors stand in gardens in which trees and shrubs grow, storerooms are filled with goods, horses eat from a feeding trough, wells and basins provide water. We can identify two shrines. The impression created is of order, abundance, and a wealth of characteristic architectural detail. But it is a projection of the inner experience of being in the city, a kind of "mental map." It is not the work of a surveyor who wanted spatial accuracy. —BK

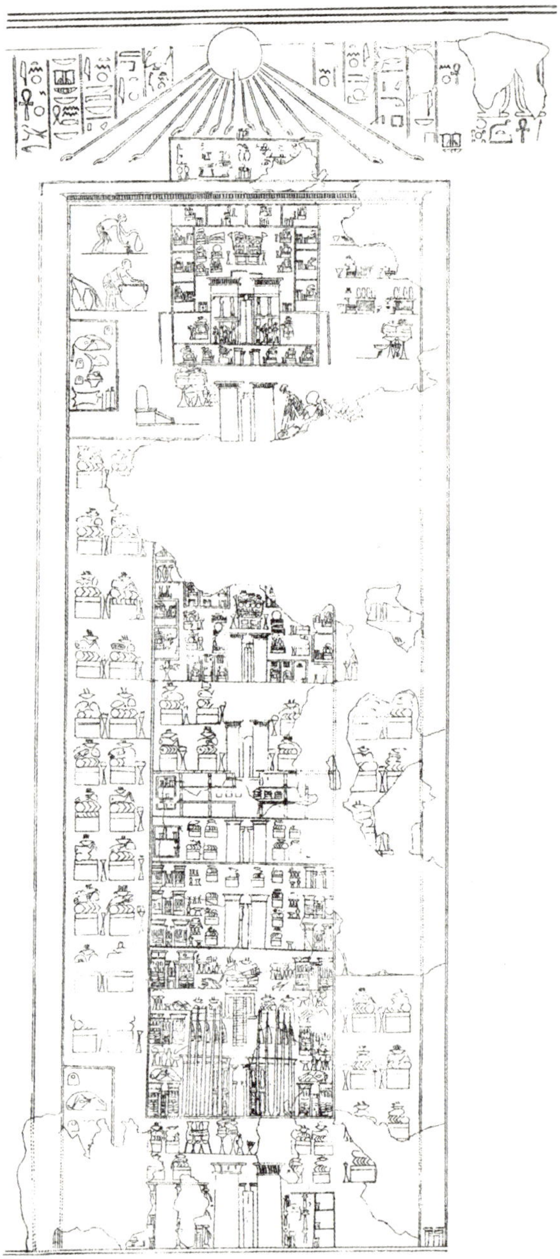

Figure 68. A remarkable, if highly abbreviated, rendering of the Great Aten Temple in the Tomb of Meryre (North Tomb 4; see p. 93). The building possibly called the Gem-pa-aten occupies most of the image, with the temple sanctuary at the top. The vast open grounds inside the temple have been omitted. After Davies, *The Rock Tombs of El Amarna*, Part 1, pl. XA. Image courtesy of the Egypt Exploration Society.

Tomb 2. Meryre (II), "Royal Scribe, Steward, Overseer of the Two Treasuries, Overseer of the Royal Harim of Nefertiti"

Meryre (II) held similar positions to Huya, owner of North Tomb 1, but in the household of Queen Nefertiti. It may be no coincidence that their tombs lie together. Meryre's tomb (fig. 69) contains an important, but poorly preserved, scene of Smenkhkare and Meritaten (Akhenaten's eldest daughter) together as king and queen. It also includes a more detailed version of the "foreign tribute" scene shown in the Tomb of Huya.

Façade. The façade of the tomb is largely destroyed, but originally had an inscribed doorframe.

Entrance to the outer hall **(1, 2)**. The sides of the entrance are badly damaged. Figures of Meryre once stood in an attitude of adoration. The texts were Hymns to the Aten. The one on the east (2) is dedicated to the setting sun.

Outer hall. Both papyrus stem columns remain intact in the outer hall. The pit in the northeast corner and the recess in the north wall may not be original.

Following the scenes counterclockwise from the doorway:

(3): A richly detailed reward scene at a Window of Appearance (see fig. 17). Akhenaten and Nefertiti appear in the Window beneath the Aten's rays, leaning on a balcony decorated with figures of bound captives. To the left are five princesses: Ankhesenpaaten, Neferneferuaten the Younger, and Neferneferure above, and Meritaten and Meketaten below, assisting with the presentation. The tomb owner, Meryre, stands at the bottom right of the Window receiving a gold collar.

To the right of the Window, rows of figures fill a courtyard. Note the foreign princes in the second register down, chariots and standard-bearers in the third and fourth, and scribes writing in the fifth register. The two lowest registers, running beneath the Window, record Meryre's homecoming. At the bottom he arrives in his chariot, female musicians behind him. Before him is his house and garden, the latter containing a T-shaped pool. Above, food rations from the palace are displayed on tables, and the household greets Meryre, as grooms tend to his chariot.

(4): The Reception of Foreign Tribute. This is a more detailed version of the scene in Huya's tomb (North Tomb 1). In the center, Akhenaten and Nefertiti sit together holding hands on a canopied platform, their six daughters standing behind them. Neferneferure holds a tiny pet gazelle.

A group of officials (one of them Meryre?) climbs the right-hand staircase to the platform. Beneath the platform stand two royal carrying-chairs with decorative lion and sphinx figures, also shown in Huya's tomb. Two registers of bodyguard troops, some of them with curved sticks and hair feathers, appear below. There are royal chariots, more Egyptian soldiers, and three sacrificial oxen further to the bottom right.

The foreign tribute appears to the right and left of the platform. On the right it occupies the top six registers, and comprises tribute from the Kingdom of Kush (in Nubia). The top register contains specimens of the gifts being offered. Note, on the left, a yoke draped with skins and gold rings, and a golden bowl from which decorative palm trees emerge. Other items include bags of gold dust, shields, and bows. More of these commodities are carried by figures in the registers below. Note also the panther and wild oxen, yoked slaves (see fig. 25), and men who may be Egyptian soldiers or more Nubians, shown wrestling and dancing.

To the left of the platform, the tribute of the other regions occupies the full height of the wall, in nine registers. At the top are specimen presents: weapons, chariots, and two horses from Syria–Palestine. Below are five more registers depicting tribute-bearers from the same area. Note the animals, including a lion, in the third register from the top; in the fourth, another chariot and horses, and two girl slaves standing at the front; elaborate vessels in the fifth; manacled prisoners in the sixth.

Below them all is a register with men dressed in long loincloths from the land of Punt (probably modern Eritrea), bearing incense in piles and modeled into fancy shapes, including that of calves. In the next register down is a row of Libyans, ostrich feathers in

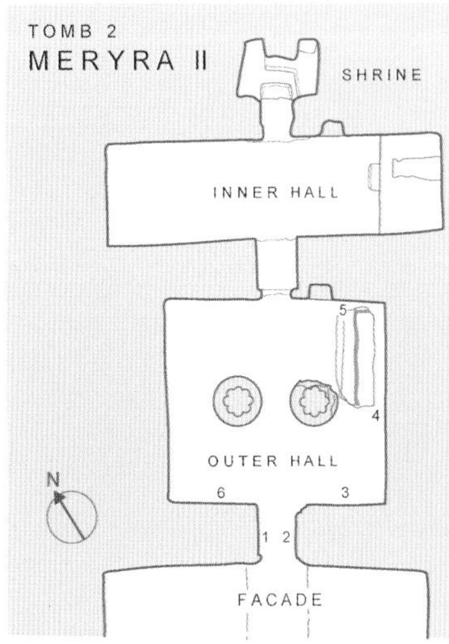

Figure 69. North Tomb 2: Meryre II. Illustration by Mary Shepperson (after Davies, *The Rock Tombs of El Amarna*, Part 2, pl. XXVIII).

their hair, who bring ostrich eggs and feathers as their tribute. The bottom register shows men bringing elaborate vessels of precious metals. These may be Hittites, Egypt's principal enemy at this time. Although the gifts are depicted as tribute, the people of Punt and the Hittites would have sent their goods as part of diplomatic gift exchange or trade. Neither country was subject to Egypt.

(5): Meryre rewarded by Smenkhkare and Meritaten. This important but poorly preserved scene is one of the key pieces of evidence for the reign of Smenkhkare near the end of the Amarna period. Meryre is on the left, above a recess cut later in the wall. The ceremony takes places at a Window of Appearance in the palace, shown in the top right corner. The royal figures, sketched in ink, are now barely visible. Traces of their cartouches can just be seen above the image of the palace. These were still readable in the 19th century and copies made at this time show that the queen was Meritaten and the king Smenkhkare.

(6): Akhenaten sits on a stool beneath an ornate canopy, holding out a cup. Nefertiti fills it with a liquid, probably wine, passing it through a strainer held in her other hand. Three daughters are present: Meritaten in front, Ankhesenpaaten above and behind, and probably Meketaten below. At the foot of the scene is a group of musicians.

Inner hall. Unfinished and undecorated, with the burial shaft roughly blocked out.

Shrine. Also unfinished and undecorated, although the stepped-out stone at the back marks the first stages in cutting a seated statue of Meryre.

Tomb 3. Ahmes, "True Scribe of the King, Fan-bearer on the King's Right Hand, Steward of the Estate of Akhenaten"

Ahmes's tomb is less ambitious than many of the Amarna tombs, but it was cut with great care and precision (fig. 70). It preserves excellent examples of artists' grids and outlines, showing the preliminary steps taken to prepare the wall reliefs.

Many Greek graffiti can also be seen scratched on the walls of the tomb. Most are thought to be from the Ptolemaic period (332–30 BC) and record the names of visitors, including several from Thrace who were perhaps mercenary soldiers. The most interesting reads: "Having ascended here, Catullinus has engraved this in the doorway, marveling at the art of the holy quarriers."

Looking down to the low desert from outside the tomb, you will see a straight strip several meters wide and edged with stones heading off in the direction of the river. This is one of the ancient roadways that Ahmes and his fellow officials would have sped along in their chariots to inspect progress on their tombs.

Façade **(1)**. The doorway was originally surrounded by a simple frame containing prayers and figures of Ahmes adoring cartouches, but these are now barely visible.

Entrance to the outer hall **(2, 3)**. Ahmes stands in an attitude of adoration with two symbols of his office slung over his shoulder: a tall fan and an axe, hanging downward. The texts are abbreviated versions of the Hymn to the Aten. Look up to see some of the original painted ceiling.

Outer hall. The wall surfaces here were given a fine coating of plaster to improve the poor-quality rock. The decoration was then drawn over this in red paint before being carved into the plaster and rock.

On the right side of the outer hall **(4)** only a few traces of paint survive. In the upper register, the royal family visits the Great Aten Temple. The scene is in yellow paint and barely visible. Opposite, on the left side of the hall **(5)**, is an abbreviated architectural drawing of the temple itself. Immediately in front of the building are two short rows of seated male musicians. Below the temple is a butchery yard and to its right a low platform supporting the sacred *benben*-stone (a symbol of the sun), with rounded top. Beyond a damaged patch to the right come four lines of soldiers in two groups, running in a stooping posture before the royal chariot. A trumpeter stands at the front and an officer with a baton runs at the back of each line. Each line contains Egyptian soldiers toward the front and a few foreign soldiers behind: Syrians (with pointed beards), a Libyan (with feather in his hair), and Nubians (with closely cropped hair and earrings). Some soldiers carry standards. Further still to the right **(6)** is the partially complete red outline of the king and queen riding in a chariot.

In the lower register, only a partially finished area at the left end survives (5). It begins with a depiction of a palace. Note the king's bedroom in the top left-hand corner, with bed, mattress, headrest, and steps carefully depicted. In the center, a group of girls relaxes, some of them playing musical instruments. To the right are traces of large-scale figures of Akhenaten (right) and Nefertiti (left), seated and eating a meal. One princess sits on the queen's lap, another on a stool below her chair.

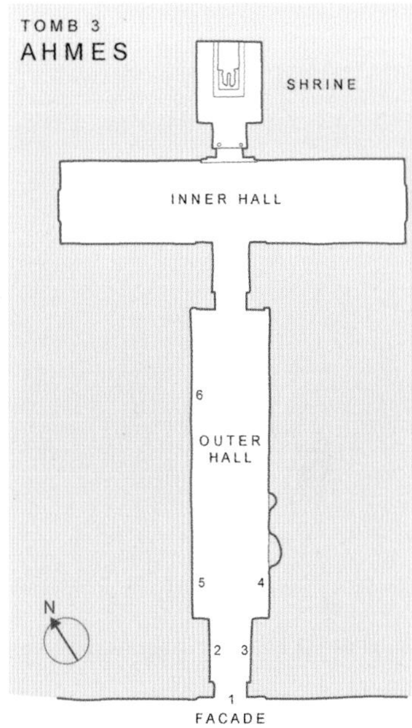

Figure 70. North Tomb 3: Ahmes. Illustration by Mary Shepperson (after Davies, *The Rock Tombs of El Amarna*, Part 3, pl. XXVI).

Inner hall. The inner hall is undecorated, but contains one finished and one unfinished burial shaft at its ends, beneath imitation doorways carved in the rock.

Shrine. A seated statue of Ahmes was carved at the back, although this is now badly damaged. Note the pivot holes in the floor of the entrance, which indicate that the shrine was once closed by wooden doors.

IN FOCUS: APPROACHING DEATH IN A TIME OF RELIGIOUS CHANGE

Egyptologists have long puzzled over how Akhenaten's religious reforms affected people's beliefs of what happened after death. It is a difficult question to answer. Most of the religious texts from Amarna concentrate on the life-giving aspects of the Aten and say little about how death was to be understood. They imply that the deceased no longer joined the gods of the underworld for eternity, with Osiris, even in his solar form, no longer appearing in tomb decoration. With him went the "judgment of the deceased," famously known from the "weighing of the heart" scenes in the Book of the Dead. The sun god seems no longer to have made his cyclical journey through the netherworld, a journey that the dead could join. The deceased appear, instead, to have remained in the world of the living, sleeping at night until they were rejuvenated at dawn to worship the sun god. Nighttime is painted in the Hymn to the Aten as a time of chaos and danger.

Rather than Osiris and the gods of the underworld, it is images of the royal family that dominate the decoration in the elite tombs, as though the tomb owner hoped the king would encourage the Aten to grant him an afterlife. In short texts, tomb owners petition Akhenaten, Nefertiti, and the Aten to receive a proper burial and offerings (fig. 71), and to see the sun god after death. The tombs contain shrines with statues of the tomb owner where offerings would be left, and some of the elite dead probably received offerings in the city's sun temples, too.

Excavation at Amarna non-elite cemeteries, where the dead were buried in simple pits in the desert sand, adds nuance to this picture. A small number of burials used painted wooden coffins. Some are decorated in a style that continued established coffin iconography, showing traditional funerary gods and texts that associate the deceased with Osiris (fig. 72). Others are decorated in a remarkable new style devoid of traditional funerary gods and texts connected with Osiris. They show, instead, human figures carrying offerings and simple offering texts, as though their owners, or those responsible for the burial, were aligning themselves with Akhenaten's version of the solar cult. Some of the dead were buried beneath a tiny stone pyramid, a solar motif, as though seeking a place in the company of the sun god after death. The non-elite dead, at least, may have had some flexibility in terms of which gods they called upon when approaching the transition from life to the afterlife at Akhetaten. —AS

Figure 71. The Tomb of Huya (North Tomb 1) is rare at Amarna for showing details of funerary rites for the deceased. Mourners lament as a huge pile of offerings is stacked in front of the mummy of Huya and a libation is poured for him. After Davies, *The Rock Tombs of El Amarna*, Part 3, pl. XXII. Image courtesy of the Egypt Exploration Society.

Tomb 4. Meryre, "High Priest of the Aten in Akhetaten, Fanbearer on the Right Hand of the King"

Meryre was the most senior priest at Akhetaten and his tomb is one of the grandest (fig. 73). The tomb includes detailed scenes of the Great Aten Temple and the royal family worshiping the sun god.

In early Christian times, stone dwellings were built in front of the tomb. Notice also the many small holes in walls inside the tomb. These were used to hold pegs and other fittings to make the tomb a more functional living space at this time.

Figure 72. A jackal-headed god, probably Duamutef, one of the four "Sons of Horus," carefully painted on a coffin from one of the Amarna cemeteries. Photo courtesy of the Amarna Project.

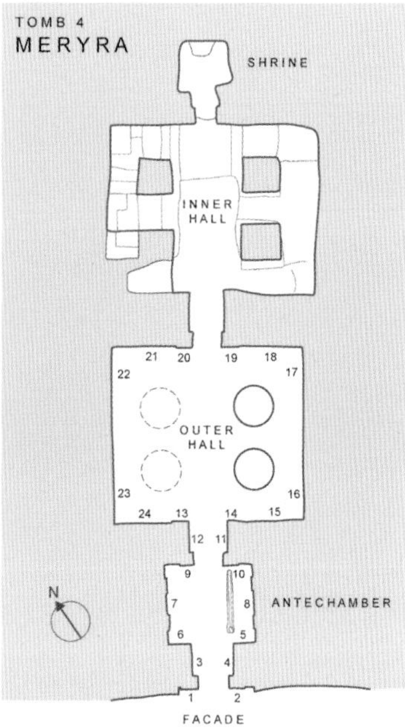

Figure 73. North Tomb 4: Meryre. Illustration by Mary Shepperson (after Davies, *The Rock Tombs of El Amarna*, Part 1, pl. I).

Façade. The façade of Meryre's tomb would once have been very impressive.

The doorway into the tomb bore prayers to the Aten and royal family **(1, 2)**; although these are now almost obliterated, their remains are protected behind the casing of the modern doorway. Notice the elaborate cornice above the door, made from a row of carved blocks set into the cliff face.

Entrance to antechamber **(3, 4)**. Meryre stands, offering a prayer to the Aten when it rises. Look up to see the remains of painted patterns on the ceiling.

Antechamber. Meryre's tomb had an extra chamber between its entranceway and outer hall, adding to the grandeur of the tomb. Around the sides of its entrance **(5, 6)**, Meryre offers a prayer to the king. Inside **(7, 8)**, false doorways have been roughly carved, bordered by panels decorated with cartouches of the Aten, Akhenaten, and Nefertiti, or with tall bouquets of flowers. Around the north doorway **(9, 10)** is a lintel, originally showing Meryre kneeling to adore cartouches.

Entrance to the outer hall. On the right side **(11)**, Meryre stands in an attitude of adoration. The accompanying text is the Shorter Hymn to the Aten. On the left side **(12)**, Meryre's wife, Tenra, offers another prayer to the Aten. She wears a tall "perfume cone" on her head.

Outer hall. Originally four columns supported the roof, each one in the form of a bundle of papyrus stems. The two on the left have been removed, perhaps in Christian times. Beside the doorway **(13, 14)** are cartouches, with a small panel at the bottom showing Meryre kneeling and offering a prayer. On the lintel, Meryre kneels to adore the cartouches of the Aten, Akhenaten, and Nefertiti, which have been defaced, presumably by Akhenaten's successors.

Following the scenes counterclockwise from the doorway:

(15): Akhenaten, Nefertiti, and two daughters (Meritaten and Meketaten) make offerings to the Aten. Meryre, as High Priest, is the first of two bowing figures beside the offerings. Note the unusual depiction of the Aten itself, where there are two arcs below the sun disc. It is not clear what they represent. Below the main scene are two narrower registers depicting priests, attendants, and, at the bottom right, a beautifully carved group of blind male musicians.

(16, 17, 18): This scene, like its companion opposite, runs along the side wall and on to the end wall. The subject matter, in two registers, consists largely of detailed architectural scenes. Above right (16) is a depiction of a palace in the Central City, with the Window of Appearance in the center of the second register from the bottom. To the left is a group of waiting chariots, shade-bearers (below), and a bodyguard (above) including Nubians, Syrians, and Libyans. Further left comes the outer court of a temple, in which Akhenaten, Nefertiti, and four princesses worship the Aten. Below a pile of offerings is a butchery yard, and underneath the princesses is a small building with its own Window of Appearance.

Below right (16), the scene begins with local city details. Above is a cattle yard, where oxen are fattened by hand (see fig. 19, left). Look for the tethering stones below the heads of the animals, and the rows of stone feeding troughs along the top. Below is the riverbank, where thirteen boats are moored to wooden stakes. Note the stepped gangways. To the left is a courtyard in which Meryre is receiving rewards of gold collars from Akhenaten and the royal family.

Above left (17) is the Great Aten Temple. At the top and bottom, thus on either side of the building, are lines of individual offering tables. The main entrance to the temple is between two pylons fitted with flagpoles and streamers. Beyond (i.e., to the left) is a courtyard containing a large altar with access ramp, then further courts and altars interrupted by a colonnade. Below left (17) are two storage buildings. The first appears to consist of two courtyards containing threshing floors piled high with grain. Behind is a line of trees, their trunks protected by low brick walls in which gaps have been left (similar structures can be seen in Egyptian villages today). The second building is a great storehouse, consisting of four rows of long chambers, their entrances shaded by colonnades and trees. In a central court stands a platform with canopy and ramp. Inside the storerooms are pottery jars, round loaves, cushion-shaped ingots of metal, chests, sacks, fish, bins of grain, and so on.

On the upper part of the northeast wall (18) is the temple sanctuary, fronted by a row of rectangular basins. In the right-hand corner is an isolated platform with a ramp supporting the sacred *benben*-stone, in front of which is a seated statue of the king. Below is a butchery yard. A group of blind male harpers occupies the top right-hand corner. The forecourt of the sanctuary contains rows of columns between which stand more statues of the king. Below this scene is another building complex set amid trees (fig. 74). The upper, and somewhat damaged, part is perhaps Meryre's own house. Note the stable with horses feeding from a trough just below the damaged area to the left, and the garden with a central pond. At the top left edge, partly damaged, is a rectangular well with steps. You can just make out the bucket, rope, and end of the long wooden arm of a water hoist (modern Arabic: *shaduf*). This is the earliest depiction of this device known from Egypt. *Shadufs* were still used into the 20th century AD. Two more rectangular pools are shown at the bottom of the scene.

(19, 20): Around the doorway are prayers and adoration by Meryre.

(21, 22, 23): This scene matches the one opposite, in that it runs across two walls. The subject is the royal visit to the Central City. (21): One object of the visit is a temple to the Aten, again probably the Great Aten Temple. It is here depicted on a small scale in a vertical diagram, with the sanctuary at the top (see fig. 68). Note the pylon entrance at the bottom, with its flagpoles, and the main altar just above, the staircase and ramp shown in a head-on view. To the left, temple staff prepare to meet the king. The uppermost two groups are female musicians. (22, 23): In the center of the scene, Akhenaten and Nefertiti arrive in separate chariots. The king's chariot, with its harness, is shown in considerable detail. A decorated case for a bow is slung on the side of each chariot. In front of the chariots are running bodyguards carrying weapons and, in the top and bottom rows, military standards (fig. 21). The men in the third row down carry flails. Behind the queen's chariot come two more chariots, each with a pair of princesses: Meritaten and Meketaten below, and Ankhesenpaaten and Neferneferuaten the Younger above (see fig. 24). Pairs of female attendants follow in more chariots. In the top left-hand corner is another depiction of a palace (see fig. 107). Note in the top right corner of the building a servant sprinkling water on the ground and a Window of Appearance in the center of the building.

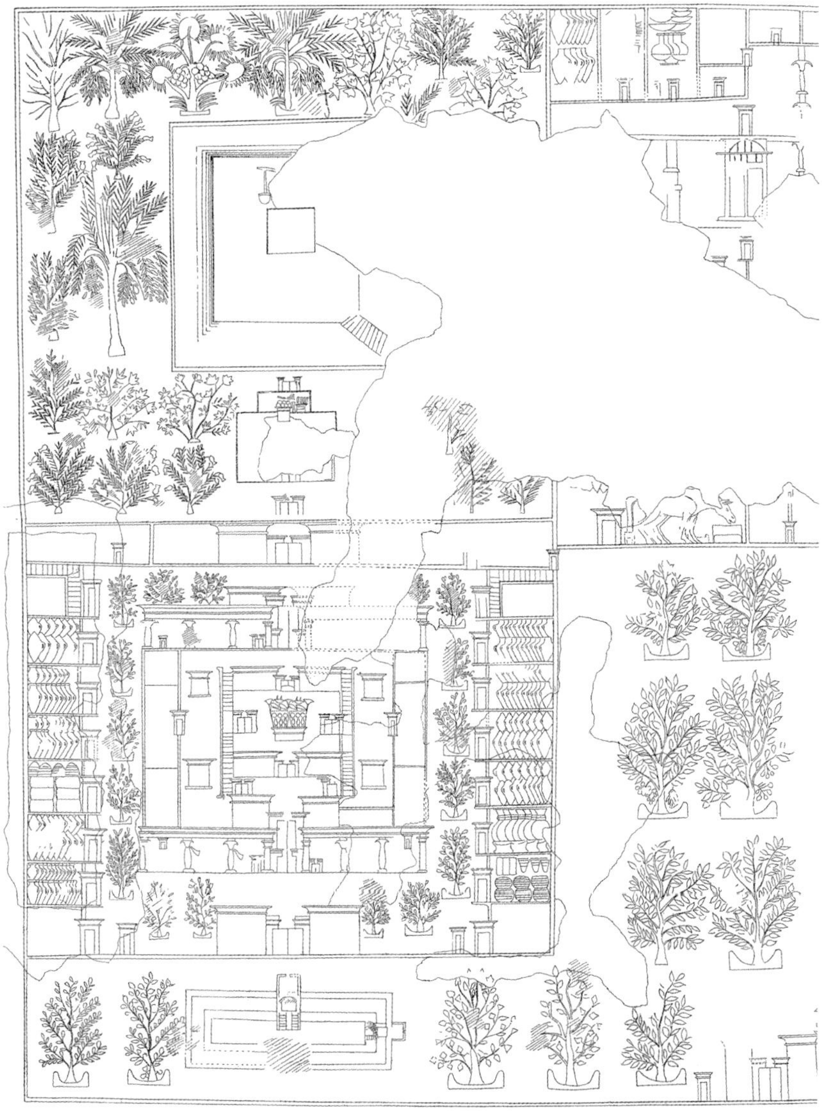

Figure 74. An elaborate garden shown in the Tomb of Meryre. Note the *shaduf*—a water-lifting device—at the top left, inside the square well. After Davies, *The Rock Tombs of El Amarna*, Part 1, pl. XXXII. Image courtesy of the Egypt Exploration Society.

On the left end wall is a large detailed Window of Appearance scene. Note the spotted cushions on which the royal family lean. Rows of attendants and scribes bow before the royal couple.

Inner hall and shrine. The intention was to cut an inner hall with four columns, but the work was abandoned at a fairly early stage. The space shows, however, how the stonecutters worked: removing the stone in complete rectangular blocks, perhaps for use elsewhere. The shrine at the back is likewise at a preliminary stage.

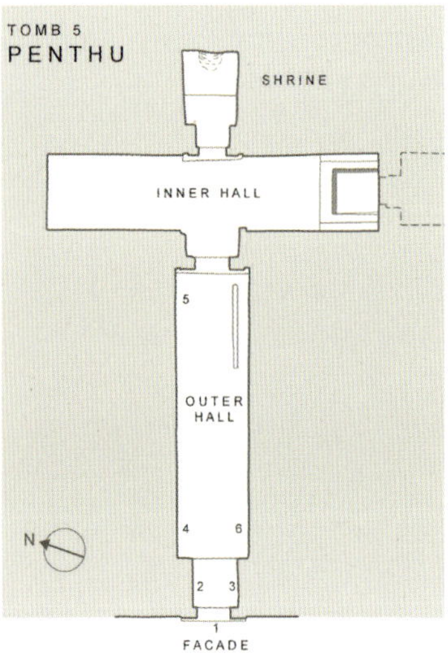

Figure 75. North Tomb 5: Penthu. Illustration by Mary Shepperson (after Davies, *The Rock Tombs of El Amarna*, Part 4, Egypt Exploration Society, pl. I).

Tomb 5. Penthu, "Royal Scribe, First under the King, Chief Servitor of the Aten in the Estate of the Aten in Akhetaten, Chief of Physicians"

The Tomb of Penthu (fig. 75) contains stylized scenes of the royal family worshiping at an Aten temple. Much of the decoration was cut into a layer of plaster that covered the poor-quality rock. Parts of the plaster have now deteriorated, but the scenes were originally of high quality.

Façade **(1)**. The doorway was once surrounded by a raised frame containing prayers and figures of Penthu adoring cartouches. Very little is now preserved.

Entrance to the outer hall **(2, 3)**. Penthu stands in an attitude of adoration before texts containing prayers to the Aten, now badly damaged. Several Greek graffiti are scratched over the figure on the left.

Outer hall. The principal decorated wall is on the left, with two registers of scenes. In the upper register **(4, 5)**, the royal family visits an Aten temple. Akhenaten is followed by Nefertiti, then by Meritaten, Meketaten, and another princess. There are attendants and waiting chariots at the left edge. Note the plumes on the heads of the horses belonging to the royal chariot. Beyond and to the right of the royal family is a simplified drawing of an Aten temple. The rays of the Aten pass through and behind the gateway. Within the temple there are many offering tables on curved legs, stacked with meat offerings. Further to the right, the royal family appears again, rewarding Penthu. Penthu stands in front of Akhenaten, as a servant adjusts the gold collars he has just received. The scene terminates (5) with a picture of the temple sanctuary.

In the lower register (4, 5), the scene begins with images of city life: 19 freight ships, identifiable by their tall masts, are moored at the waterfront. There were once houses, gardens, and chariots above. Further to the right is a badly damaged courtyard in which the king and queen reward Penthu again, under the Aten's rays. Following a damaged area, the scene ends (5) with a depiction of cattle stalls within the courtyard.

The right (south) wall **(6)** had also been laid out in two registers, but only the right end shows traces of decoration. In the upper register, a few patches of paint survive from a scene of the king and queen seated at a meal. Akhenaten was the left figure, eating a pigeon. In the lower register is another reward scene, this time inside the palace. The king sits in a columned hall, the diminutive figure of Penthu in front of him, with an attendant adjusting his gold collars. Details of the palace appear at the far right. Note the depiction of a painted pavement with plant designs around a rectangular basin, above the two talking figures at the bottom. The two niches cut into this wall belong to the sixth to seventh centuries AD, when the tomb was lived in by a Christian community. The long slot in the floor is a loom emplacement from this time.

Inner hall. The inner hall is undecorated but at its right end is a parapet surrounding a shaft, nearly 12m deep, leading to the burial chamber.

Shrine. A rock-cut statue of Penthu was intended at the back, but this has been destroyed.

Follow the path around to the last of the decorated northern tombs, belonging to Panehesy. On the way, you will see some very well-preserved stone structures dating to the early Christian reoccupation of the landscape.

IN FOCUS: CHRISTIAN USE

Two thousand years after the abandonment of Akhetaten, the desert cliffs at the northern perimeter of the site were repopulated by a Christian monastic community. At around the same time, a separate community built a walled monastery just inside the desert to the south of the ancient city at the site of Kom al-Nana. Each community had a very different approach to creating a settlement. The northern monastic group preferred greater isolation, both from the everyday world and from each other. Their individual self-contained dwellings, some reusing dynastic tombs, were scattered from the low desert immediately below the cliffs to the high desert beyond them.

Each of the dynastic tombs provided ready-made interior (usually just the outermost room) and exterior spaces for each monastic dwelling, both of which were modified according to need. In some cases this was minimal, inserting niches (Penthu, North Tomb 5) or a setting for water jars (Meryre, North Tomb 4). More drastic action was taken in the tomb of Huya (North Tomb 1), where one of the columns supporting the roof was removed to provide more light for a loom emplacement on the east side of the outer hall. The numerous loom emplacements that can still be seen throughout the settlement (the long slots cut in the floors and ceilings of the tombs) suggest that weaving went beyond personal needs and was an economic activity for this community. The exterior space was often partially subdivided into rooms built of undressed stone, best seen on the pathway between the tombs of Penthu (North Tomb 5) and Panehesy (North Tomb 6). These were lightly roofed with palm logs and palm leaves, a technique still used in Egyptian villages today. It can be imagined that the monks, just like modern villagers, moved their household tasks between interior and exterior spaces according to the daily and seasonal rhythms of light and heat.

The spiritual and spatial heart of the community was the church, located in the outer hall of the tomb of Panehesy (North Tomb 6). This space, originally organized and decorated according to the conventions of Amarna-period elite funerary monuments, required extensive remodeling. The southern part of the outer hall (the left side on entry) became the nave of the church. The two southern columns were removed, the south wall was cut back, and the southern false door was remodeled into the apse. The floor and remodeled walls were plastered, and the apse and surrounding wall painted with appropriate Christian images, which, in a late phase, focused on a unique six-winged eagle in the semi-dome. The monks probably gathered at the church for weekly and special services but otherwise lived alone or in small households, separated by the challenging landscape. Although isolated, they were interlinked by barely visible physical footpaths and staircases, lines-of-sight between dwellings, and a sense of spiritual community. —GP

Figure 76. An ancient revetted stone pathway separates two early Christian residences at the North Tombs settlement. Photo courtesy of Gillian Pyke/The North Tombs Settlement Project.

Tomb 6. Panehesy, "Chief Servitor of the Aten in the Temple of Aten in Akhetaten"

Panehesy held the great responsibility of preparing offerings for the sun god in the Great Aten Temple. He owned a large house beside the temple and another in the Main City. His tomb (fig. 77) includes scenes showing Panehesy being rewarded by the king, a detailed representation of the Great Aten Temple, and a lively image of the king and queen in their chariots.

In the sixth to seventh centuries AD, the outer hall was made into a church by enlarging it on the northwest side and adding an apse at the end. Several layers of painted wall plaster survive from this period. The ruined building outside the tomb dates to the same time.

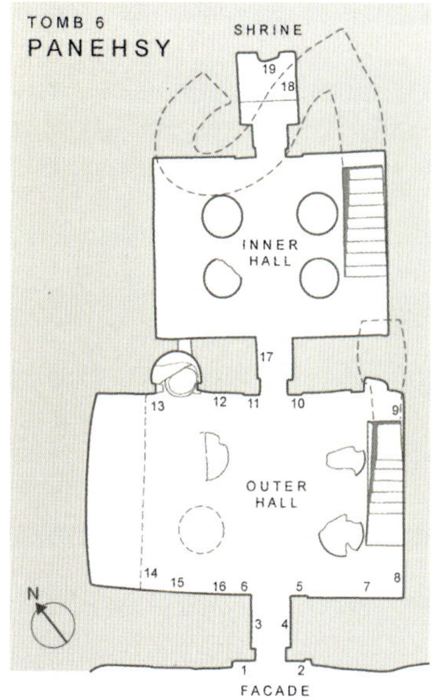

Figure 77. North Tomb 6: Panehesy. Illustration by Mary Shepperson (after Davies, *The Rock Tombs of El Amarna*, Part 2, pl. II).

Façade **(1, 2)**. Around the entrance are scenes of the royal family worshiping the Aten, now protected by the iron facing of the modern door.

Entrance to the outer hall **(3, 4)**. The royal family worships the Aten on each side of the entrance. Below this is a narrow band of figures centered on Nefertiti's sister, Mutnodjmet, accompanied by dwarfs. Beneath, Panehesy offers a prayer to the Aten and to the king.

Outer hall. Around the doorway **(5, 6)** are prayers, while above Panehesy kneels to adore the cartouches of the Aten, Akhenaten, and Nefertiti. Following the scenes counterclockwise from the doorway:

(7): The royal family worships the Aten as chariots and an escort (including Panehesy?) wait below.

(8, 9): The left-hand part of the scene remains unfinished, but the remainder depicts the royal family driving in chariots, accompanied by running soldiers (see fig. 101). Note the harness details on the king's horse. In the top right-hand corner is an image of a palace. In the floor below, a flight of steps leads to a small undecorated burial chamber.

(10, 11): Around the doorway to the inner hall are prayers and adoration by Panehesy.

(12): Akhenaten and Nefertiti make offerings to the Aten, while Panehesy bows underneath. The scene is partly obscured by painted plaster applied in early Christian times when the tomb was used as a church.

(13, 14): The lower part of the wall was also cut away during the early Christian reuse. The surviving upper scene contains an important depiction of an Aten temple, seemingly the Great Aten

Temple. Note, from left to right, the main pylon with flagpoles and the butchery yard above. Akhenaten makes offerings to the Aten on an altar with a ramp, while the rear of the temple (13) is shown as a separate building of courts and offering tables, entered through a columned porch with statues of the king. Above and to the left is an isolated platform with a ramp supporting the sacred *benben*-stone, with a seated statue of the king beside it.

(15, 16): The royal family is shown at a Window of Appearance, rewarding Panehesy. At the bottom, Panehesy is greeted by his household.

Inner hall. This is undecorated except for the left side of the entrance **(17)** where Panehesy appears with his daughter. On the right side of the hall a flight of steps leads down to an undecorated burial chamber.

Shrine. Originally a rock-hewn statue of Panehesy stood at the back, but only the scar remains **(19)**. On the right wall **(18)** is an offering scene. Panehesy sits before a table of offerings accompanied by female members of his family. An unnamed man waits on them.

IN FOCUS: LABORING FOR THE KING?

Near the North Tombs, there are at least three large pit-grave cemeteries for the ordinary people of Akhetaten. All are important for what they tell us of the experiences of everyday life at the ancient city, but one of the cemeteries is particularly remarkable. Those things that make it unusual also help us understand the people who were buried there and what their lives were like.

Lying in the valley that opens between the tombs of Meryre (II) and Ahmes (North Tombs 2 and 3), the North Tombs Cemetery (figs. 78, 79) includes burials of an estimated 3,500 to 5,000 individuals, nearly 75 percent of whom fall into the restricted age range of 11–18 years old at the time of death (fig. 80). In itself, this age distribution sets the cemetery apart from other burial grounds at Amarna, which contain individuals from all age groups from fetuses to old adults (c. 40+ years), as expected of a regular urban population. Another interesting feature of the North Tombs Cemetery demography (the study of population characteristics) is that among the adults in the excavated sample, there are just over three times more females than males. In fact, only 23 adult males have been identified in the cemetery, and everyone older than 20 years old is a female.

Many of the burials here also contained more than one person, probably placed in the grave at the same time, while the burials are very poor, with very few grave goods. This evidence, taken from a widespread sample of graves, suggests that these individuals were part of a specific community at Akhetaten. The marks on the skeletons suggest this selected population was likely a work group performing heavy labor.

The skeletal remains of the young individuals here reflect a life filled with hard work. About 25 percent of the individuals in the excavated sample show signs of joint breakdown, commonly called arthritis, with examples in children as young as six to seven years old. In modern populations, arthritis is not a common condition until mid- to late adulthood. Nearly one-third of the individuals suffered from at least one broken bone in life and most of these fractures occurred in the spine as a result of compression and extension of the back. The youngest individual to exhibit a spinal fracture is six years old. Spinal fractures of these types, compression fractures and spondylolysis, are not typical in otherwise healthy individuals. These are viewed as evidence the population buried here was performing heavy labor including, but not limited to, carrying weighty objects, swinging heavy tools, long-term repetitive use of tools, and possibly being subject to occupational falls due to hazardous work conditions.

Considered together, the demographic characteristics and skeletal remains of the individuals buried here, along with the burial practices, suggest this is the burial ground for a selected group of individuals who may have been separated from their families in a work group situation, and that the work performed was extremely hazardous to individual health, resulting in high frequencies of broken bones, joint degeneration, and early death. The exact nature of the duties performed by this population is not yet known, but it is possible the young people of the North Tombs Cemetery were working in the limestone quarries situated on the high cliffs above their final resting place, among other tasks connected with building and maintaining the city on behalf of the king. —GD

Boundary Stela U

On the way to the Royal Tomb, make sure to stop by Boundary Stela U, one of 16 territorial markers Akhenaten had inscribed around the perimeter of Akhetaten (fig. 81). Looming out of the cliff face, Stela U is one of the most impressive monuments at Amarna (see fig. 8), a testament to the king's efforts to impose order on the natural landscape.

Stela U is the largest of the Boundary Stelae. It reaches nearly 8m in height and has statues of the royal family projecting from the rock

Figure 78. Simple, closely packed pits provide the setting for the burials of young people at the North Tombs Cemetery. Photo courtesy of the Amarna Project.

Figure 79. Archaeologist Wendy Dolling excavates a group burial of three subadults at the North Tombs Cemetery. Photo courtesy of the Amarna Project.

face at its base. The inscription reveals Akhenaten's vision for Akhetaten. He lists the institutions he wants to establish, and events and endowments planned for the sun god. He states that Akhetaten was built on land not previously owned by any other god and vows to repair the Boundary Stelae should they be damaged. He also promises not to extend Akhetaten's boundaries, a statement sometimes misunderstood to mean that he himself would never leave the city.

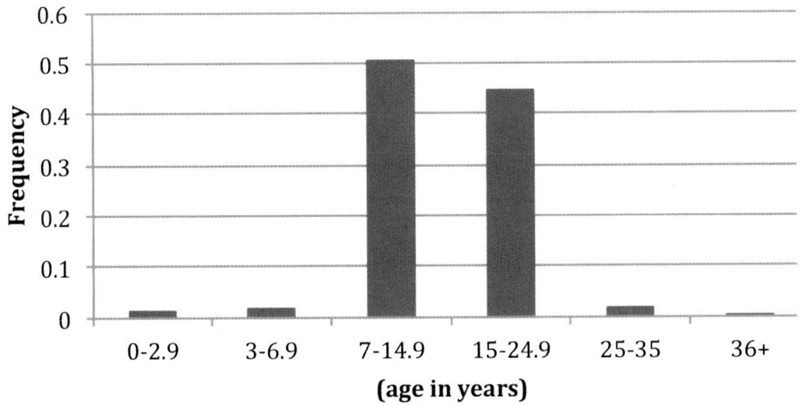

Figure 80. Age distribution of individuals buried at the North Tombs Cemetery. Notice the very high numbers of young individuals. Courtesy of the Amarna Project.

The stelae were inscribed in two phases, in year 5 and year 6 of Akhenaten's reign. Stela U, like most examples, was carved in year 6 and includes a short renewal text dating to the king's eighth year of rule. The dates are listed at the beginning of each text.

Most of the Boundary Stelae are now poorly preserved, having suffered from weathering, the carving-out of images for illegal sale, and damage resulting from the mistaken belief that there is treasure behind the rock face.

Another well-preserved stela (Stela A) can be visited at the west-bank site of Tuna al-Gebel near Mallawi.

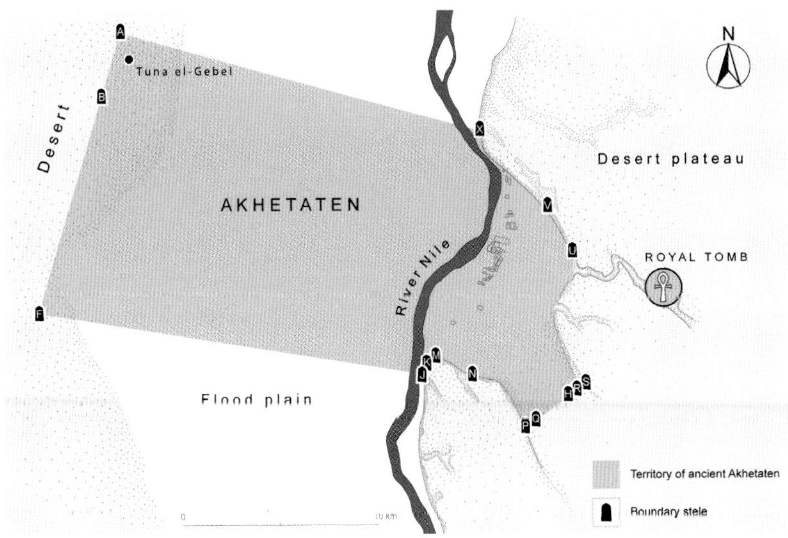

Figure 81. The Amarna Boundary Stelae. Illustration by Mary Shepperson (after Kemp, *The City of Akhenaten and Nefertiti*, fig. 1.6).

Royal Wadi and Tombs

An evocative drive through a winding rocky valley takes you to the original burial place of Akhenaten himself, hidden in the eastern cliffs (figs. 82, 83).

The Royal Tomb lies off the main valley in a smaller side valley. The tomb was badly looted shortly after its discovery in the late 19th century and has since suffered from vandalism and flooding. Many objects from the tomb are now in museums, including those in Cairo, the UK (Fitzwilliam Museum, Royal Scottish Museum, Petrie Museum, Ashmolean Museum, and others), and the USA (Brooklyn Museum, Metropolitan Museum of Art, and others).

Moving the royal burial ground from the Valley of the Kings at Thebes to Akhetaten was one of Akhenaten's most radical moves, although the tomb itself is generally of traditional design. A long sloping corridor leads to the main burial chamber, where Akhenaten himself was buried. Many pieces of burial equipment for the king have been recovered from the tomb, including pieces of sarcophagus, a canopic chest for his internal organs, and over 200 *shabtis* (funerary figurines). The king's burial equipment is also quite traditional, although with certain modifications, such as the removal of images of goddesses on his sarcophagus and of the prayer to Osiris on his *shabti* figures.

A second prominent, unfinished suite of rooms is a more unusual feature of the tomb. It was perhaps intended for Nefertiti, although it is unlikely that she was ever buried here. Only a single *shabti* bearing her name has been recovered from the tomb. Another suite likely served the burial of Princess Meketaten, who is apparently shown being mourned by the royal family in striking and poignant wall reliefs. Two images show nurses holding a baby, suggesting the princess may have died in childbirth. Pieces of a sarcophagus for Meketaten have been recovered from the tomb. The tomb also yielded burial equipment for Queen Tiye, suggesting she, too, might once have been interred here.

Probably in the reign of Tutankhamun, the Royal Tomb was opened and its contents partly transferred to Thebes for reburial in the Valley of the Kings. Several Amarna-period mummies and pieces of burial equipment have been recovered from tombs here, such as KV55.

The Amarna Royal Wadi contains three additional unfinished tombs, presumably intended for other members of the royal family, and a small chamber that was perhaps a store for embalming materials. These are not accessible to the public. One of the tombs, in the main valley, has a steep entrance staircase leading to a large, impressive corridor. The two other tombs, in a side valley, are less complete, one consisting of a long straight corridor passing down through four doorways. There

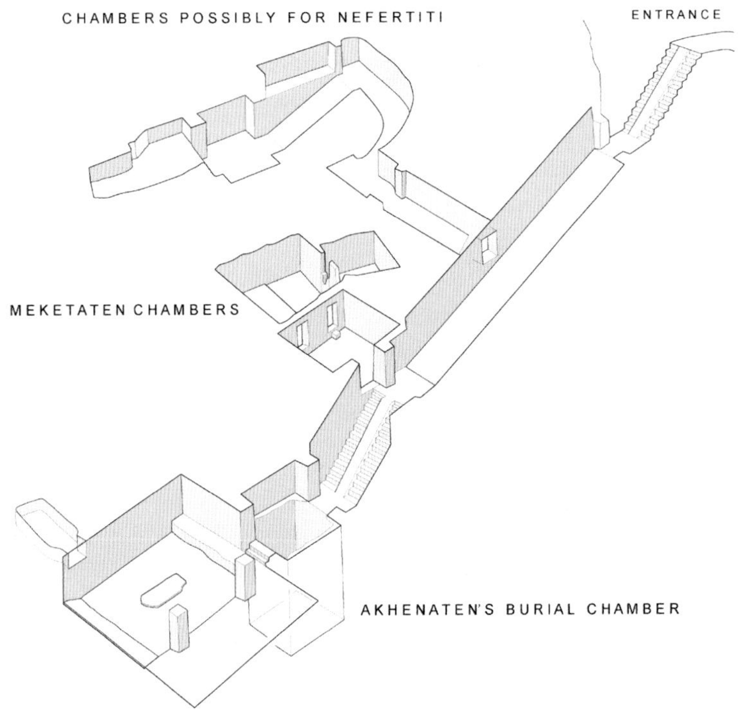

Figure 82. The Amarna Royal Tomb. Illustration by Mary Shepperson (after S. D'Auria, "Preparing for Eternity," in Freed, Markowitz, and D'Auria, *Pharaohs of the Sun: Akhenaten, Nefertiti, Tutankhamun*, fig. 127).

Figure 83. Clearance of the Royal Wadi by the Egypt Exploration Society in the 1930s. EES Amarna Archive Negative 1931–2.A.138. Photo courtesy of the Egypt Exploration Society.

are no inscriptions or reliefs to help us identify which royal individuals the tombs were intended for, but Smenkhkare, Neferneferuaten, Tutankhaten, and Meritaten are among the obvious candidates.

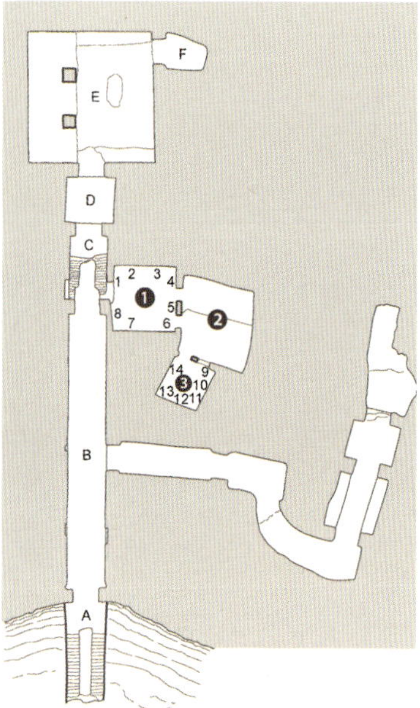

Figure 84. Key to decoration in the Amarna Royal Tomb. Illustration by Mary Shepperson (after G.T. Martin, *The Royal Tomb at El-'Amarna*, vol. 2, *The Reliefs, Inscriptions, and Architecture*, pl. 11A).

The Royal Tomb

The Royal Tomb (fig. 84) is entered by a flight of modern steps, which cover a steep ancient ramp **(A)**, leading to a long sloping corridor **(B)**. Around halfway down the corridor, on the right, a doorway opens onto a long string of corridors and chambers, all unfinished and undecorated. This is the suite possibly intended for Nefertiti, although seemingly never used for a burial.

Continuing down the sloping corridor you will come to a second doorway on the right, just before a flight of steps **(C)**. The doorway leads to the chambers of Meketaten, the first and third of which are decorated. Watch your head as you move through the chambers!

Chamber 1. Following the scenes clockwise:

(1): Remains of seven registers of foreigners raising their arms in adoration of the Aten.

(2, 3): The king, queen, and princesses worship the Aten in a temple as the sun sets in the west, with courtiers below.

(4): Nine registers of soldiers and chariots. Note that in some cases the heads of the horses are in frontal view, rare in Egyptian art.

(5): Originally seven registers of soldiers, some of them foreign, raising their hands in adoration of the Aten, depicted on the adjacent wall.

(6, 7): The king, queen, and princesses worship the Aten in a temple as the sun rises over the eastern horizon (fig. 85). Attendants and chariots wait outside. Birds and animals rejoice in the sun's rays at the left end, beyond the temple.

(8): Two registers (fig. 86) originally showed the king and queen mourning a deceased female lying on a bier (bottom left). The figure is not named here, but she is usually assumed to be Princess Meketaten, who is named in a similar mourning scene in chamber 3. The king and queen weep over the corpse, with distraught attendants behind. In the upper part of the scene, a nurse holds an infant, usually assumed to be the princess's baby. The mourning scenes in the Meketaten chambers in the Amarna Royal Tomb convey a depth of royal emotion that is unique in Egyptian art.

Chamber 2. On two levels and left undecorated.

Chamber 3. Following the scenes clockwise:

(9): Remains of pictures of funerary furniture beside the doorway.

(10, 11): A second scene of mourning a dead princess on a funerary bed (fig. 87). Mourners, including two princesses (?), lament beside

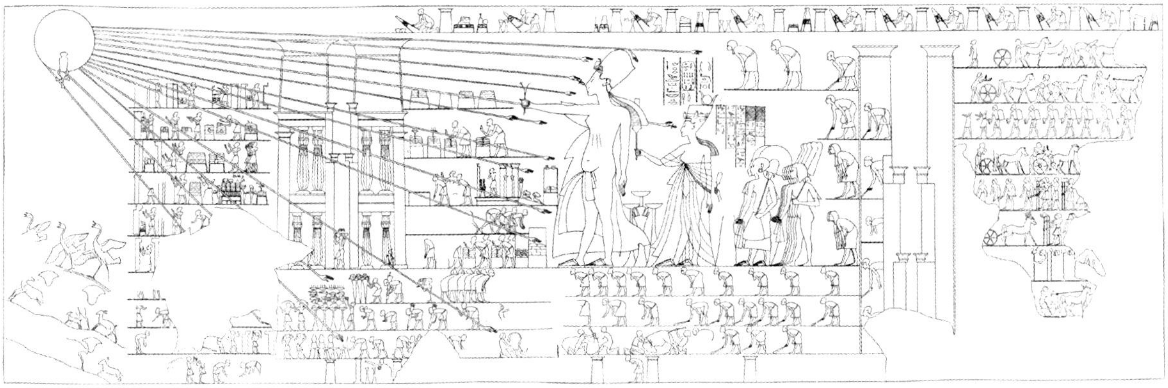

Figure 85. Akhenaten and Nefertiti worship the Aten as it rises in the eastern horizon. After U. Bouriant, G. Legrain, and G. Jéquier (1903), *Monuments pour servir à l'étude du culte d'Atonou en Egypte. Tome premier. Les tombes de Khouitatonou* (Cairo: Imprimerie de l'Institut français d'archéologie orientale), pl. 1.

Figure 86. The royal family mourns a reclining figure, usually thought to be Meketaten, as an attendant holds a child. After Bouriant, Legrain, and Jéquier, *Monuments pour servir à l'étude du culte d'Atonou en Egypte*. Tome premier, pl. 6.

the bed. Funerary offerings are shown. One of the standing attendants in the middle register again held a child, no longer clearly visible.

(12, 13): The deceased Meketaten stands on a pedestal beneath a canopy decorated with leaves (fig. 88). The king, queen, princesses, attendants, and courtiers stand in front. The style of the canopy is similar to examples shown in scenes of birthing rituals, raising the possibility that Meketaten died while giving birth to the child shown in the previous scene. (13): Further scenes of mourners, mostly male and in animated postures of grief, and in the lowest register offerings of food and drink.

Figure 87. An early copy of the poorly preserved scene of mourning attendants in chamber 3 of the Royal Tomb, showing one of them cradling a child in her arms—perhaps the same infant as shown in chamber 1. After Bouriant, Legrain, and Jéquier, *Monuments pour servir à l'étude du culte d'Atonou en Egypte*. Tome premier, pl. 7.

Figure 88. Meketaten, seemingly deceased, stands in a shrine decorated with floral motifs of fertility and regeneration, as the royal family looks on in distress. After Martin, *The Royal Tomb at El-'Amarna*, vol. 2, pl. 68. Image courtesy of the Egypt Exploration Society.

Continuing back down the main corridor you reach a shaft 3.5m deep **(D)**. Faint traces of decoration survive on the walls above the shaft: the side walls showed Akhenaten and Nefertiti making offerings to the Aten and the end walls depicted one or more of the princesses.

Beyond the shaft is Akhenaten's burial chamber **(E)**, with raised platform on the left, and the remains of two square pillars. Note also the rectangular plinth in the middle of the room, now below the level of the modern floor, where the king's sarcophagus once stood. In the far right-hand corner when you enter is a further unfinished chamber. The rock is of poor quality, so that much of the decoration was wholly or partly cut into a thin layer of gypsum plaster. Very little of the decoration is preserved now. The clearest scene is on your left as you enter, where large-scale figures of Akhenaten and Nefertiti worshiping the Aten can be seen.

North Suburb

Head back from the cliffs through the town of al-Till to reach the temples and palaces of the Central City. Note the turnoff to the Visitor Centre just before you cross the large drainage channel.

Al-Till is built over the North Suburb, the modern name given to one of the main residential areas of Akhetaten (fig. 89). Driving through al-Till, areas of ruined ancient houses can still be seen, interspersed with large spoil heaps left from archaeological excavations in the early 20th century. In part, the North Suburb may have housed scribes and bureaucrats who worked in the Central City, just to the south.

Figure 89. An aerial photograph of the North Suburb taken by the Royal Egyptian Airforce in 1932. Photo from B. Kemp, *The City of Akhenaten and Nefertiti*, fig. 5.6.

Figure 90. A colorful reimagining of life in the North Suburb by Richard Leacroft, based on the ground plan of excavated houses and an original reconstruction drawing by Seton Lloyd (see H. Frankfort and J.D.S. Pendlebury, *The City of Akhenaten*, Part 2, *The North Suburb and the Desert Altars*, pl. XVII).

Figure 91. The area of the North Suburb on which the reconstruction drawing (fig. 90) is based. Notice the well-preserved ancient staircase leading down to a desert channel (which, contrary to the reconstruction drawing, is unlikely to have held water). EES Amarna Archive Negative 1930 1.A.140. Photo courtesy of the Egypt Exploration Society.

Figure 92. This huge stone lintel once spanned a doorway in the villa of the "chief builder" Hatiay in the North Suburb. On the lintel, Hatiay is shown worshiping the cartouches of the Aten, Akhenaten, and Nefertiti. The cartouches of Akhenaten were later hacked out. EES Amarna Archive Negatives 1930–1.O.70, 114. Photos courtesy of the Egypt Exploration Society.

With over 1,000 houses excavated, Amarna is one of Egypt's most important archaeological sites for learning about everyday life in the past (figs. 90, 91). Only rarely can we identify the owners of individual houses, although important officials tended to inscribe their names and occupations around the doorways of their homes. The North Suburb included the home of Hatiay, one of Akhenaten's chief builders, whose house was excavated in the 1930s (fig. 92). Officials like Hatiay lived in large villas with walled courtyards, although most people lived in far more modest houses, of which there are many examples in the North Suburb.

CENTRAL CITY

The road between the towns of al-Till and al-Hagg Qandil takes you through the ancient Central City (figs. 93, 94), the hub of Akhetaten and, by far, the most intact urban center to survive from ancient Egypt. The huge mud-brick ruins along the riverbank mark the Great Palace, with temples, a smaller palace, workshops, and offices opposite.

From here, Akhenaten and his court maintained the cult of the Aten, administered Egypt, and negotiated international trade and diplomacy, connecting Akhetaten to the world beyond. Imagine the air thick with the sounds of construction and industry as Akhenaten's temples and palaces took shape, bakeries and butchery yards churned out offerings for the sun god, and workshops produced decorative faience and glass for the king's buildings.

The ruined appearance of the Central City today is a result of the stonework being removed after Akhenaten's death, although the mud-brick buildings survive in better condition. The stylized scenes of the city's temples and palaces in the rock-cut tombs provide invaluable clues to the original appearance of these important complexes, although the images are often difficult to link precisely with buildings and features on the ground.

Great Aten Temple

Your first point of call in the Central City is the Great Aten Temple (fig. 95). This was the ritual centerpiece of Akhenaten's city: a vast open-air complex designed to sustain the Aten. The temple was, in some ways, of traditional design, formed of a series of courts leading to the sanctuary. But while temple courts usually led to a dark enclosed sanctuary with a statue of the patron god, the effect at the Aten temples was the opposite.

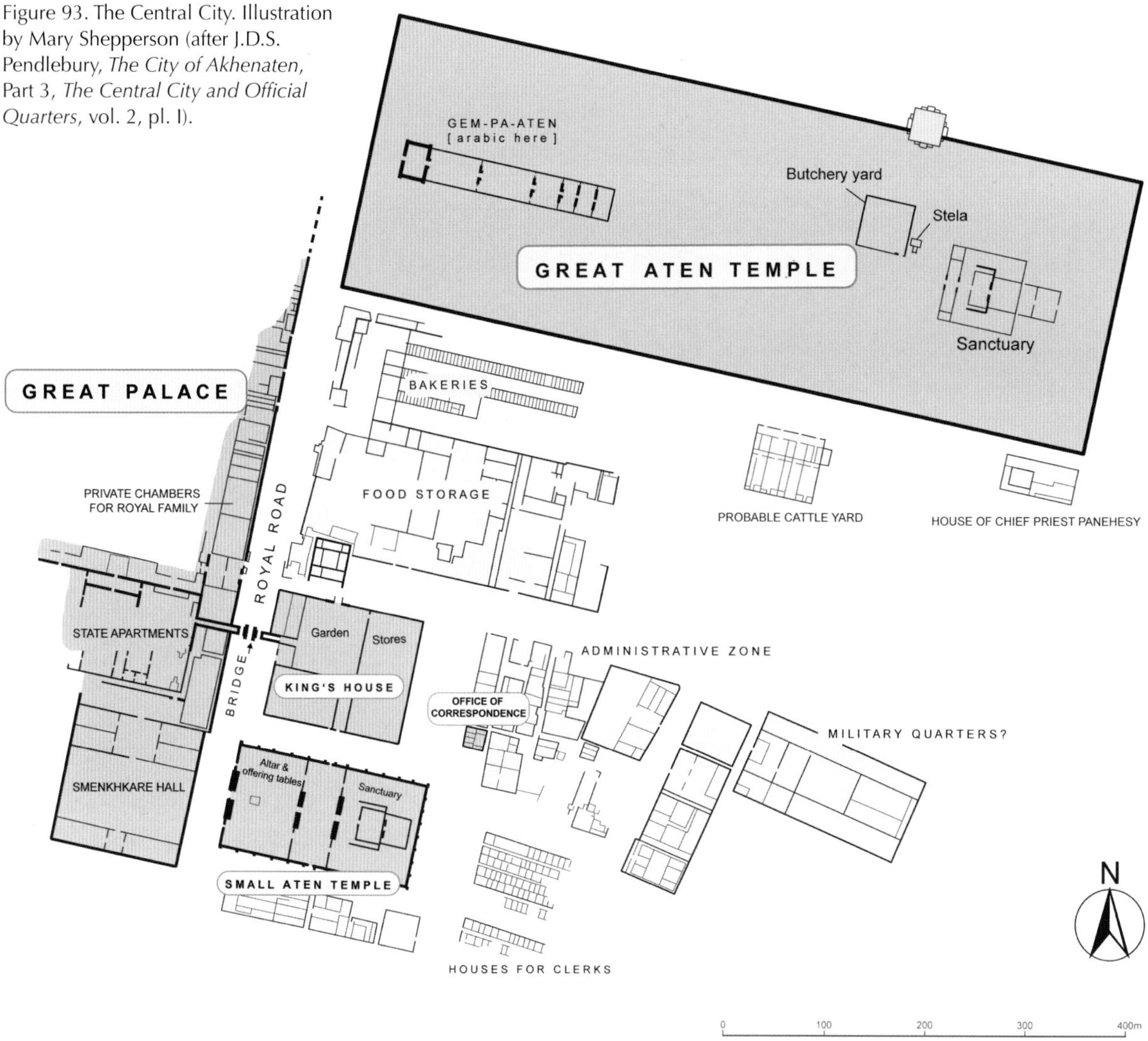

Figure 93. The Central City. Illustration by Mary Shepperson (after J.D.S. Pendlebury, *The City of Akhenaten*, Part 3, *The Central City and Official Quarters*, vol. 2, pl. I).

The complex had no roofs, so that the light of the sun god penetrated the temple, and no statue of the god was required.

While not a lot of the Great Aten Temple is visible above ground today, archaeological excavations and scenes in the rock-cut tombs help us envisage how this great complex functioned. At the front of the temple, now partly reconstructed, stood a building probably known as the Gem-pa-aten ("Discovery of the Aten"), one of the buildings listed on Akhenaten's Boundary Stelae. It was built of talatat blocks, carved and brightly painted. A façade fronted with flagpoles led to several

Figure 94 A model of ancient Amarna showing the buildings of the Central City. The huge white complex is the Great Palace—viewed here from the northwest—running along the banks of the river. The model was created by Tetra (Andy Ingham Associates) to designs by Mallinson Architects. It can be seen in the Amarna Visitor Centre. Photo courtesy of David Grandorge.

sequential courts filled with offering tables. Many hundreds more offering tables originally flanked the courts outside. The huge open space in the temple begs the question: did the people of Akhetaten gather here to leave gifts for the sun god?

Some 800m beyond this—behind the modern structures—lay the sanctuary (fig. 96), a place for the king and sun god to communicate. It originally featured a grove of trees and a mud-brick altar, but later in Akhenaten's reign a stone building was erected and filled with open-air offering tables. In front of the sanctuary stood a quartzite stela (probably the sacred *benben*-stone, symbol of the solar cult) listing offerings for the Aten. Statues of the royal family in ritual poses filled the sanctuary. There is little to see above ground at the sanctuary today.

The Great Aten Temple also had its own butchery yard (fig. 96), and huge bakeries in the grounds just to its south. The sounds and smells of food production and animal keeping must have filled the temple air, mingling with the incense sent skyward to please the god.

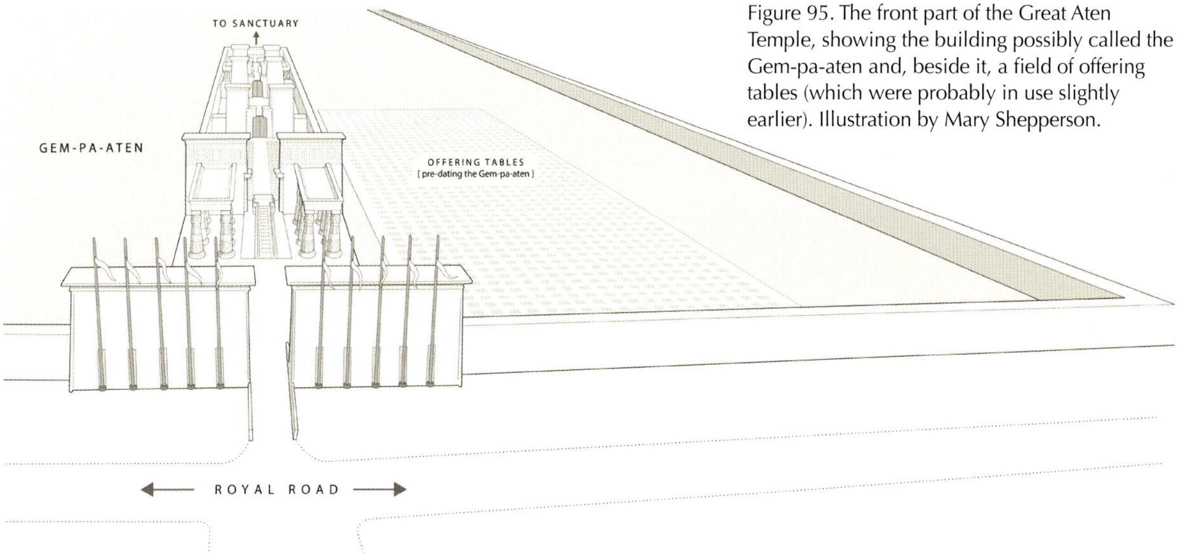

Figure 95. The front part of the Great Aten Temple, showing the building possibly called the Gem-pa-aten and, beside it, a field of offering tables (which were probably in use slightly earlier). Illustration by Mary Shepperson.

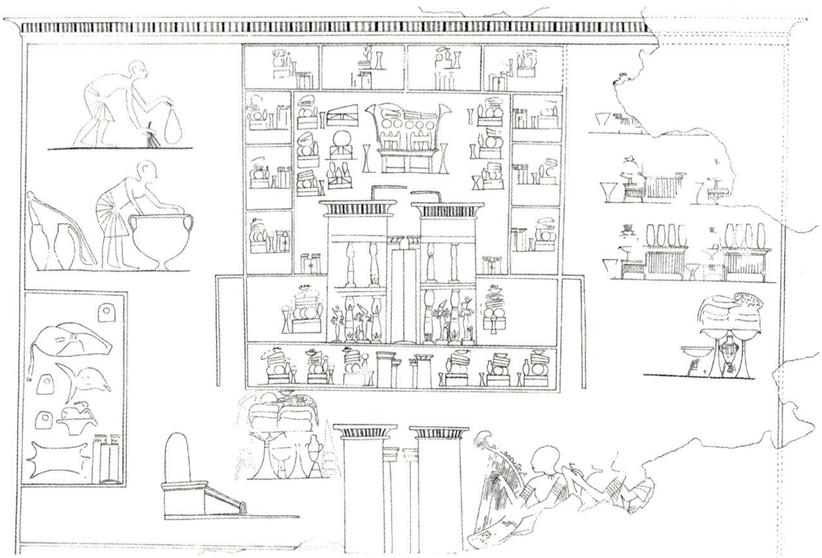

Figure 96. The sanctuary of the Great Aten Temple as represented in the Tomb of Meryre. Notice the butchery yard just outside the sanctuary to the left, and the great round-topped stela to the right of the yard. After Davies, *The Rock Tombs of El Amarna*, Part 1, pl. XI. Image courtesy of the Egypt Exploration Society.

IN FOCUS: WHAT WERE AMARNA'S TEMPLES FOR?

We can recognize at Amarna two temples intended specifically for the cult of the Aten as conducted by the royal family. They are both in the Central City, about 600m apart. Both face toward the place of sunrise in the east. The larger was given the name "House of the Aten," the smaller was the "Mansion of the Aten." Their modern names are the Great and the Small Aten Temple. They were extensively rebuilt during the Amarna period.

Both temples were designed to give maximum space to a performance by the king (fig. 97) at the moment of sunrise when, sometimes accompanied by members of his family, he would climb the steps to a platform on which was a table laid out with offerings of food, drink, flowers, and incense. From this elevation, he would greet the appearance of the sun with a hymn, to the accompaniment of male and female musicians and singers.

Both temples were also provided with numerous small offering tables at ground level, built from mud bricks or from stone blocks. The sanctuary at the Small Aten Temple, for example, contained at least 150 in stone. In the main part of the Great Aten Temple, their number probably reached 750. When the Great Aten Temple was first laid out, more than a thousand offering tables, many of mud brick, were arranged in long rows on the ground outside the main temple building (probably called the Gem-pa-aten), within the outer enclosure. Officials in their rock-tombs recorded the desire to share in the offerings of the main temple. This might explain the large numbers. A proportion of the offerings, blessed by the direct rays of the sun, was presented as a way of commemorating the dead (those making the commemoration subsequently consuming the food). The numbers of tables imply that the temple enclosure at least was accessible to many people. A link to non-royal dead might also be seen in the provision of rectangular platforms surrounded by narrow basins, the whole construction plastered with gypsum which was periodically renewed. Circular reservoirs provided a source of water. Laying out the dead for a ceremony of washing is one possible interpretation.

These constructions nevertheless covered only a small part of the huge open space that separated the main parts of the Great Aten Temple from the outer enclosure wall. Sample areas of excavation have uncovered postholes from wooden buildings and other holes where pottery jars were set into the ground. The possibility should be kept in mind that these ephemeral buildings represent periodic festivals drawing in large crowds.

Excavation of the ground in front of the temple (fig. 98) has yielded a varied range of objects in stone and gypsum which do not look as though they derive from a cult sponsored by the king. They include roughly made circular plates of gypsum into the top surface of which fragments of designs have been deeply scooped out, and the whole sometimes quickly splashed or daubed with paint. Other pieces, carved from limestone, show worshiping figures, the name of the king (poorly carved), and in one case a human ear. Some or all perhaps derive from opportunities for the expression of private emotions, in an atmosphere altered by the king's wishes and in which formal traditions were still being developed. —BK

Figure 97. Akhenaten sacrifices a duck for the Aten on a talatat block that probably once formed part of an Amarna temple. MMA 1985.328.2. Photo courtesy of the Metropolitan Museum of Art.

Figure 98. The remains of the Great Aten Temple are re-recorded during modern excavations, after being rapidly cleared in the 1930s. Photo courtesy of the Amarna Project.

IN FOCUS: TEMPLE STATUARY

It may be difficult to imagine now, but the Great Aten Temple, like all the temples of Akhetaten, was once vividly decorated. Brightly painted and inlaid reliefs brought life and color to the temple walls. Statues were also a crucial part of temple imagery. They stood throughout the open-air Gem-pa-aten at the front of the temple, in the sanctuary, and in certain other parts of the large precinct, serving jointly as decorative and ritual images.

Unlike gods in other periods, the Aten was never shown in a statue. The god was present as the sun in the sky and only otherwise represented by the disc with rays. But the king, queen, and their daughters were depicted. Hard stones, naturally colored brown, black, speckled, or white, were used, and also softer stones such as limestone, often painted in lifelike fashion. Eyes, crowns, and sashes are sometimes inlaid in bright materials. Wooden statues may also have existed, but are not preserved.

The destruction of the Great Aten Temple by later pharaohs has left the temple statuary in small puzzling fragments for archaeologists to try to reconstruct. Comparisons with better preserved statues from other periods can help to identify the forms. We see that the temple held statues of Akhenaten seated on a throne, striding with one leg forward, or holding an offering table (fig. 99)—much like any ancient Egyptian king. But the artists of Akhetaten also developed unusual types of statuary. Evidence from elsewhere at the city, including the Boundary Stelae and relief scenes, point toward some reconstructions. One of the most surprising fragments revealed during excavations at the Great Aten Temple was part of a painted limestone torso of Nefertiti with a large forward projection attached to her chest. Along with a second fragment that preserves part of an inscription, the finds reveal that royal statues holding pillars with the Aten names stood in the Gem-pa-aten, like those at the Boundary Stelae.

The sanctuary was the first part of the Great Aten Temple to be finished. Predictably, relief scenes in Akhenaten's buildings at Karnak in Thebes (modern Luxor), carved shortly before he left that city to start the new capital, illuminate the statuary fragments from the sanctuary. Some of these statues enact the ceremonies shown in scenes carved at Karnak, as, for example, one that depicts the king presenting the new god Aten's formal name enclosed in cartouches (fig. 100).

By this time in ancient Egypt, it had become fairly common practice for wealthy elites to donate statues of themselves to temples. There is no clear evidence for this practice at the Great Aten Temple. Probably the king's plans took precedence. But those who could afford it would have participated in the maintenance of temples in other ways, including through provision of images and equipment via the artists' workshops dispersed through the city. —MH

Royal Road

The unpaved road running through the Central City is part of the ancient Royal Road, the great processional route that linked Akhetaten from north to south.

The Royal Road helped shape the rhythm of urban life. It may have channeled workers through the city on foot or donkey-back, making way as officials hurried by in their chariots. But the road was far more than just a thoroughfare. It provided an axis along which the most important buildings in Akhetaten were aligned. And it also served a ceremonial role. As the king sped along in his golden chariot on his way to worship at the Aten temples (fig. 101), his divine authority was on public display.

Figure 99. A fragment of sculpted stone in the shape of an offering table with a hand beneath, likely to come from a standing royal offering statue like that on the left. Sketch of Cairo JE 43580 (left) after J. Dittmar, "Ein Bruchstück einer opfernden Figur in der Tübinger Sammlung," *Göttinger Miszellen* 41 (1980): 31 no. 14, with inserted offering table fragment, L. 19 cm. Petrie Excavations, 1891–92. MMA, Harris Brisbane Dick Fund, 1957 (21.9.573). Image courtesy of the Metropolitan Museum of Art.

Figure 100. Two finely carved Aten cartouches once held as offerings by a royal statue, recalling scenes of the ceremonial presentation of Aten cartouches as in the drawing on the left. Drawing by Sara Chen after Robert Vergnieux (1997), *Aménophis IV et les pierres du soleil: Akhénaton retrouvé* (Paris: Arthaud), 178. Petrie Excavations, 1891–92. MMA, Gift of Edward S. Harkness, 1921 (21.9.431). With joined cast of British Museum EA 58471, EES Excavations, 1926–27. Image courtesy of the Metropolitan Museum of Art.

Figure 101. The royal family race through the city in chariots under the protective rays of the sun god and accompanied by their military escort. Scene in the Tomb of Panehesy (North Tomb 6). After Davies, *The Rock Tombs of El Amarna*, Part 2, pl. XIII. Image courtesy of the Egypt Exploration Society.

He followed the road north–south as the Aten moved simultaneously east–west in the sky above.

There is no evidence that the road was ever paved, but it must have been kept clear of stones to allow chariots a smooth ride.

Bridge to the King's House

Among the most intriguing structures in the Central City are two mud-brick foundations on either side of the Royal Road. These are supports for a bridge which once spanned the road, joining the Great Palace to the King's House (fig. 102).

The bridge seems to have offered the king private passage between the two buildings, avoiding the street below. Perhaps it was also used to help control traffic passing along the Royal Road. Reconstructions of the bridge are largely speculative, although pieces of painted wall plaster found nearby suggest it was at least partly enclosed and painted.

Passing by overhead, Akhenaten would have descended at the King's House into a courtyard filled with trees, before continuing into what were perhaps his private daytime chambers in the Central City. One of the most famous scenes to survive from Amarna, showing two princesses relaxing on cushions, was found by Flinders Petrie in the King's House in the 1890s (fig. 103). The preserved fragment was part of a larger scene of the royal family. The sandaled feet of Akhenaten and Nefertiti can be seen, along with the lower parts of three additional princesses. To the left, on a much smaller scale, a servant bows beside a painted column. The painting is a masterpiece of Amarna art, typifying the languid style of Akhenaten's reign—completely at odds with traditional representations of royal figures. It is now in the Ashmolean Museum, Oxford.

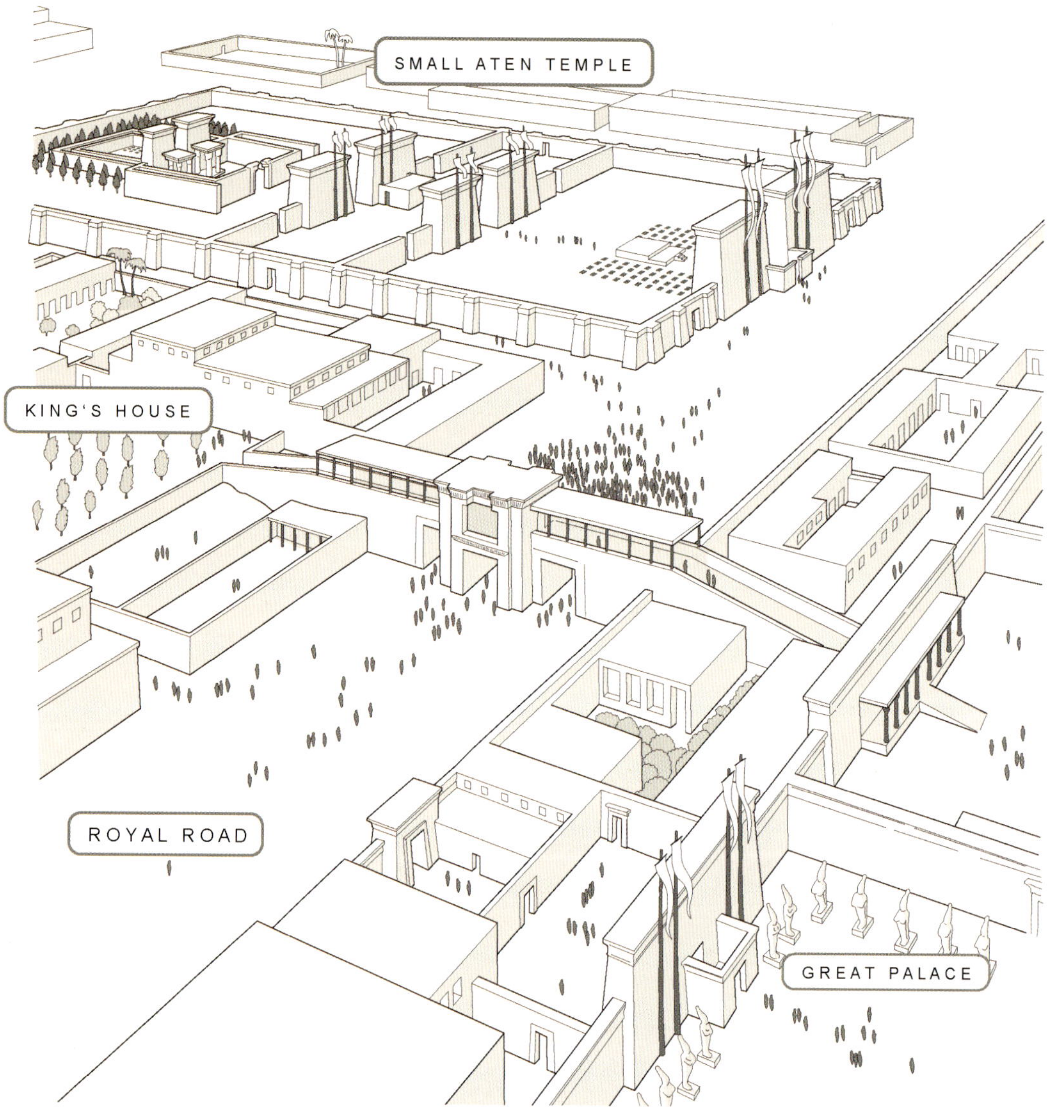

Figure 102. A view along the Royal Road and onto the bridge that passed between the Great Palace and King's House. The reconstruction of the upper part of the bridge is speculative. Illustration by Mary Shepperson (after R.S. Lavers, in Pendlebury, *The City of Akhenaten*, vol. 2, pl. II).

Figure 103. The Amarna Princess Panel is part of a wonderful colored scene of the royal family at leisure that once decorated the King's House. Ashmolean Museum AN1893.1–41.267. Photo courtesy of the Ashmolean Museum.

Great Palace and Smenkhkare Hall

The mud-brick ruins along the riverbank in the Central City are the remains of the Great Palace (figs. 104–107). This huge complex, nearly 600m long, was the center of royal life and court business, once lavishly decorated with statues, wall inlays in faience and hard stones, and colorful wall and floor paintings.

The eastern part of the palace, surviving today, was built largely from mud brick. It contained mostly service areas and storerooms. One suite of rooms, perhaps for royal women, had a sunken garden and beautifully painted pavements showing scenes of river life.

Nearer the river, stone-built apartments provided the setting for court business. A huge courtyard was lined with colossal statues of the king in "Osirid" pose with crook and flail, emblems of pharaonic power, crossed on his chest. Designed to impress the viewer with the king's power, 144 such colossi were intended to line the courtyard, although only perhaps a dozen were ever installed. The courtyard led to a series of formal courts and halls. There was probably a Window of Appearance for the king to hold ceremonial audiences.

The mud-brick walls lying opposite the Small Aten Temple represent the only known monument for King Smenkhkare, who ruled briefly near the end of the Amarna period. They mark out a large hall that was added to the southern end of the Great Palace late in the occupation of the city. Its ceiling was partly decorated with grapevine motifs and its walls faced with colored faience tiles. Stamped bricks give the name Smenkhkare. Little is known of the function of the hall, although some suggest it served the king's coronation ceremony.

Small Aten Temple

The Small Aten Temple, originally called Hut-Aten ('Mansion of the Aten'), was the second largest temple at Akhetaten, at around one-tenth of the size of the Great Aten Temple (fig. 108). Its function is not well understood. Perhaps, lacking the large, possibly public courts of the Great

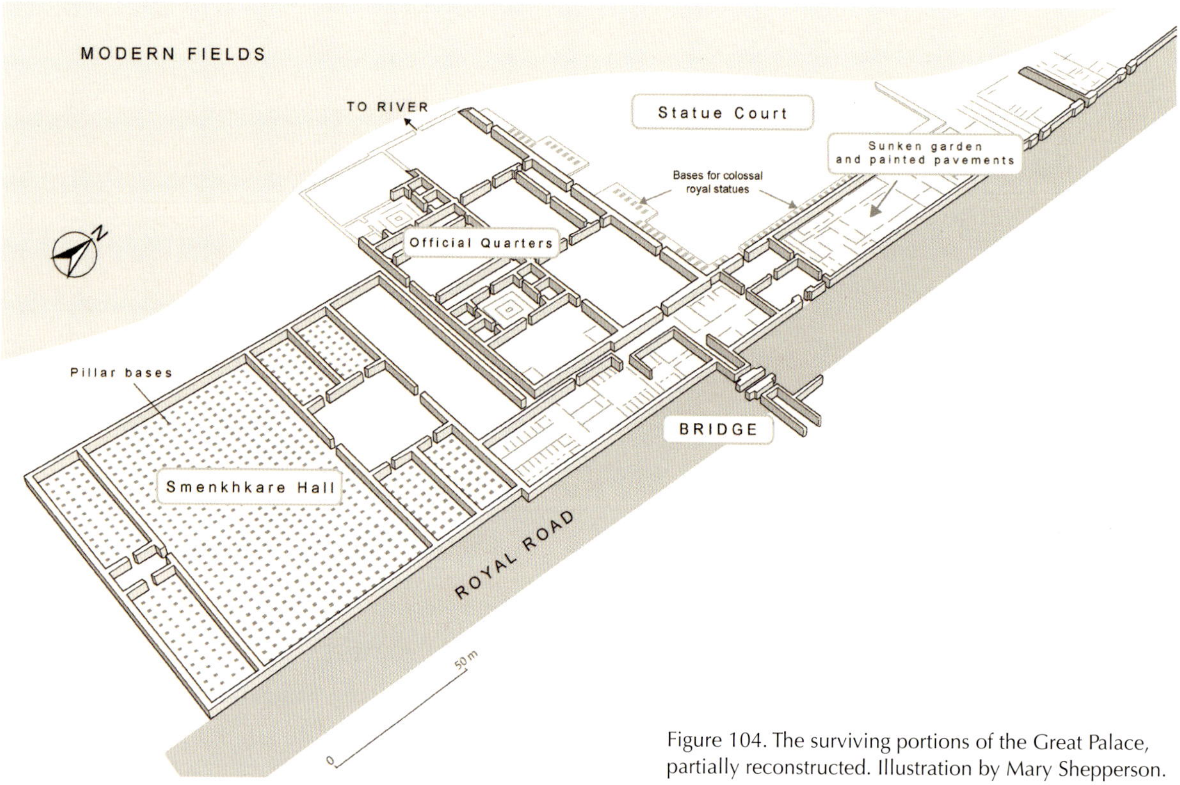

Figure 104. The surviving portions of the Great Palace, partially reconstructed. Illustration by Mary Shepperson.

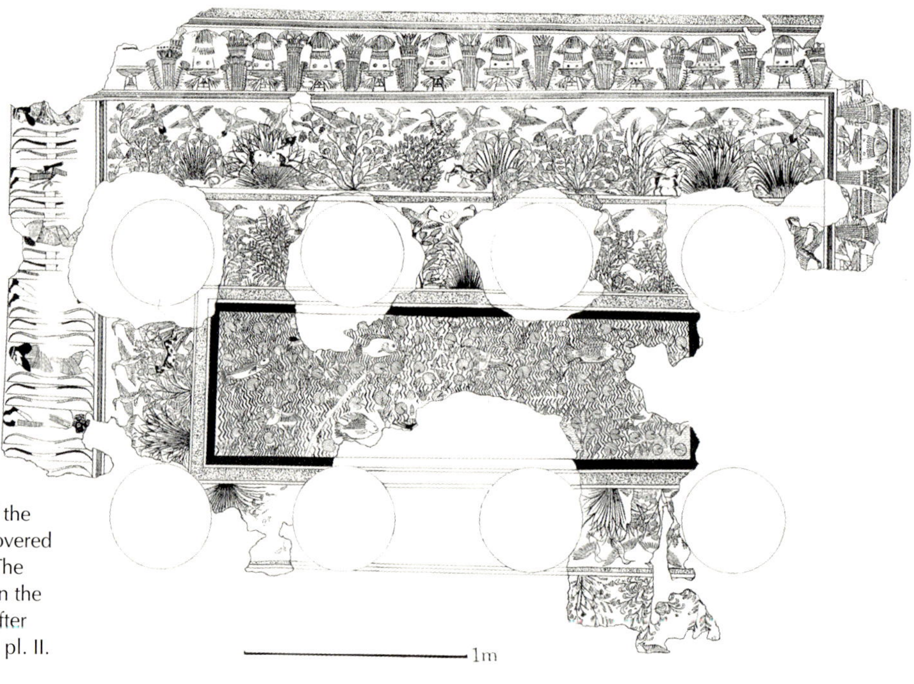

Figure 105. A line drawing of the grand painted pavement uncovered in the Great Palace in 1891. The pavement is now on display in the Egyptian Museum in Cairo. After W.M.F. Petrie, *Tell El Amarna*, pl. II.

Aten Temple, it was a place where the king worshiped the Aten privately. It is also striking how closely the temple lines up with the Royal Wadi in the eastern cliffs—visible behind the reconstructed columns—where the royal family was buried (see fig. 9; also fig. 109). The Small Aten Temple might instead have been a kind of mortuary temple where the royal family joined the sun god after death.

Much of the temple has been capped with modern mud brick and stone to protect what remains of the original building. The entrance was once flanked by flagpoles. In the middle of the gateway is a raised platform and just inside lies the base of an altar with foundations for steps or a ramp, flanked by smaller rectangular altars (fig. 109). Scenes in the rock-cut tombs show altars of this kind heaped with offerings for the sun god.

In the second court is a small building that resembles a house, perhaps used by the king during rituals. It contains a brick platform fronted by a narrow staircase that might be a throne base or an altar.

The sanctuary at the far end was an open-air stone building surrounded by gardens (fig. 110). It would have been decorated with carved and brightly painted scenes, and statues in hard, colored stones. Two columns have been reconstructed in the sanctuary using cement and original stone. Look up at the columns when you are inside to get a sense of the original height of the temple. Other pieces of carved stone left behind when the temple was dismantled are also on display.

Just outside the Small Aten Temple, to its south, was a large industrial complex where bread was made, in part for the temple cult; faience and glass decorative items may have been produced here, too.

Figure 106. Watercolor reproductions of portions of the painted pavement from the Great Palace. After Petrie, *Tell El Amarna*, pl. III.

Figure 107. An insider view of life in one of the Amarna palaces as shown in the Tomb of Meryre (North Tomb 4). Notice the servants sweeping and sprinkling water to keep the dust down, while in the top left corner is an image of the king's bedroom. After Davies, *The Rock Tombs of El Amarna*, Part 1, pl. XVIII. Image courtesy of the Egypt Exploration Society.

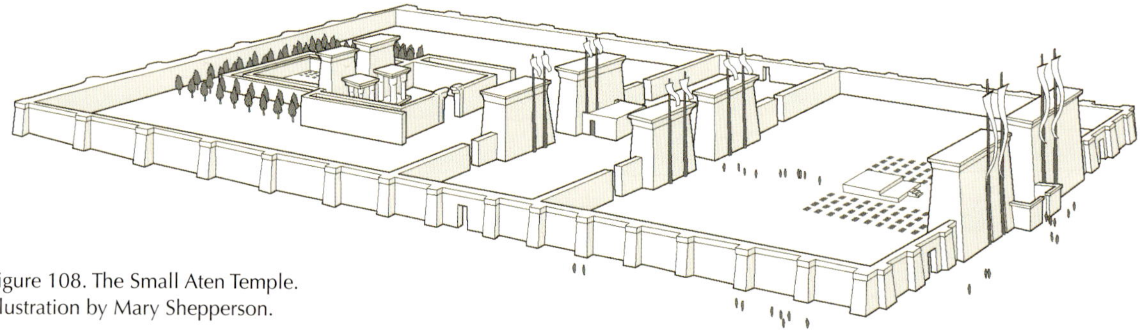

Figure 108. The Small Aten Temple. Illustration by Mary Shepperson.

Figure 109. A view along the axis of the Small Aten Temple. In the foreground is the reconstructed base of an altar-like structure that was probably once used in offering rituals. Photo courtesy of the Amarna Project.

Figure 110. Regularly spaced tree pits form the ephemeral archaeological traces of a sacred garden that once encircled the sanctuary in the Small Aten Temple. EES Amarna Archive Negative 1931–2.A.189. Photo courtesy of the Egypt Exploration Society.

Administrative Quarters

Walk through the Small Aten Temple, and veer left after exiting at the rear, to reach the sprawling administrative zone where teams of scribes and military men put into action the king's instructions.

Stamped mud bricks provide the names of some of these buildings. The House of Life was a place for learning, where priests were trained to read and copy sacred texts, and scribes and children of the elite might also have been educated. The House of the King's Statue seems to have been a chapel where the king himself was worshiped as a god. A complex behind the Small Aten Temple resembles a housing estate and perhaps provided working space and living quarters for lower-ranking scribes, while a large building on the eastern outskirts contains possible horse stables, perhaps identifying it as the headquarters of the armed forces.

One of the most famous buildings, just beyond the Small Aten Temple, is the Records Office. From this inconspicuous mud-brick building, Akhenaten's scribes translated, copied, and archived letters from the king's foreign allies and dependents. In the late 19th century, an extraordinary collection of diplomatic correspondence (the Amarna Letters) was discovered here, one of the most important sets of written material from the ancient world.

The Amarna Letters are a group of around 400 clay tablets incised with Akkadian cuneiform (wedge-shaped) script from ancient Mesopotamia (fig. 111). Most are correspondence from lands to the north, as distant as Turkey and Cyprus. The letters reveal the complexities of foreign relations in the ancient Near East, including diplomatic marriage and gift exchange. Access to gold left Egypt in a powerful position: "gold is in your land like the dust" writes one Assyrian king. The letters show Egyptian dominance over the city-states of the Levant. The kings of other regions—Babylon, Hatti, Mitanni, and Assyria—write as equals to the Egyptian king.

Figure 111: One of the Amarna Letters. In this example, the newly crowned Assyrian king Ashur-uballit sends a chariot, two horses, and lapis lazuli as a diplomatic greeting gift to the Egyptian pharaoh. MMA 24.2.11. Photo courtesy of the Metropolitan Museum of Art.

IN FOCUS: INCENSE AT AMARNA

While Akhenaten changed many aspects of religious beliefs, he still retained the use of incense in religious and ceremonial rituals. Sweetly scented resins were said to have come from the gods, and burning incense was intended to make offerings suitable for them. Given this link to the gods, it is perhaps unsurprising that the most common ancient Egyptian word for incense was *senetjer*, which means "to make divine."

The walls of some of the tombs at Amarna are decorated with depictions of temple and palace scenes that show Akhenaten holding a censer before tables with heaps of food offerings. Often these offerings also have small bowls of burning resin and charcoal placed among them, a practical way of censing the offerings without coating them with sticky resin. These bowls have been found in many areas of Amarna, not only in temples and royal buildings, but also in homes of the officials and even of the workmen (fig. 112). This leaves open the question of whether the resin also had a secular use simply to scent the air.

Since Egypt has few sources of resins, these aromatic products would have been imported from areas to the north and south. Chemical analysis of samples of resin in the bowls has indicated that it came from trees of the genus *Pistacia,* a relation of the non-resin-producing trees that are the source of pistachio nuts. At Amarna, large pottery storage jars, known as amphorae, sometimes still have deposits of pistacia resin remaining inside.

Microscopic study of the minerals in the clays used to make the jars containing resin has revealed that they came from the southern coastal Levant to Egypt's northeast. Inscriptions on some of the jars not only specify that the contents are *senetjer,* but even mention the name of the ship's captain who delivered them.

Given that censing was a crucial part of many religious rituals, and the vast numbers of temples in ancient Egypt, it is easy to guess that demand for incense would have been high. This undoubtedly remained the case in the Amarna period. As a ritual substance, pistacia resin was also sometimes brushed over the decoration on coffins and funerary objects in the New Kingdom to emphasize the need to make the deceased divine. Traces of such a coating, likely containing pistacia resin, can also be seen on some coffin fragments found in the cemeteries at Amarna.

These uses demonstrate a fundamental need to maintain access to supplies of incense through trade or military control. We know, for example, that, during the reign of Thutmose III, over 800 jars of *senetjer* were shipped to Egypt in a single year. The intricacies of sustaining international relations, amid sometimes volatile political circumstances, are evidenced by the diplomatic correspondence found at Amarna (the Amarna Letters). The remarkable discovery of a shipwreck off the coast of Turkey near Uluburun offers a direct attestation of the scale of Mediterranean trade in the Bronze Age (fig. 113). The shipwreck dates slightly later than Akhenaten's reign. The ship's diverse cargo included ten tons of copper, 170 glass ingots, and a gold scarab of Nefertiti, but also nearly 150 amphorae containing pistacia resin. It is estimated that

Figure 112. Used widely in temples to the sun god, incense is also commonly found in houses at Amarna, as solid lumps (above right) or still attached to pieces of charcoal (above left) and to the fragments of pottery bowls in which it was burned. Photo courtesy of the Amarna Project.

this would have amounted to almost a ton of resin. We can speculate, although it is far from certain, that this cargo was destined for Egypt; regardless, it must certainly attest to the scale of the incense trade. We can wonder, too, how the loss of such a cargo would have affected supplies of this essential product across Egypt. —MS

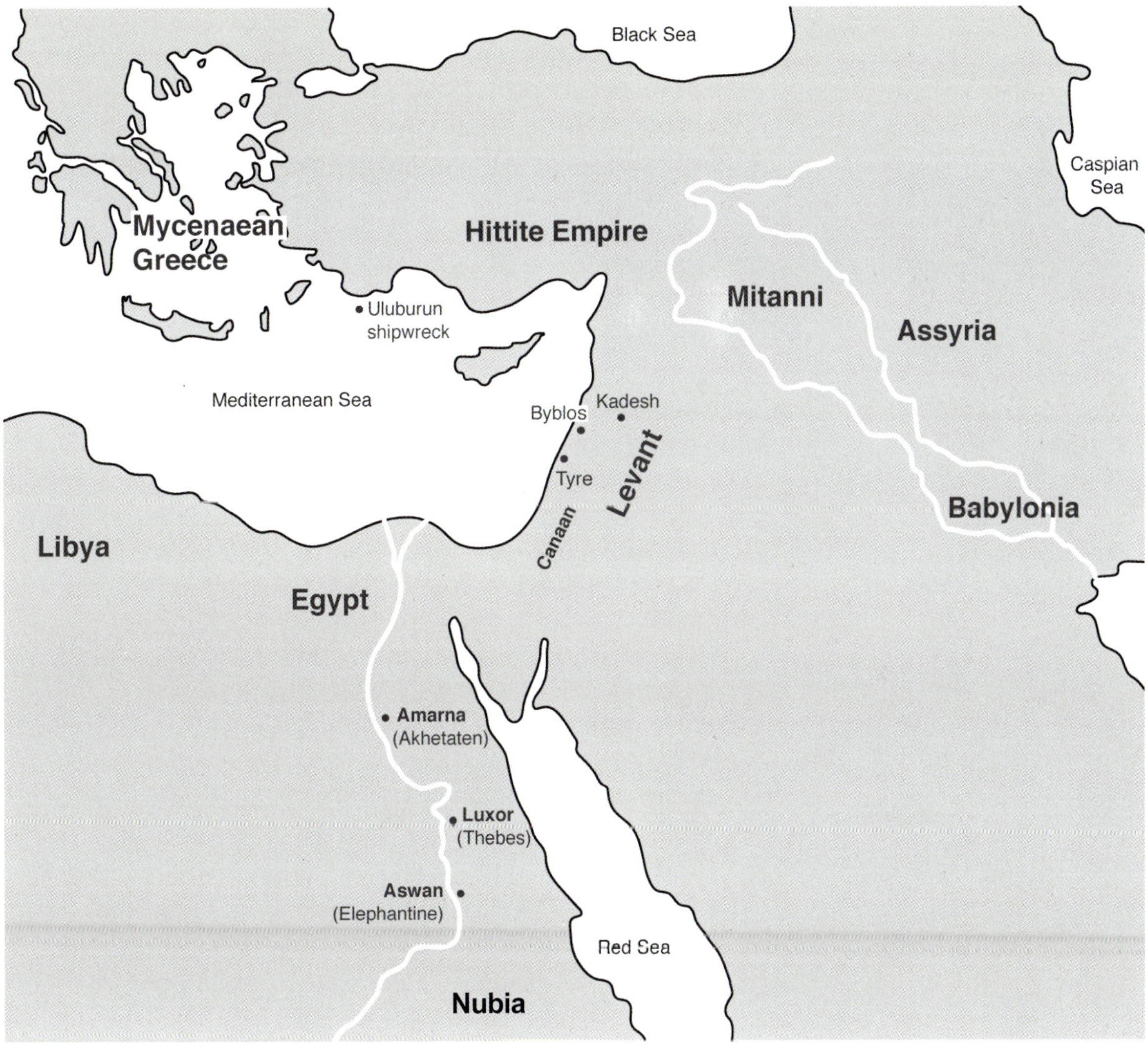

Figure 113. Map of the Mediterranean, showing the location of the Uluburun shipwreck. Illustration by Mafdy Mansour.

SOUTHERN CITY AND TEMPLES

An Ancient Villa

Head south again, past the back of the Small Aten Temple, toward the wedge-shaped viewing platform a couple of hundred meters away to your left. The viewing platform marks the location of a partially reconstructed villa. Excavated in 1923, it represents a typical house for a well-to-do official (fig. 114). It would have been at least two stories high.

Grand houses of this kind were both a home and a place of business. The upper floors were probably devoted to family and private space. The ground floor, visible here, was arranged around a central room containing, between two brick piers, a bench for seating. Visitors were received here after passing through a columned hall, giving a sense of formality and grandeur. Inscriptions around the doorways announced the name and occupation of the house owner.

The owner of this house is no longer known, but he was undoubtedly prosperous. His estate enclosed all the land contained within the wire fence. Although no longer visible, excavations have revealed many granaries for storing barley and emmer wheat and a chamber lined with feeding troughs and paved with stone cobbles for keeping cattle (fig. 115). Servants would have helped with the never-ending tasks of processing food, collecting water, and tending to livestock. In his garden, this official built a chapel to the royal family and Aten, with a small sacred lake. This showed his loyalty to the king and perhaps gave his ancestors a place to live on after death, with the sun god.

The villa marks the beginning of a huge residential area that stretches southward from the Central City, where the landscape opens up to a plain

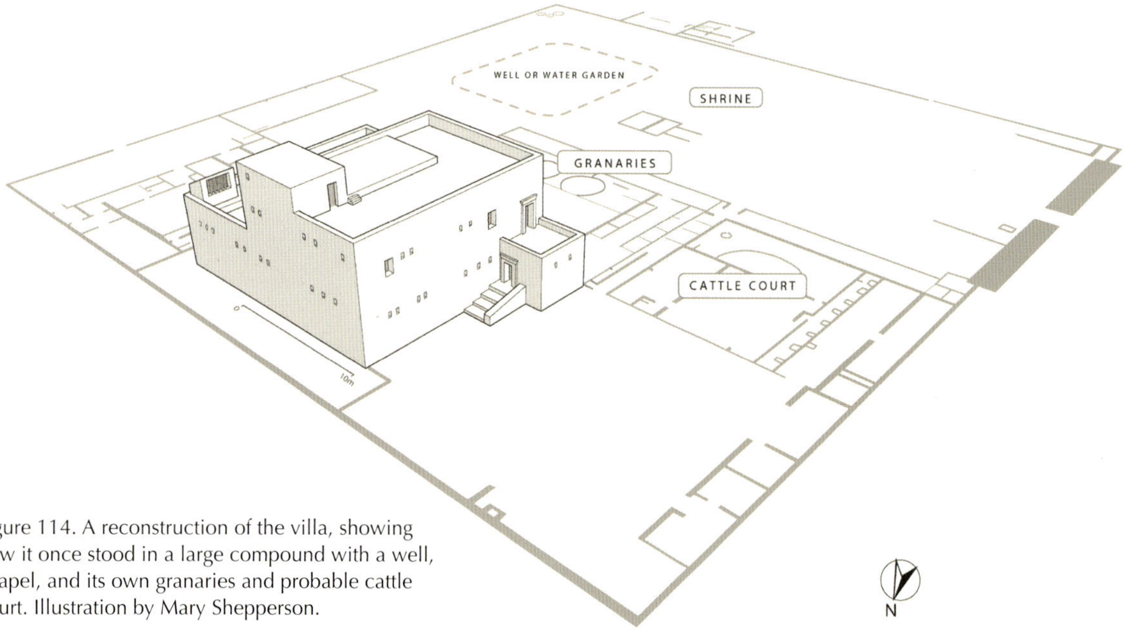

Figure 114. A reconstruction of the villa, showing how it once stood in a large compound with a well, chapel, and its own granaries and probable cattle court. Illustration by Mary Shepperson.

Figure 115. Mud-brick structures thought to have been feeding bins for cattle in the courtyard of the villa. (Note the similar constructions, in stone, at the North Palace.) EES Amarna Archive Negative 1923.31. Photo courtesy of the Egypt Exploration Society.

of low mounds covered in potsherds and mud-brick rubble. Today called the Main City, this was the largest residential area of ancient Akhetaten.

Main City

Much of the city's population, rich and poor, lived side by side in the Main City (fig. 116). Standing mud-brick walls of excavated houses can be seen, but many more remain buried under the desert and fields, probably running all the way to the riverbank.

Figure 116. A view across the ancient houses of the Main City, as reconstructed in the model of Amarna on display in the Visitor Centre. Photo courtesy of David Grandorge.

Most houses at Akhetaten were small mud-brick buildings, packed closely together, with floors of brick, plaster, or trampled earth (figs. 117, 118). Windows were placed high in the walls to keep out the sun and dust. Interior walls were sometimes painted white to increase the reflected light. There might be a bench for seating and a fireplace for light and heat (figs. 119, 120). Low stone tables provided flat surfaces for working on. Squat stone stools would be padded with wads of textile or cushions, and mats of palm rib, sedge, and grasses lined the floors. Keeping the household running was a major undertaking. Grain had to be ground on stone querns, and bread baked in small pottery ovens. Constant supplies of water were needed and houses were swept out regularly with palm-fiber brushes to keep them free of dust and rubbish.

The Main City was a place of busyness and production. Around the large walled villas of officials—Akhenaten's middlemen—grew neighborhoods of smaller houses whose owners provided labor in exchange for grain and other supplies. Many houses were the setting of small-scale industries using glass, faience, metal, stone, and wood. The end products were often directed into state building schemes. The Main City provided a vast pool of semi-organized labor for the king.

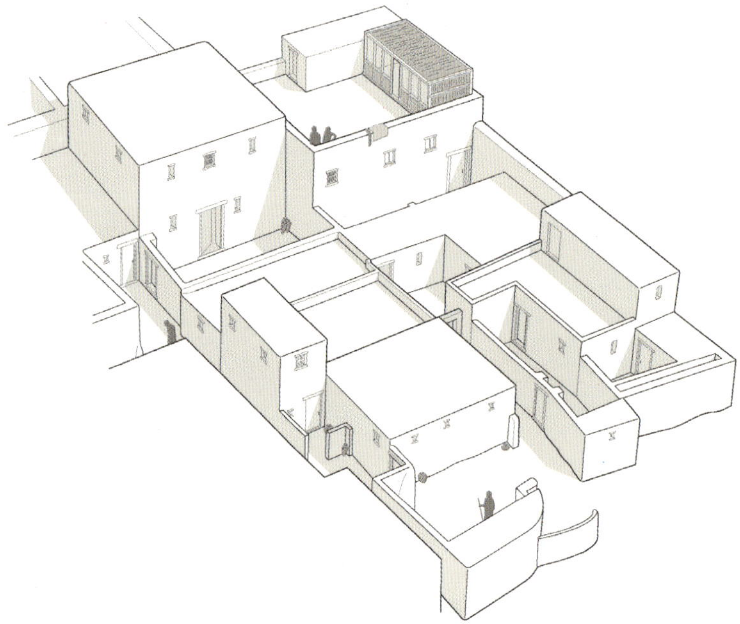

Figure 117. Reconstruction of part of a neighborhood of closely packed houses in the Main City. Illustration by Mary Shepperson (after an illustration by Barry Kemp in B. Kemp and A. Stevens, *Busy Lives at Amarna: Excavations in the Main City*, vol. 1, *The Excavations, Architecture and Environmental Remains*, p. 509, fig. 10.13).

Figure 118. The archaeological remains of the houses on which the reconstruction drawing (fig. 117) is based. Photo courtesy of the Amarna Project.

Figure 119. Ancient baskets are scattered on the floor of an Amarna house, left by the inhabitants over 3,000 years ago. Also visible are the remains of a circular hearth (lower right) and a stone slab for grinding grain (below the basket to the left). EES Amarna Archive Negative 1922.13. Photo courtesy of the Egypt Exploration Society.

Figure 120. Stone furniture used in the ancient houses: a basin, pot stands, low stool (lower left), and a headrest (lower right), which would have been placed under the neck. EES Amarna Archive Negative 1924–5.18. Photo courtesy of the Egypt Exploration Society.

IN FOCUS: HOME OR WORKSHOP? AMARNA'S URBAN INDUSTRIES

As Akhetaten grew and more people moved to the city, the need for luxury and everyday goods grew. These included objects manufactured from glass and faience, especially jewelry and decorative vessels, metal tools, sculpture, and smaller items from stone, including agate (fig. 121). With this growing demand for products, a number of workshops sprang up throughout the city. Most are found in the Main City, the sprawling suburb south of the Central City.

Activities using fire and heat, and the working of raw materials into finished objects, usually took place in the courtyards of houses, and in some cases perhaps on the roofs, in order not to pollute the interiors. Many buildings at Amarna have the character of both domestic houses and workshops. Depending on the nature and scale of the output, these workshops could be deemed more or less specialized. Most glass workshops, for example, focused on the production of finished objects from raw glass rods and bars, using very simple firing structures, but a few contained large kilns for the production of raw glass itself.

Technological skills and resources were often shared across neighboring workshops. Copper oxide, for instance, a major component of bronze and therefore a common raw material, was also used as a colorant in glass and faience to achieve a light blue or turquoise color. Cobalt, which was mined in Egypt's western desert and so somewhat valuable, was used to give both glass and faience a dark blue color. Cobalt-colored glass imitated the highly valued lapis lazuli, providing a more accessible alternative. An example of the sharing of technological skills is the cold-working of glass by grinding and carving, in the same manner as stoneworking. This technique is seen especially in the production of colorful and detailed glass and stone inlays for the decoration of items such as coffins and furniture. Workshops could be multi-functional, manufacturing more than one product at a time. A good example is the workshop of Thutmose, the main output of which was sculpture—most famously, the painted bust of Nefertiti—but which also produced faience inlays and jewelry, in part probably for the decoration of sculptural items.

An industrial network can be reconstructed for Akhetaten whereby workshops in small and mid-sized domestic buildings were probably loosely controlled by leading neighborhood officials, their main outputs perhaps delivered to the royal court or other elite houses for redistribution. By contrast, other workshops, often closer to the Central City, may have reported directly to the royal court. —AH

IN FOCUS: NEFERTITI AND THE SCULPTORS' WORKSHOPS

Among the most striking outputs of the Main City workshops were stone statues of the royal family, used to decorate the king's temples and palaces. Made in the new artistic style of Akhenaten's reign, they were carved from beautiful hard stones: granite, granodiorite, quartzite, travertine, and marble-like indurated limestone. Some statues were designed to impress the viewer with the king's power, such as the colossal figures in the Great Palace. Others were more ritualistic in function, like the figures of Akhenaten and Nefertiti piously holding offering tables that stood in the Great and Small Aten Temples (see fig. 99). The unusual artistic emphasis on the royal family in Akhenaten's reign was also reflected in more informal group statues of the royal couple and their daughters, and of the princesses holding hands.

After the abandonment of Akhetaten, most statues of the royal family, both finished and unfinished, were broken up into fragments in the attempt to destroy all traces of their existence. Archaeological excavations at the city have shown that hundreds of statues had already been installed in temples and palaces, in houses, or were in preparation in workshops.

Some statues were made in royal workshops near the palaces and temples (fig. 122). Part of one of these workshops was located in the 1930s by the Egypt Exploration Society, opposite the Great Aten Temple. Another seems to lie just south of the Small Aten Temple. Private workshops also supplied royal statuary. The best-known is the workshop of a sculptor probably called Thutmose, where the famous painted head of Nefertiti was found by Ludwig Borchardt and his team of excavators in 1912. Thutmose and the other owners of private workshops settled in an area to the north and south of a broad channel that divides the Main City roughly in half, creating a kind of workshop district. The scant surviving evidence suggests that sculptors like Thutmose made relatively small statues of the royal family destined for the Sunshade Temples to the south of the city, such as Kom al-Nana and the Maru-Aten. Their workshops line one of the main north–south roadways, which may have provided access for the delivery of statuary to these southern temples.

The painted bust of Nefertiti (fig. 123), stunning though it is, probably served a purpose not for public display, but as a model for Thutmose's artists. It may be the most famous output of the Thutmose workshop, but this and other workshops nearby contained other remarkable and sometimes innovative pieces. These include beautiful, unfinished heads and limbs of quartzite, nearly ready to be attached to garments made separately of white stone. The resulting composite statues were an innovation of Akhenaten's reign.

Today, the most extensive displays of statue fragments from Amarna can be seen in Cairo, the Egyptian Museum in Berlin, and the Metropolitan Museum in New York. —KT

Figure 121. The colorful leftovers of suburban industry: beads, chips, and rods of glass, as well as part of a glass ingot placed in a cylindrical pottery mold; molds for making faience jewelry; faience pendants, scarabs, and beads; and at the bottom right, part of a crucible for metalworking. Photo courtesy of Anna Hodgkinson.

Figure 122. A busy scene inside a sculptors' workshop where the chief sculptor, Iuti, creates a statue of Baketaten, the daughter of Queen Tiye. Tomb of Huya (North Tomb 1). After Davies, *The Rock Tombs of El Amarna*, Part 3, pl. XVIII. Image courtesy of the Egypt Exploration Society.

IN FOCUS: WHAT DID THEY WEAR?

Textiles and footwear preserved in Egypt's dry climate, along with pictorial evidence, offer unique insight into everyday life and fashion in cities like Akhetaten. Clothing items were traditionally woven from linen, the Egyptian sovereign fiber. Weavers used spindle whorls to spin fibers into yarn, which was then woven into cloth on horizontal or vertical looms by professional male workers in state-controlled workshops, and also by the whole family in domestic contexts. The predominant structure was the plain weave, the simplest and most universal weave, produced by passing the weft across the warp twice. Amarna has produced much evidence for textile production, particularly from households, including spindle whorls, spinning bowls, and loom fittings. Identifiable garments are less common here, as is often the case at settlement sites, although the dry climate at the two desert workers' villages has preserved several pieces of clothing that are important for showing what the non-elite would wear.

Clothes were usually left in their natural off-white color or were bleached. This was due partly to the poor suitability of linen for dyeing, but also to the Egyptian taste for white garments as a sign of hygiene and purity, and as an indication of social status. In the New Kingdom, a standard clothing item worn by men, women, and children alike was the bag-tunic. It was made of a large rectangular piece of cloth, folded over and stitched up the sides, with a slit or a keyhole-shaped cut for the neck opening. Bag-tunics could be worn with or without sleeves and adjusted with a belt, sometimes pleated, which would be knotted on the belly.

For men, the kilt was another principal item of clothing, and, at Akhetaten, the fashion was to wear it low under the belly at the front and very high at the back, as a sign of wealth and high social rank. In the fields, workers wore only loincloths, a sort of triangular-shaped underwear that was adjusted and knotted around the waist and the crotch. For women, another fashion of the time was to wear a large piece of cloth, sometimes pleated and fringed, that they draped around their body and secured by a knot or belt under the chest. Children went mostly unclothed.

Those who could afford footwear in New Kingdom Egypt most often wore sandals, although open shoes (basically sandals with a low upward projection to protect the sides of the foot) were quite common as well. Most known sandals and open shoes are made of plant materials, such as palm leaf, grasses, and papyrus. Less frequently worn, but by no means uncommon, were leather sandals. Depending on the social status of the owner, footwear was more or less delicately made and/or elaborately

Figure 123. The bust of Nefertiti, shown in its original excavation photograph in 1913. Photo © Deutsche Orient-Gesellschaft, Archive no. 13.69.

decorated. Highly decorative or very finely made sandals were only worn by a small, select group of people. As far as we can determine, men and women wore the same kinds of footwear, with occasional exceptions for some of the more unusual types. Children's sandals were smaller versions of adult footwear. There were probably many very poor members of society, however, who mostly went barefoot.

Amarna has produced a fair number of items of footwear. Only a few sandals made of vegetal materials have been found. This is surprising, considering it is the most commonly used material in ancient Egypt. A fair number of leather sandals have been excavated at the site over the years (fig. 124). These consist mostly of single-layer soles with cut-out loops at the back to attach simple leather straps that ran between the two first toes to keep the sandal tight on the foot. There are also examples with two layers of sole. Several small fragments and one complete child's version of a decorated leather sandal have also been found, perhaps once colored red and green, and used by people from the higher echelons of society. —AM, AV

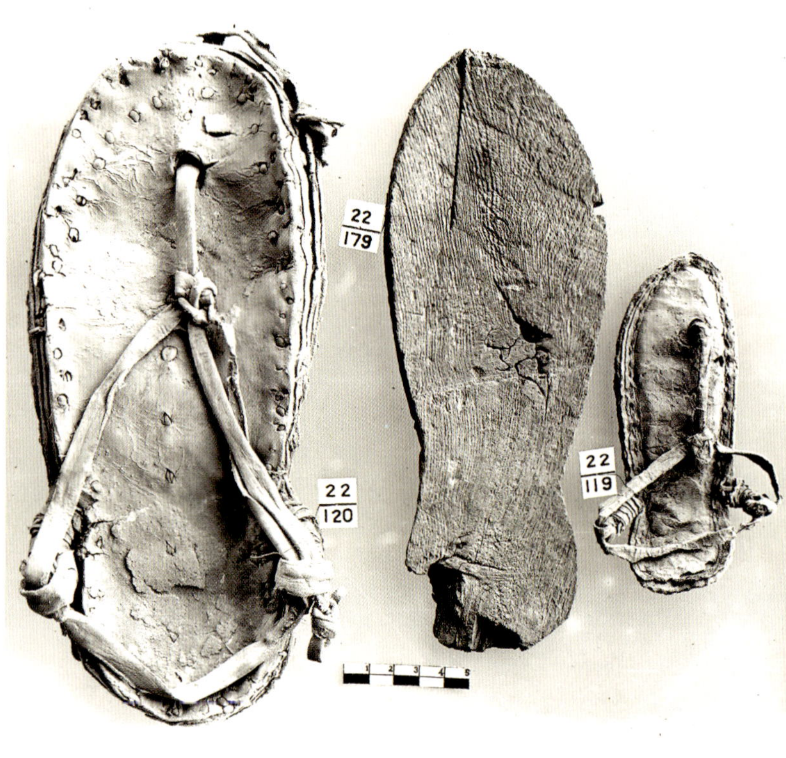

Figure 124. Leather sandals, for an adult and a child, from the Workmen's Village, where the dry desert environment preserved organic materials particularly well. The purpose of the wooden sole-like object in the center is unclear. EES Amarna Archive Negative 1922.45. Photo courtesy of the Egypt Exploration Society.

IN FOCUS: WATER FOR AN EGYPTIAN CITY

Although Akhetaten was located close to the Nile, the river does not seem to have been the main water source for the city, as it was for most Egyptian settlements. Instead, Amarna has the highest concentration of wells discovered in any ancient Egyptian city to date. Almost 100 wells have been identified, more than half located in the courtyards of larger houses, and the rest in open spaces.

The excavated wells are all constructed in two stages (fig. 125). Cut into the desert surface, the upper part was a wide pit, either rectangular or circular, and about 4m broad, with inward-sloping walls. A flight of steps or ramp gave access to the lower level a couple of meters down, where the shaft became a narrow off-center circle that descended to the water table. Some more elaborate versions, found mainly in the courtyards of larger houses, had mud-brick casing walls and mud-brick or stone steps.

The private wells in the large elite estates at Amarna are, so far, unique for ancient Egypt. Located so close to the house, the well provided convenient access to a water source for the household (fig. 126), and gave the elite independence regarding their water supply. This was a remarkable situation: before, and even after, the Amarna period, the central administration seems to have been largely in charge of the water supply for the population, through a redistribution system.

There must have been consequences for the poorer inhabitants of the city, who may no longer have benefited from organized water deliveries. They may have taken charge of the situation by coming together in small groups to cut wells that served clusters of small houses. Digging a well was probably not a very difficult task as the ground at Amarna is mainly composed of sand and gravel. The simple nature of the wells in public spaces, which lack mud-brick or stone staircases or ramps, could support the idea that they are the work of people with limited resources.

Why there are quite so many wells in Amarna remains somewhat unclear. The size of the city, some 7km long, could be one factor. Access to a private or public well meant avoiding having to go every day, if not more often, to cart water from the Nile. Accessibility to the river may also have been a factor: perhaps some of the palaces and other official buildings on the Nile partially or totally obstructed access to the river. In any case, wells seem to have been the simplest solution to meet the daily water needs of the population at Akhetaten. —DD

Figure 125. A well in the courtyard of an official named Ranefer. Note the large circular granaries nearby—another marker of his wealth. The well had been filled in before the granaries were built. EES Amarna Archive Negative 1921.73. Photo courtesy of the Egypt Exploration Society.

Figure 126. Large houses of Akhenaten's officials had elaborate bathrooms. This stone slab was probably used much like a modern shower basin, with water poured over the bather from a jug, which then ran into the adjacent basin. Some installations like this had drains that funneled the waste water directly into the street. This bathing slab was uncovered in the house of the sculptor Thutmose in 1912 (but is now destroyed). EES Amarna Archive Negative 1922.176. Photo courtesy of the Egypt Exploration Society.

South Tombs

The South Tombs are reached from a turnoff on the main road south of the Central City. Just after the turnoff, on the left, is the Dig House used by archaeological teams today. The road to the South Tombs also gives a good view of the Great Wadi on your left, a striking valley in the eastern cliffs that closely resembles the hieroglyphic sign for horizon. Did this prompt Akhenaten to choose this stretch of land for the sun god?

Kom al-Nana, location of both a Sun Temple to Nefertiti and a later monastery, is also reached via a turnoff on the road to the South Tombs. Take the dirt track just before the small bridge over the canal, a couple of hundred meters after the Dig House, and follow it through the cemetery and fields to reach the temple site.

The South Tombs represent the second group of tombs for Akhenaten's officials (fig. 127). These men were mostly (although not entirely) of lower standing than the owners of the North Tombs. Their tombs are generally smaller and simpler, and occupy a less prominent position in the landscape, but they still contain many important and characterful scenes. There are 19 numbered tombs (nos. 7–25) and several unnumbered chambers. The most frequently visited tombs are 7, 8, 9, 10, 14, 23, and 25. Like the North Tombs, few were used for burial.

Nearby, there is a huge cemetery containing several thousand pit-graves for the city's non-elite citizens. Their burials are very simple, with few grave goods.

Figure 127: A view across the South Tombs. Photo courtesy of Gwil Owen/ The Amarna Project.

IN FOCUS: CREATING TOMBS

An ambition for many of the city's elite inhabitants was to have a tomb cut into the rock of the eastern cliffs. It would offer a secure place for their burials (including burial equipment). Its decoration would show their loyalty to Akhenaten and his cult of the Aten. A chapel at the back would, by means of a statue and accompanying scenes, provide a place of eternal commemoration for themselves and their families.

To finish a decorated tomb of reasonable size was a large undertaking. It required access to several groups of workers and craftsmen. Stonemasons cut out the rock to create the chambers, columns, and other architectural features (fig. 128). They often removed the stone in blocks which could be used in buildings in the city. The finished surfaces were frequently given a coat of gypsum plaster, the local rock being of poor quality. Over this, a draftsman drew the outlines of the decoration in black ink. Sometimes this was corrected with red lines. A sculptor then converted the outlines into carvings in shallow-sunk relief. The final stage was painting in bright colors. The tomb of Ay (South Tomb 25) illustrates all stages, although little paint had been applied.

It is common, as in Ay's tomb, to find that some or all of the stages of tomb preparation had been started, sometimes in the same chamber. The likely explanation is that, even for the elite, there were not enough workers and craftsmen available to allow a tomb to be completed in a single, logical sequence of specialist operations. Craftsmen were engaged

Figure 128. An elegant column emerges from the limestone bedrock in one of the Amarna tombs (South Tomb 8). Photo courtesy of the Amarna Project.

for limited periods as and when they could be persuaded to work on a particular tomb.

The tomb of the royal scribe Any (South Tomb 23) is the one most likely to have been used for the burial of its owner. Six small stelae (now in Cairo) were found in front of the tomb entrance. Those who knew him left them to honor him. His burial would have been at the bottom of a shaft cut into the floor of the tomb. The tomb would have remained open so that offerings could continue to be made before a statue of Any, carved in the rock at the back. The surfaces of the walls and ceiling are smoothly finished, but bear no linear decoration. If Akhetaten had continued to be occupied, perhaps a descendant would have paid to have more decoration added. —BK

IN FOCUS: CHILDHOOD HEALTH AT AKHETATEN

An invaluable source for examining health in ancient cities is human skeletons, through the science known as bioarchaeology. The skeleton itself is often the only direct source of information on individual health available from ancient societies, with medical records rarely available. Our skeletons reflect the sum total of our individual lives, showing evidence of disease, nutrition, activity, and even psychological stress. Over 400 individual skeletons have been excavated and analyzed from a huge pit-grave cemetery near the South Tombs (fig. 129), providing unparalleled information on life at ancient Akhetaten for the average citizen.

The individuals represented in the sample reflect the expected population of Akhetaten, with males and females present in equal proportions and all ages represented, from fetal remains to the very old (i.e., 51+ years). Many of the people buried here may have lived in the Main City, the huge residential suburb south of the Central City. The bioarchaeological study of their skeletons suggests they had difficult lives that were full of heavy work, disease, and poor nutrition. These conditions were likely present throughout life, from childhood onward.

Hardships in childhood, whether nutritional, physical, or psychological, can have lasting effects throughout life. One way to examine generalized childhood stress in ancient populations is to examine adult height across the population, because when children experience stress, growth often slows or stops to allow resources to be reallocated toward stress management. The adults at Amarna were shorter than during any other time period in Egyptian history (for which comparative skeletal assemblages are available for study), suggesting life was difficult from an early age (fig. 130). The average adult male was 163cm tall (5'4") and the average adult female was just 153cm (5'0").

Further indicators of stress are linear enamel hypoplasias, horizontal grooves in the enamel of the teeth, which reflect extremely severe stress events during childhood (fig. 131). These grooves show bioarchaeologists that the child was fighting for its life, but recovered from whatever stress event had occurred (commonly disease or malnutrition). More than three-quarters of the individuals examined from the South Tombs Cemetery have at least one linear enamel hypoplasia, suggesting they were near death at least once during childhood.

Reduced adult stature and linear enamel hypoplasias are what bioarchaeologists call non-specific indicators of stress, meaning that we know the individual was stressed by something, but we cannot identify whether that stress was a disease, a physical or nutritional hardship, or some combination of all three. On the other hand, some conditions cause recognizable skeletal modifications that allow bioarchaeologists to identify their cause, such as nutritional deficiencies. At the South Tombs Cemetery, nutritional deficiencies were common (fig. 132). We have skeletal evidence of individuals with scurvy (18 percent of the sample), which results from a lack of vitamin C in the diet, and anemia (41 percent), which can be caused by low-iron diets, iron loss via parasites, and folate and other vitamin deficiencies.

Was life more difficult for the average citizen at Akhetaten than other cities? This is a difficult question to answer, in part because we have few large sets of human remains available for comparison from elsewhere. The citizen cemeteries are among the most modest of Amarna's ancient monuments, but the richness of information they provide on life in the past is almost unparalleled. —GD

Figure 129. An imagined funerary procession at one of the Amarna cemeteries, where the deceased were buried mostly in simple pits probably covered with piles of stones. Reconstruction by Fran Weatherhead. Image courtesy of the Amarna Project.

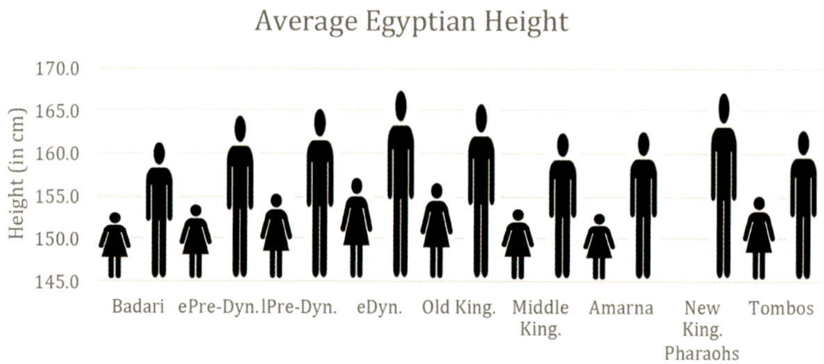

Figure 130. Average heights for males and females in different time periods throughout ancient Egyptian history, including the people buried in the cemetery near the South Tombs. Image courtesy of Gretchen Dabbs.

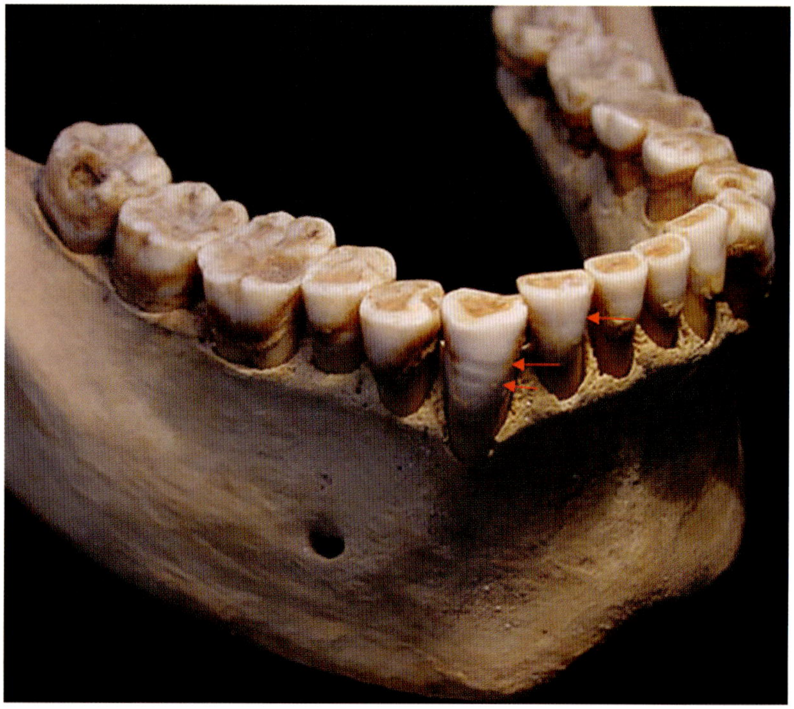

Figure 131. An adult mandible (lower jaw) with linear enamel hypoplasias on the canine (two) and lateral incisor (one). Image courtesy of the Amarna Project.

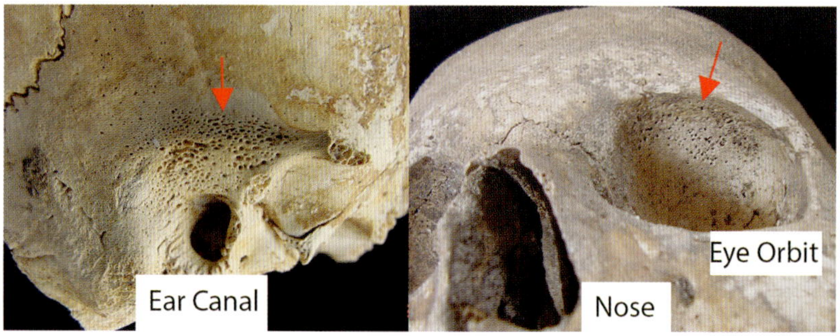

Figure 132. Skeletal manifestation (holes, or porosity) of scurvy (left) and anemia (right). Image courtesy of the Amarna Project.

IN FOCUS: HAIRSTYLES AT AKHETATEN

The way we wear our hair can reflect status, occupation, circumstance, and identity. Hundreds of samples of hair have been recovered from the Amarna cemeteries, including beards and eyebrows. Even eyelashes and nose hair have survived. Most important, though, is the sample of head hair, both styled and unstyled, which prompts a series of technical and social questions. Who dressed the hair of the dead, and how was this done? How skilled were the hairdressers? And how does hair analysis contribute to the understanding of the social positions of the people of Akhetaten?

Most women buried in the Amarna cemeteries who had hair preserved had it styled into braids, each around 2.5cm thick (fig. 133). This made a coiffure of 20 to 40 braids, hanging on either side of the head. The hair of young women was often styled into much thinner braids, less than 1cm across, resulting in over 60 to 90 braids per individual. Adults used extensions to increase their volume or hair length (fig. 133). Extensions were used on such a scale that, on occasion, hairstyles are found with more than 60 extensions, set in at different lengths of the hair. Extensions were braided into the hair, but also tied onto loose strands. They were made by folding swatches of hair and tying them with thin hair strands. Extensions were perhaps worn with pride: no attempts were made to hide the extension bulbs. Men usually wore their hair short without braids. No wigs have been found in the Amarna cemeteries.

Was the hair of the dead styled purposefully before burial? This is a distinct possibility. If so, the simple nature of the styles suggests that they could often have been produced by non-professional hairdressers, as though the dead were cared for by their relatives in the privacy of their homes. Taking care of the appearance of the dead in this way may have been part of the mourning rituals of the people of Akhetaten. Implements used in hair care, like combs and mirrors, have also occasionally been found in the Amarna burials. How far the styles reflect those worn in life is unknown, but it seems likely to at least some degree. Future research on the hair may tell us even more: about people's diet and health, for instance, and the socioeconomic importance of hair as we examine the origin of donor hair in the extensions. Study of hair from the Amarna cemeteries adds a new social dimension to our understanding of the people of ancient Akhetaten. —JB

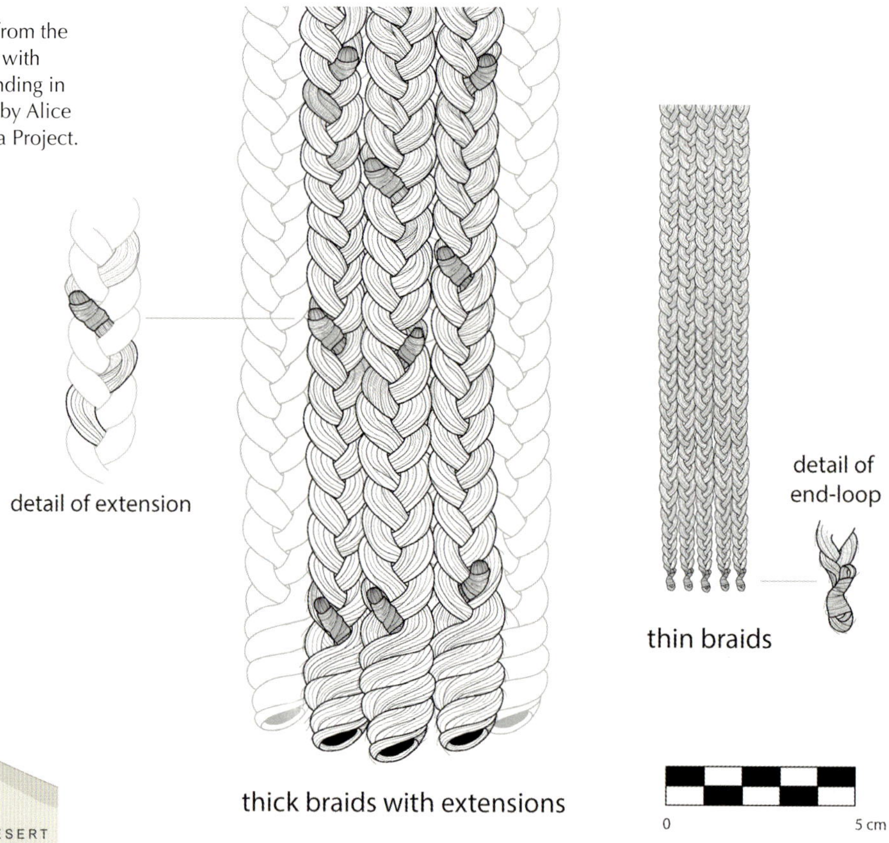

Figure 133. Common hairstyles from the Amarna cemeteries: thick braids with extensions, and thinner braids ending in a carefully tied loop. Illustration by Alice Salvador. Courtesy of the Amarna Project.

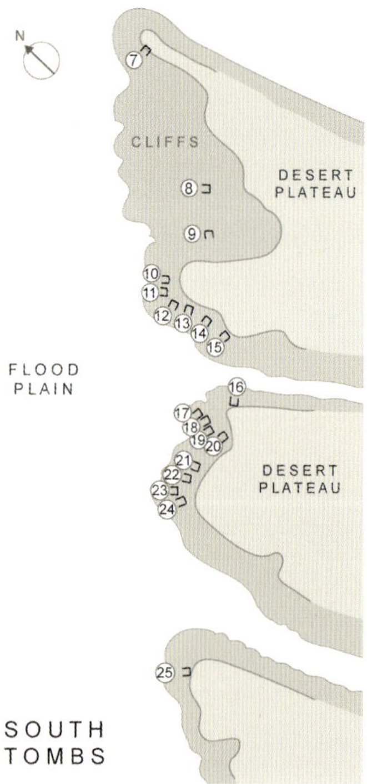

Figure 134. The South Tombs. Illustration by Mary Shepperson (after Davies, *The Rock Tombs of El Amarna*, Part 4, pl. XIII).

Tomb 7. Parennefer, "Royal Craftsman, Washer of Hands of His Majesty"

Parennefer's tomb (fig. 135) is quite simple, but it does have a fully decorated façade showing the royal family worshiping the Aten. Other images of the royal family and tomb owner survive inside, including what was once a detailed Window of Appearance scene.

Façade. On either side of the doorway into the tomb are the remains of scenes showing the royal family worshiping the Aten **(1, 2)**. Below the left-hand scene (1) is a narrow register with chariots, bodyguards, and, to the right, Parennefer kneeling in adoration, apparently of the king above. A further scene of the royal family worshiping occurs on the lintel above the door **(3)** and there are cartouches beneath the sun's disc on each doorjamb **(4, 5)**.

Entrance to the hall **(6, 7)**. On the north side (6), the royal family is depicted as if entering the tomb. Accompanied by shade-bearers, Akhenaten and Nefertiti embrace as they walk, with three of their daughters behind them, Meritaten and Ankhesenpaaten below, and Meketaten above. A narrower scene below shows bowing attendants. The third figure from the right, carrying a large water jug and towel, may be Parennefer himself. On the south side (7), Parennefer, facing outward, stands in an attitude of adoration and offers a prayer to the Aten.

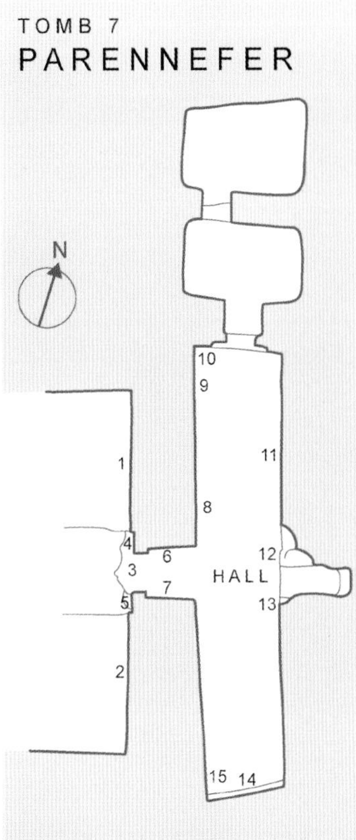

Figure 135. South Tomb 7: Parennefer. Illustration by Mary Shepperson (after Davies, *The Rock Tombs of El Amarna*, Part 6, pl. II).

Hall. The interior of the tomb, including the floor, is rough and unfinished. At the north end is a door leading to two low undecorated chambers of uncertain purpose. The decoration of the hall is partly carved and partly remains at the stage of outline sketches in ink. Following the scenes in a clockwise direction from the doorway:

(8, 9): Originally a detailed and lively scene of reward at the Window of Appearance, now partly destroyed. Akhenaten and Nefertiti, leaning on a cushion with lozenge pattern, stand at the Window, which is decorated beneath with bound foreign captives attached to the symbolic plants of Upper and Lower Egypt, an interwoven lotus and papyrus. Behind the Window, in a vertical arrangement, are details of the palace and three princesses. Nefertiti's sister Mutnodjmet originally stood at the far left. To the right of the Window is a courtyard filled with activity. In the second register from the bottom, Parennefer appears wearing several gold collars, while servants hand others to him from a casket. Presents in the form of foodstuffs in jars and sacks are carried off in the bottom register. To the right (9) is an ink sketch in five registers of Parennefer's homeward journey. Parennefer in his chariot was apparently greeted by his wife and by groups of musicians in the central register.

(10): The scene continues around the corner, in ink. Only traces at the bottom remain, evidently depicting Parennefer's house and garden.

(11): Traces of a further scene outlined in ink occupy the rear wall at the north end. In the original composition, the king sat beneath a canopy and the rays of the Aten. Two courtiers can be seen bowing before him. Behind them stand dishes, jars, and tables, and groups of musicians.

(12, 13): On the jambs of the intended entrance to the shrine or inner hall are traces of inscriptions in ink.

(14): On the end wall a false door has been outlined in ink.

(15): The remains of hieratic graffiti in red, almost illegible and of uncertain meaning. They are not part of the original decoration.

Tomb 8. Tutu, "Chamberlain, Chief Servitor of Neferkheperura-waenra (the King) in . . . (damaged text) . . . of the Temple of the Aten in Akhetaten, Overseer of All Works of His Majesty, Overseer of Silver and Gold of the Lord of the Two Lands," etc.

Tutu's titles and the extensive inscriptions in his tomb (fig. 136) show that he was one of the most important men in Akhenaten's court. He is perhaps named in the Amarna Letters as an official who served as intermediary between the king and foreign princes. Note the prominent position of his tomb in the local landscape. His tomb shows him being rewarded by the king. Look also for the behind-the-scenes glimpse of domestic activity in the Great Palace.

Façade. This was left plain except for the surround to the doorway, where prayers to the Aten were carved on the jambs **(1)** and a scene of the royal family added to the lintel **(2)**, now almost entirely weathered away.

Entrance to the outer hall **(3, 4)**. On the left (3), the royal family worships the Aten before a table of offerings. The faces of the king and queen, and figures of princesses, were carved on separate slabs of finer limestone, now lost. Below, Tutu kneels and offers a prayer, the shorter hymn to the Aten. A longer prayer originally occupied the right side (4), but this was largely destroyed late in the last century. Note also the bands of inscription on the ceiling.

Outer hall. Two rows of columns divide the outer hall into three aisles. The back row of columns are linked together in two groups by a low screen wall, the only Amarna tomb to have this architectural feature (see fig. 128). At either end of the hall, the intention was to cut three niches to contain statues of Tutu. Much is unfinished, however, providing a good opportunity to examine the methods of the ancient stonecutters. Following the scenes and points of interest in a counterclockwise direction from the doorway:

(5, 6): Tutu is appointed as Chief Servitor at the Window of Appearance (5). He stands in front of the Window, long formal speeches carved above him. Details of the palace are carved below and to the right of the Window, and over the lintel of the entrance doorway. Note, in the portion on the lintel, the separate chambers for girls, who are shown relaxing. To the left of the Window are rows of figures in the courtyard outside the palace: foreign emissaries at the top, soldiers, and then scribes below.

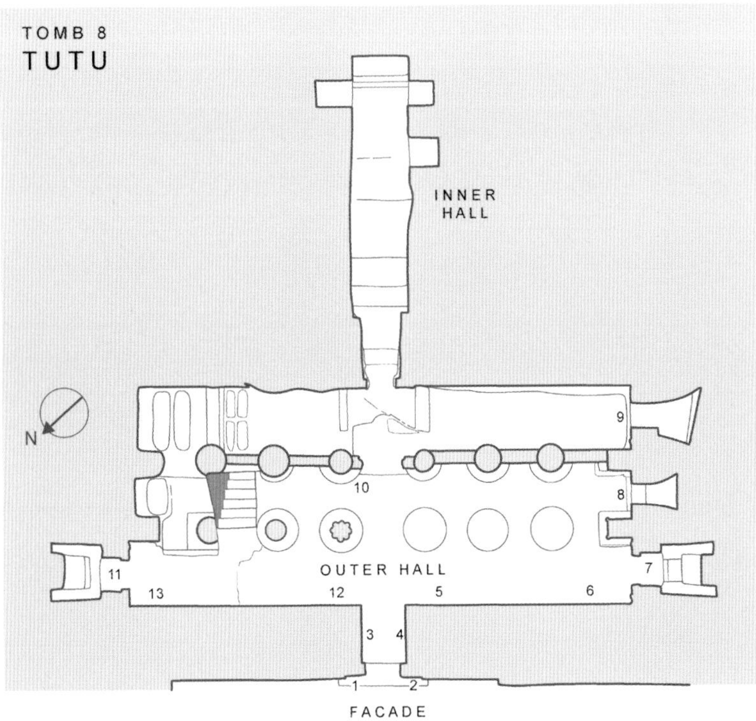

Figure 136. South Tomb 8: Tutu. Illustration by Mary Shepperson (after Davies, *The Rock Tombs of El Amarna*, Part 6, pl. XI).

At the far left end (6) is a simplified image of one of the Aten temples surrounded by trees, the only full temple depiction in the South Tombs. The space between this and the Window of Appearance shows Tutu emerging from the courtyard of the palace and then driving to the temple in a chariot. There are soldiers and musicians below, servants and soldiers above, and at the top a picture of military stables. Note the horses feeding from mangers and the military standards set in altar-like stands. Below this, to the right, is a long prayer in honor of the king.

(7–9): Three statue niches were intended here. Only in (7) has a start been made on blocking out the statue. Note the decorated panels above the entrances to (7) and (9).

(10): This column illustrates the decorative scheme of some of the columns in this hall. Akhenaten and Nefertiti are shown on a panel, while the rest of the column shaft and capital is decorated with motifs that include groups of hanging ducks. There are further depictions of the royal family and, at thc bottom, Tutu praying on the attached door jamb. The rear of the outer hall is undecorated and most of the northeast end is unfinished. One of the statue chambers **(11)**, however, has a rough block-out of the statue.

(12, 13): Tutu is appointed to be in charge of tax collection. Akhenaten and Nefertiti are shown seated, apparently outside the palace (12). Nefertiti originally held some of her daughters on her lap, but much of this group was carved on a separate inlaid slab, now lost. Behind the queen, and on the lintel of the entrance doorway, are details of the palace. Long speeches accompany Tutu's appointment. To the right (13) are rows of figures in the courtyard and sacrificial cattle with decorated horns (see fig. 19, right). Similar figures are shown outside, to the right, with female musicians at the bottom. Tutu addresses them with another loyal speech. A short prayer and figure of Tutu are carved beneath this scene.

In the floor of the hall, steps lead down to where the burial chamber was intended. Fifty-four steps were carved, in three flights, but the chamber was not cut.

Inner hall. Only a low gallery has been cut, with a start made on blocking out the columns toward the back.

Tomb 9. Mahu, "Chief of Police of Akhetaten"

This small and inconspicuous tomb (fig. 137) is the most complete of the South Tombs and contains unusually detailed scenes of Mahu's duties as police chief. He is shown apprehending a group of men trespassing on the city's border and taking stock of supplies that were perhaps intended for a desert work site. Another group of scenes shows the royal family in their chariots on a possible tour of inspection.

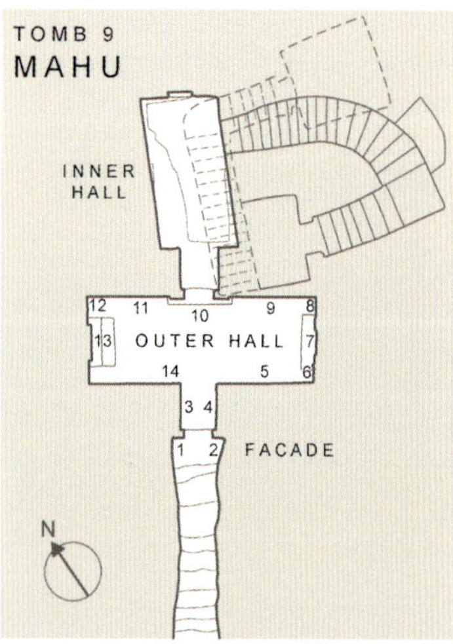

Figure 137. South Tomb 9: Mahu. Illustration by Mary Shepperson (after Davies, *The Rock Tombs of El Amarna*, Part 4, pl. XIII).

Façade. The façade occupies only the width of the narrow stairway, but the doorway was surrounded with the usual inscribed jambs **(1, 2)** and decorated lintel, the latter almost weathered away.

Entrance to the outer hall. On the left **(3)** the royal family offers to the Aten. Here, and throughout this tomb, only their eldest daughter, Meritaten, is shown. Below this panel is another one depicting Mahu in an act of adoration. In front of him is a short hymn to the Aten being spoken by the king. On the right **(4)** the decoration consists of a similar figure of Mahu and a duplicate of the hymn.

Outer hall. The T-shaped design of the tomb, with a transverse outer hall leading to a longitudinal hall, is derived from a standard pattern used in the Eighteenth Dynasty at Thebes (modern Luxor). The two ends of the outer hall are carved with stelae. The decoration in the outer hall is unfinished. Notice how the scenes remain in almost every stage of production, from the initial ink sketch to the finished relief.

Following the scenes counterclockwise from the doorway:

(5, 6): Scenes concerned with Mahu and his duties. Unfortunately, the lack of inscriptions leaves much of the meaning ambiguous. The central feature of the upper scene (5) is a fortified building containing weapons and stores. The location is not known. To the right of this building, men and women bring produce on their shoulders and by donkey, some of which is stored in vessels on wooden stands to the left (see fig. 31). Further goods are piled above and inspected by Mahu. At the top, he is shown again, talking to two senior officials, the first of whom is evidently the vizier. The meaning of the lower register of (5) is clearer. At the right is a building in ink, outside of which stands a damaged group of leading officials and army commanders, the vizier at the head. Mahu greets them, leading three foreign-looking prisoners wearing manacles: are they "desert dwellers" caught trespassing on the city's perimeter? Further to the left, Mahu rides in his chariot. In the next register up, he stands beside a brazier (fireplace) observing more of his men and his chariot.

At (6), in the narrow space beside the upper part of the stela, Mahu stands talking to a scribe, accompanied by his dog. Below this is an interesting little sketch in ink, now very faded, showing the interior of a building, perhaps Mahu's own house. A man squats inside warming his hands over a fire.

(7): A stela set within a false-door frame. The royal family, including Meritaten, offer trays of food to the Aten while, below, Mahu kneels before a prayer to the Aten spoken by the king.

(8, 9): Two main scenes are present. The upper scene (9) depicts the royal family driving in a chariot from a temple, with police running in front. The temple is rendered only in the form of a pylon entrance with columned portico and flagpoles from which streamers flutter. At (8), in the narrow space beside the stela, Mahu himself leads his men, being the solitary figure in the second register from the top. The destination of the royal chariot drive is above the lintel of the stela. It is a fortified building with towers and battlements, standing between and beside what seem to be four lines of fences or a double roadway. It might represent the North Riverside Palace, or even one of the two workers' villages, which are both surrounded by roadways.

The scene below seems to be a continuation of this. The royal family is again shown in the chariot (9), their figures largely destroyed. Mahu is shown both kneeling behind them and standing in front in an attitude of praise, while his men run forward to the left. Above them is a group of six enigmatic structures, which have been suggested as watch posts, representations of Boundary Stelae, or rock-cut tombs (fig. 138). Below the whole scene, the fence or roadway appears again, interrupted by more possible sentry posts or tombs. At (8) Mahu appears twice, in each case behind a more prominent official. The meaning of the scene is not clear. Is the Royal Family making a ritual visitation of the territorial limits of Akhetaten, or a more pragmatic inspection of the city's cliffside monuments?

(10): Around the doorway to the inner chamber are brief hymns, while the lintel depicts Mahu adoring Aten cartouches.

(11, 12): An impressive ink drawing originally depicting two separate scenes. Of the upper one, only the central part remains (11). It belongs to a reward scene in three registers, with a Window of Appearance at the right end. The preserved area portrays figures waiting in the courtyard outside. In the upper register are chariots, bowing courtiers are seen in the middle register, and in the lower register Mahu himself stands with arms upraised before a group of his men, while another man holds a military standard. Mahu was perhaps given the standard as a sign of his appointment during the reward scene.

In the lower scene, Mahu visits a temple. At the right edge is a depiction of the temple pylon raised on a pedestal. Mahu

Figure 138. The king and queen on a tour of inspection, shown in the Tomb of Mahu (South Tomb 9). After Davies, *The Rock Tombs of El Amarna*, Part 4, pl. XXII. Image courtesy of the Egypt Exploration Society.

is shown twice in front of it, standing in the upper register and kneeling in the lower. Behind Mahu are processions of his policemen, who were Medjay, originally a Nubian desert tribe. In the narrow space beside the stela (12), the lower scene continues with a lively image of men with a chariot. There are traces of female musicians above.

(13): The end wall is occupied in the center by a round-topped stela. The royal family worships the Aten above, while Mahu kneels below before a hymn to the Aten spoken by the king.

(14): A reward scene was intended here, but all that survives is part of an ink sketch of the royal family at the Window of Appearance.

Inner hall. An unfinished chamber. At the back is a partly carved doorway intended to open into the shrine. On the left side is an incomplete false door, matching the entrance to the burial chamber in the opposite wall. This leads to a winding staircase of 47 steps to a burial chamber.

Tomb 10. Ipy, "Royal Scribe, Steward"

Although small and largely undecorated, this tomb includes some of the best-preserved portraits of the king and queen at Amarna. They are shown on the left of the entrance with Princesses Meritaten, Meketaten, and Ankhesenpaaten presenting votive figures to the sun god (see fig. 5). Below, there was once a short dedication to the Aten written in ink. On the right side of the entrance is a well-preserved example of the shorter Hymn to the Aten. The doorway into the tomb was also originally framed with texts and a scene of royal worship.

Tomb 11. Ramose, "Royal Scribe, Commander of the Soldiers of the Lord of the Two Lands, Steward of the Estate of Nebmaatra (Amenhotep III)"

This small, simple tomb is of interest mainly for the decoration in the entranceway and the carved statues in the shrine.

Entrance. On the left side is a damaged scene of Akhenaten and Nefertiti offering to the Aten, and Princess Meritaten. On the right side is a kneeling figure of Ramose accompanied by a prayer for the king, praising his generosity.

Hall. At the back is a niche surrounded by a decorated frame. Inside is a pair of seated statues carved from the rock and finished in plaster, depicting Ramose and his sister or wife Nebet-iunet. Be careful of the open shaft on your left.

Tomb 12. Nakhtpaaten, "Prince, Chancellor, Vizier"

As vizier, Nakhtpaaten was one of the most important officials at Akhetaten, although very little work was done on his tomb. Only the façade and the entrance were completed, with the beginnings of three columns in the main hall.

The house of Nakhtpaaten, excavated in 1922, was one of the largest villas at Amarna. The remains of the house, now almost entirely destroyed, lie on the river side of the Main Road adjacent to the turnoff to the South Tombs.

Tomb 13. Neferkheperu-her-sekheper, "Mayor of Akhetaten"

This tomb is only half finished, but well preserved. The burial chamber has been cut, perhaps indicating that the tomb owner died before the tomb was finished. There is little decoration apart from around the doorway, where hastily cut inscriptions gave Neferkheperu-her-sekheper's name and titles, perhaps to commemorate him upon death.

Tomb 14. May, "Fan-bearer on the Right Hand of the King, Royal Scribe, Scribe of Recruits, Steward of the House of Sehetep-Aten, Steward of the House of Waenra in Heliopolis, Overseer of Cattle of the Estate of Ra in Heliopolis, Overseer of All the Works of the King, General of the Lord of the Two Lands"

May was a very high official early in Akhenaten's reign (fig. 139). Before the king's death, he had fallen from grace and most instances of his name have been carefully erased. Interestingly, he also had offices in the sun temples at Heliopolis, near Cairo.

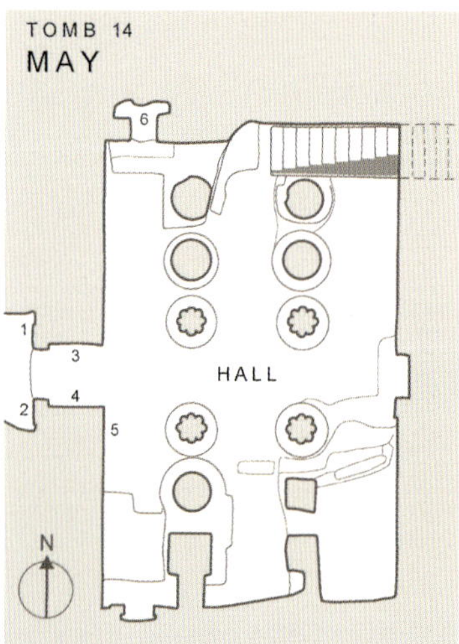

Figure 139. South Tomb 14: May. Illustration by Mary Shepperson (after Davies, *The Rock Tombs of El Amarna*, Part 5, pl. I).

Façade. The doorjambs **(1, 2)** are inscribed with funerary prayers and the lintel shows the royal family adoring the Aten, although the scene is almost destroyed.

Entrance to the hall **(3, 4)**. On the left side (3) is a panel depicting the royal family worshiping the Aten. Akhenaten and Nefertiti are followed by three daughters, Meritaten and Meketaten in the lowest register and Ankhesenpaaten above. Nefertiti's sister Mutnodjmet can be seen with her two attendant dwarfs in the register further above. Below the scene are 17 columns of hieroglyphs containing a prayer to the Aten. Note how the kneeling figure of May to the right has been hacked out and plastered over. On the right side of the entrance (4) five columns of hieroglyphs contained a brief description of May's career, emphasizing his promotion from humble birth. May's figure stood to the left, but this has also been defaced.

Hall. This was intended to contain 12 papyrus columns, but was never finished. A start has been made on carving out a door to an inner hall at the back. Statue niches were also intended in both sides of the hall; that on the north **(6)** contains a roughed-out standing figure of May. A stairway of 19 steps leads to an unfinished burial chamber.

The only decoration in the hall is on the south side of the west wall **(5)**, and is in ink. It belongs to a reward scene at the Window of Appearance, which was shown in the upper right-hand part. Below it ran a colonnade, underneath which is an unusual scene of the riverfront (see fig. 49). A sloping path leads down the vegetation-covered bank and a line of moored boats. The two principal boats belonged to the king and queen: notice their crowned heads carved on the ends of the steering oars. At the right edge of the scene are piles of oars, ropes, and spars. A man sits nearby making a net.

Tomb 15. Suti, "Standard-bearer of the Guild of Neferkheperura (Akhenaten)"

Tomb 16

The owner of this tomb is no longer known. There is no decoration in the tomb, but it does have a handsome and finely carved columned hall brought almost to completion.

Tomb 17

A small unfinished tomb preserving only the entrance and outer hall. There is no decoration to indicate its owner.

Tomb 18

Only the façade of this tomb was completed, but very little of this now survives. The inscriptions give adorations to the king, the queen, and the Aten. The name of the tomb owner is lost.

Tomb 19. Setau, "Overseer of the Treasury of the Lord of the Two Lands"

This is another unfinished tomb. Inside the entranceway there was once an inked image of the royal family worshiping the Aten, with a figure of Setau and a prayer below.

Tomb 20

The inner chambers have been partly cut, but the owner of the tomb is unknown. The only part of the tomb to be decorated was the lintel, which bears a partly finished scene of the royal family worshiping the Aten.

Tomb 21

The tomb owner is unknown. The outer hall of the tomb has been partly cut, with a portico-like arrangement of columns inside.

Tomb 22

Another unfinished tomb, its owner no longer known. The lintel of the main doorway has a scene of the royal family worshiping the Aten.

Tomb 23. Any, "Royal Scribe, Scribe of the Offering Table of the Aten, Steward of the Estate of Aakheperura (Amenhotep II)," etc.

This tomb (fig. 140) is unusual for the round-topped niches just inside its portico-like entranceway. These originally contained small memorial stelae for Any (fig. 141). Inside, the tomb is largely undecorated apart from the statue of Any in the shrine, with painted figures of him on the walls on either side. The dedicatory stelae and the care taken to finish Any's statue, his body substitute after death, leave little doubt that this tomb was used for his burial.

Figure 140. South Tomb 23: Any. Illustration by Mary Shepperson (after Davies, *The Rock Tombs of El Amarna*, Part 5, pl. VIII).

Façade **(1, 2)**. On either side of the door three columns of hieroglyphs give the cartouches of the Aten, Akhenaten, and Nefertiti, as Any offers a short prayer below. The lintel is very eroded, but depicts the royal family worshiping the Aten.

Entrance to hall **(3, 4)**. The decoration has been set out in red paint on a yellow ground. Large figures of Any stand on each side, that on the left (3) facing outward and offering a prayer, and that on the right (4) shown entering the tomb.

Hall. The surfaces of the walls have been prepared, but no decoration was added apart from a cornice, bright with paint, along the top. The now filled-in shaft in the floor leads to a burial chamber beneath the shrine.

Shrine. At the back sits a rock-hewn statue of Any at the top of a little flight of steps. Both sides of the shrine are decorated in paint only. On the left **(5)**, Any sits before a table of offerings, attended by a servant called Meryre. In a similar scene on the right **(6)** he is joined by his wife, whose name is not preserved.

Tomb 24. Pa-aten-em-heb, "Royal Scribe, Overseer of Soldiery, Steward, Overseer of Works"

Only the entrance to the tomb is preserved, once decorated with inscriptions giving the name and titles of the tomb owner.

Tomb 25. Ay, "God's Father, Fan-bearer on the Right Hand of the King, Overseer of Horses of His Majesty," etc.

Ay briefly became king at the end of the Amarna period, after the death of Tutankhamun. As king, he had a tomb cut in the Western Valley at the Valley of the Kings at Thebes, but his Amarna tomb (fig. 142) was cut when he was still a senior official in Akhenaten's court. It includes a Window of Appearance scene in which the figures of the royal family are the best preserved at Amarna. Inside the entrance hall is a scene of the royal family worshiping the Aten, with beautifully carved images below of Ay and his wife, a lady named Tey. The most complete example of the longer Hymn to the Aten also appears in Ay's tomb, on the right side of the entrance.

Figure 141. A drawing of one of the memorial stelae that was once set into the entrance of Any's tomb. At the top, Any is shown with the donor of the stela, a scribe called Nebwawi. Below, Nebwawi leads a sacrificial ox, probably to be slaughtered and offered to the sun god on behalf of Any. After Kemp, *The City of Akhenaten and Nefertiti*, fig. 3.29. Image courtesy of Barry Kemp.

Façade **(1, 2)**. The doorjambs were originally decorated with prayers and the lintel with a scene of the royal family, but these are very worn.

Entrance to the hall **(3, 4)**. On the left (3) an upper panel depicts Akhenaten and Nefertiti worshiping the Aten in front of a table of offerings. Behind them, on the bottom register, are three daughters, and, in the register above, the queen's sister Mutnodjmet accompanied by two dwarfs, now damaged, each ironically called "the vizier." Below this panel is the text of a long prayer and beautifully modeled but damaged figures of Ay and his wife. The right side (4) is taken up with the text of the famous Hymn to the Aten. This is the longest copy of the Aten hymns in any of the Amarna tombs, although many shorter versions occur.

Hall. This was planned on an ambitious scale, but less than half was completed. Three rows of eight columns were intended, set very closely together except for the central aisle, leading to the door of the inner hall. Most of the southwest side of the hall remains to be carved from the rock, while only four of the columns flanking the central aisle have been fully carved in detail. On the finished columns, raised panels depict Ay and his wife adoring cartouches. The ceiling has the remains of a painted pattern with lines of prayers.

Proceeding clockwise from the entrance:

(5, 6): The only completed scene in the tomb (5, 6) is the standard reward scene at the Window of Appearance. Note the quality of carving and relative lack of mutilation of the royal figures, which make this one of the most important examples of this scene at Amarna. The figures of the royal family are carved on blocks of high-quality limestone, inserted into the wall. Three princesses accompany

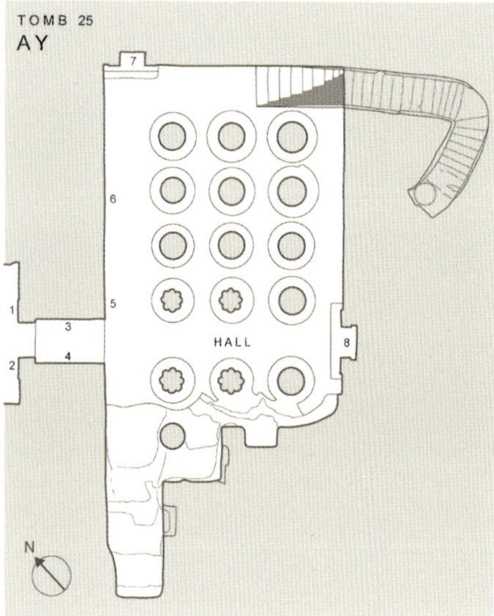

Figure 142. South Tomb 25: Ay. Illustration by Mary Shepperson (after Davies, *The Rock Tombs of El Amarna*, Part 6, pl. XXII).

Akhenaten and Nefertiti: Meritaten at the left, shown throwing a collar to Ay, Meketaten above her, and Ankhesenpaaten between the royal couple. The entire family appears to be naked. Note the tiny hands of the Aten's rays clasping the king's body.

Behind the Window (5), and stretching over the entrance doorway, is a particularly clear and detailed picture of the palace. Note the figure of Mutnodjmet, Nefertiti's sister, the second figure from the bottom on the right. The king's bedroom contains a bed and three footstools at the top, there is a servants' house to the left, and a separate house for girl musicians is located above the doorway, in which the girls are shown hairdressing, eating, and playing instruments, with a separate instrument store beside. Further to the left, this part of the scene is repeated in reverse, as the beginning of an intended repetition of the whole reward scene.

To the right of the Window is the courtyard of the palace. Ay and his wife stand at the bottom receiving their gifts, which included not only collars, but also dishes of precious metal and, on top of the pile of gifts in front of them, a pair of gloves. Five registers of figures fill the courtyard behind them: two royal chariots at the top, scribes with a small group of foreign representatives at the back, two rows of officials and soldiers, and a group of comic dancers at the bottom. Further to the right (6) is a scene outside the courtyard. At the top sit a group of soldiers beside standards in special supports. Below come the chariots and servants of Ay's homeward procession. Just outside the gateway from the courtyard, which is itself illuminated by the Aten's rays, Ay himself stands, drawn only in ink outline. He wears his gold collars and the gloves, painted in solid red.

(7, 8): At (7) is the doorway to an intended statue niche, never completed. At (8) is a similar doorway to a planned inner hall. The decorated jambs and lintel are now almost totally destroyed. In the northeast corner of the hall, notice the steps leading down into the rock. Twenty-nine steps in two flights tail off into a shallow, unfinished burial chamber.

Kom al-Nana

Kom al-Nana is a huge religious complex on the southern outskirts of Amarna (fig. 143). It preserves both a Sunshade Temple for Queen Nefertiti and the remains of an early Christian monastery. There were originally four probable Sunshade Temples in the area, places where the king would be connected to the regenerative powers of the sun god. The

Kom al-Nana complex is the only one that now survives. Although the visible ruins are somewhat difficult to understand, archaeological excavations have yielded a wealth of information on both phases of use.

Most of the walls visible in the northern end of the complex belong to the monastery, which was built in around the fifth to sixth centuries AD, and included a small church decorated with colored wall paintings. At the other end of the complex, walls from the Amarna-period Sunshade Temple can be seen. The temple complex was divided into two large enclosures with open-air altars and shrines (fig. 144). It also contained facilities for supporting temple staff and cult: houses, a well, garden plots for growing food, and a bakery/brewery.

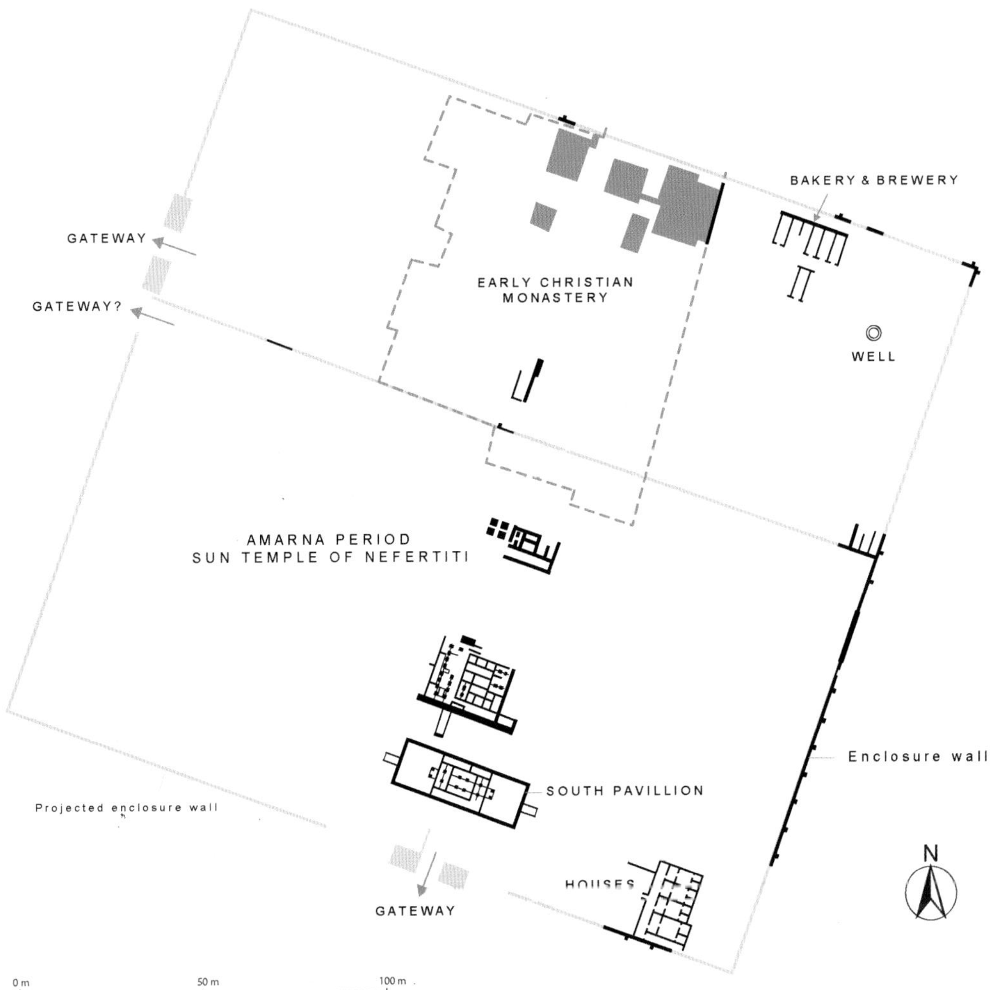

Figure 143. Kom al-Nana. Illustration by Mary Shepperson (after Kemp, "Outlying Temples at Amarna," fig. 15.14).

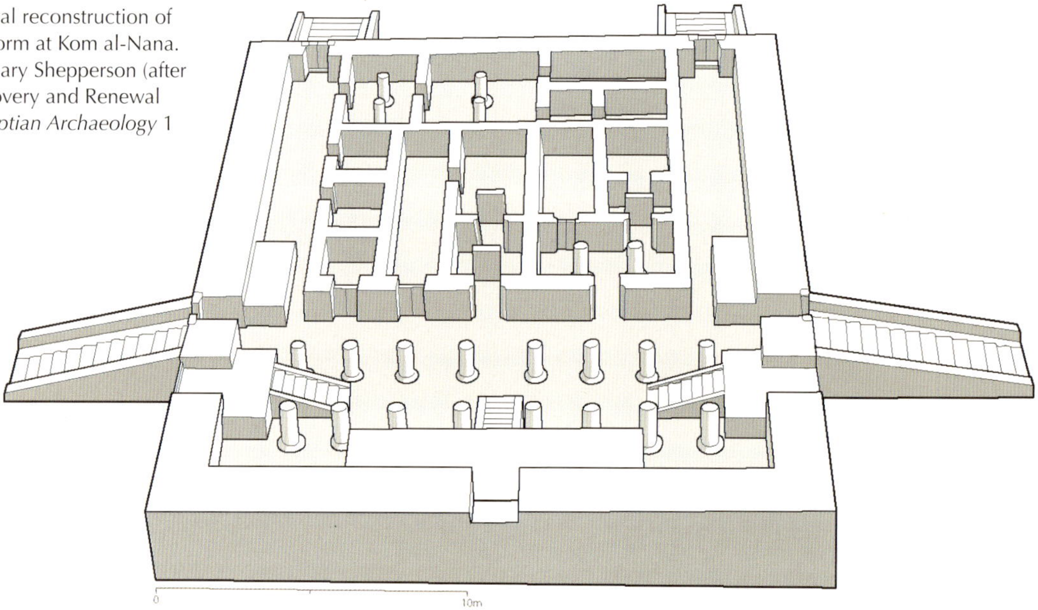

Figure 144. Partial reconstruction of the central platform at Kom al-Nana. Illustration by Mary Shepperson (after B. Kemp, "Discovery and Renewal at Amarna," *Egyptian Archaeology* 1 (1991): 19–22).

IN FOCUS: AMARNA'S LOST TEMPLES

The grand temples of the Central City were not the only important cult buildings at Akhetaten. Around the southeast outskirts of the city, Akhenaten constructed at least four huge ritual complexes, creating something like a southern cult zone. These had a very special character. They were called "Sunshades of Re," and were places for the worship of the solar cult, but with an added divine presence: the royal women of Amarna. Sunshade Temples in ancient Egypt were ritual hubs for the king's divine renewal and daily rebirth. They drew upon the attributes of Hathor, the solar goddess of sexuality, fertility, and celebration, and of Isis, the goddess who safeguarded the king. At Amarna, royal women served as stand-ins for these goddesses, who could not be worshiped under Atenism. The large number of Sunshade Temples at Amarna is highly unusual. Most kings had only one, but Akhenaten may have had as many as seven (if not more). Queen Nefertiti, the king's mother, Tiye (fig. 145), and the royal daughters Ankhesenpaaten and Meritaten (reusing a temple for Kiya) all had Sunshades. The Sunshade for Nefertiti is listed on the foundation texts in the Boundary Stelae. Akhenaten clearly considered these temples to be a crucial component of the Aten cult.

Perhaps the most evocative of the Amarna Sunshade temples was called the Maru-Aten in ancient Egyptian (fig. 146). Excavated rapidly in the 1920s, inscriptions reveal that this was the Sunshade for Meritaten,

Akhenaten's eldest daughter. She was not the first owner, however—her name seems to have been carved over that of Kiya, a prominent secondary wife of the king. Like the Sunshade for Nefertiti, the temple had two enclosures, one containing a large shallow lake surrounded by gardens and orchards. There were also a raised viewing platform and solar altars standing on an artificial island. Excavations at the Sunshade of Meritaten produced many beautiful pieces of ritual architecture, including finely carved and painted columns. The Sunshade also featured pavements painted with colorful scenes of the natural world, such as ducks emerging from papyrus clumps with their wings flapping. The artificial lake, the extensive gardens, and the painted scenes all, very purposefully, showcased the beauty of nature. The Sunshade formed an architectural example of the regenerative aspects of the Aten cult. It advertised that belief in the Aten would bring about abundance and beauty. Many of the elaborate architectural pieces and floor paintings from Amarna that are now housed in museum collections originated from this site.

Unfortunately, most of Amarna's Sunshade temples, isolated on the outskirts of the archaeological site, have been unable to withstand the desire for agricultural land over recent centuries, the Sunshade of Meritaten included. The only one that survives is at Kom al-Nana, the Sunshade of Nefertiti. This makes Kom al-Nana of unparalleled importance for our understanding of how Sunshade Temples functioned, not only at Amarna but generally in ancient Egypt. —JW

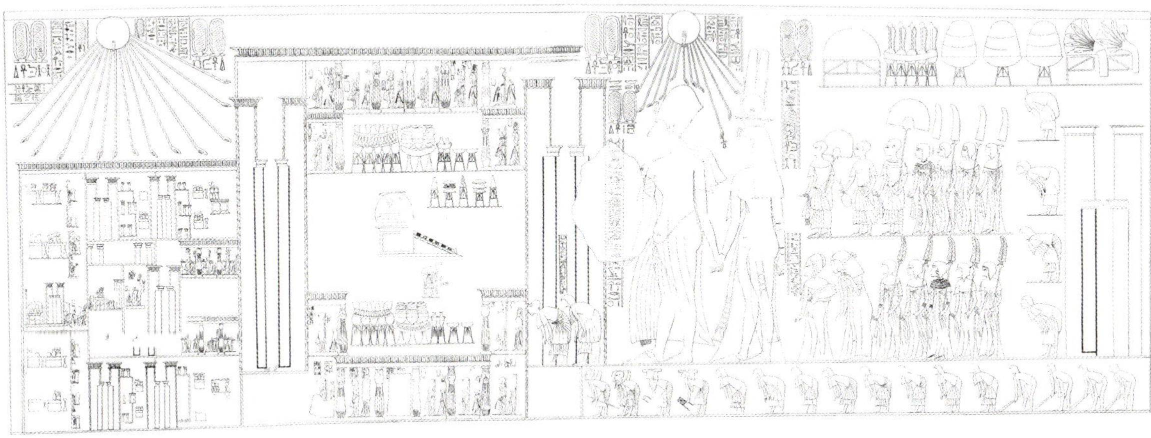

Figure 145. The Tomb of Huya (North Tomb 1) contains a scene of Queen Tiye and her son Akhenaten visiting Tiye's own Sunshade of Re Temple at Akhetaten. After Davies, *The Rock Tombs of El Amarna*, Part 3, pl. VIII. Image courtesy of the Egypt Exploration Society.

Figure 146. One of the Maru-Aten shrines when excavated in 1922, including parts of the elaborately decorated columns showing plants, fruit, and hanging ducks. EES Amarna Archive Negatives 1922.75, 78, 87. Photos courtesy of the Egypt Exploration Society.

IN FOCUS: RECONSTRUCTING NEFERTITI'S SUNSHADE

The site of Kom al-Nana, perhaps meaning "mound of mint," was excavated in the 1960s by the Supreme Council of Antiquities of Egypt and again in the 1980s and 1990s by the Egypt Exploration Society. The excavators documented a huge walled compound that held many different structures inside. In addition to an industrial-scale brewery (one of only three at Amarna), there were two shrines built of stone talatat blocks and several mud-brick structures, one of which is likely to be a Window of Appearance.

Kom al-Nana is unusual in that much of its decorated stonework was left behind. The demolition teams who dismantled Akhenaten's city after his death removed the main decorated blocks from the temple, but left many stone chippings, which fell to the ground not far from their original locations. Careful excavation and analysis of these fragments allows for something of the decorative scheme of the temple to be reconstructed (fig. 147). It is, in fact, the only one of Amarna's surviving temples where wall reliefs can be matched fairly closely to the architectural footprint of the ancient building. But the task is not without challenges! All that remains are tiny snippets of the original scenes. Using proportions and comparing the fragments with more intact ritual scenes—especially those in the Amarna tombs—it is possible to gradually reconstruct something of the original decoration of Nefertiti's Sunshade. The scenes show a familiar set of motifs, dominated by the royal family worshiping the Aten. Unlike in her famous Karnak reliefs, Nefertiti is not an especially dominant figure in these scenes: it is her role within the family and as Akhenaten's divine consort that seems to be important here.

Inscriptions from the temple also reveal insights into how it functioned. They show, for example, that it played an important role in the mortuary cults of the elite at Akhetaten. Deceased officials visited Nefertiti's Sunshade as spirits to obtain offerings to sustain them for eternity. This is a valuable piece of information on mortuary religion at Akhetaten, of which we know relatively little.

Another surprising aspect of the site is the near-absence of evidence for *damnatio memoriae* (iconoclastic destruction). The damage to the temple seems to have been aimed primarily at dismantling the buildings, not at defacement. Usually the pattern of destruction at Kom al-Nana indicates that large, fairly imprecise tools were driven straight into the wall with a heavy mallet. Only in a couple of cases does the damage seem to have been done to deliberately carve out royal names. Here, the tool used was one of the finer carving instruments applied at an angle to gouge out only the upper surface of the stone.

Why was such destruction minimal at Kom al-Nana, compared to other areas of Amarna? The South Tombs, for example, show ample evidence of *damnatio memoriae*. The tombs are more remote than Kom al-Nana, so isolation is unlikely to be a factor in the irregular pattern of destruction. Perhaps, if Nefertiti was still alive at the end of the Amarna period, the temple's affiliation with her household helped to preserve it from the post-Amarna-period backlash. —JW

Figure 147. Pieces of broken-up relief work are scaled and compared against known scene types to reconstruct the decorative program of Nefertiti's Sunshade of Re at Kom al-Nana. This scene shows the Aten being venerated by Akhenaten and Nefertiti, and nourished by food offerings. Reconstruction by Jacquelyn Williamson.

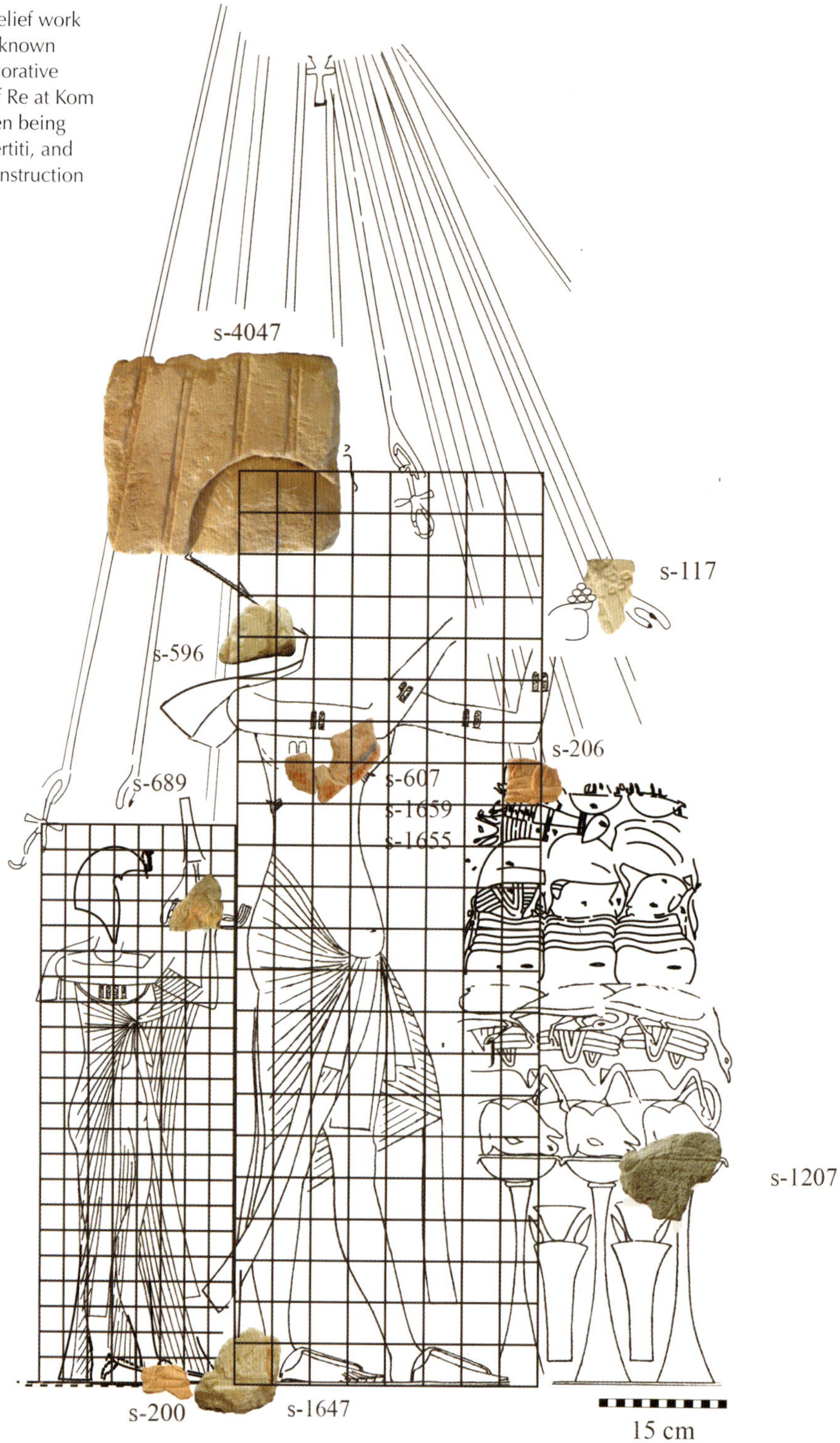

IN FOCUS: MONASTIC LIFE

The Kom al-Nana monastery, probably called Teclooce by its residents, was like a small village (fig. 148). It was built at the desert edge at a distance from where most people lived, with a wall around it to separate the religious space from the outside world. The buildings included a small church with a scene of the Apostles and Christ Triumphant in the sanctuary (fig. 149), a kitchen and animal pens, living and working spaces, refectories for communal eating, and two multi-story towers. Most of the buildings were in white-plastered mud brick, some spaces with simple painted decoration. The courtyard next to the church is unusual because it had a stone floor.

We know about how the monks lived from the things they left behind or threw away, such as pottery, cooking waste, and a few texts. The pottery includes highly polished red- and cream-colored bowls and cups with stamped decoration, the height of fashion around the Mediterranean at the time. The examples here were made both in Aswan and probably also at nearby Sheikh Ibada. Other vessels, often highly decorated, were probably also for food service and preparation. Large basins and storage vats are similar to the *magur* and *sawami'* still used in Egypt in recent times. The many water-lifting jars (*qawadis*) show that there must have been a well nearby with a complex lifting device *(saqya)*. Transport jars (like modern *balalis*) for wine, oil, soft cheese, pickle, fish sauce, and other food items were abundant. Most were made in Egypt, but some came from North Africa, Cyprus, Lebanon, and Gaza.

The plants and animal bones in the cooking waste show that the monks ate quite well, despite the image of self-denial presented in monastic literature. Like in modern Egyptian villages, the basic food was bread. The monks also ate lentils, seasoned their food with coriander, dill, and cumin, and enjoyed fruit that included figs, peaches, mulberries, and dates. Their diet also contained many kinds of meat, such as beef, pork, sheep/goat, chicken, duck, and pigeon, as well as several types of fish. The most common was catfish, which was also used to make a preserved fish sauce. The monks ate their meals together in the refectory. This monastery is unusual in having two refectories. One refectory located near the kitchens was perhaps used by the monks themselves and the second might have been reserved for visitors, who stayed in the adjacent tower.

The few brief surviving documents, written on fragments of pottery—the ancient equivalent of text messages!—tell us that although living physically and spiritually separated, the monastery still had dealings with the local communities. They made and received payments relating to agricultural land and also paid various taxes, one text recording a payment of two jars of wine. These records, and a painted prayer on the walls of the monastery, give the names of some of the monks, including its head Apa (abbot) Phib, Eisak, Phoibammon, and Aroou the Younger. A visitor, Kirakos, from a place called Kej, also left a prayer in the courtyard. —GP

Figure 148. The Monastery at Kom al-Nana during excavations in the 1990s. Photo courtesy of the Amarna Project.

Figure 149. Part of the painting from the apse of the church inside the Kom al-Nana Monastery. It shows one of the Apostles, probably John, holding a large book representing his Gospel. Photo courtesy of the Amarna Project.

FURTHER INFORMATION

The most complete study of Amarna is Barry Kemp's book, *The City of Akhenaten and Nefertiti: Amarna and Its People*. The website of the Amarna Project (www.amarnaproject.com) provides information on the site and its research history, while the Egypt Exploration Society website (www.ees.ac.uk) gives details of their early work at Amarna and links to important online resources, including archives of fieldwork photographs and film footage. The Deutsche Orient-Gesellschaft website also gives information on their excavations at the site in the early 20th century (http://www.orient-gesellschaft.de/forschungen/projekt.php?a=36).

Akhenaten and the Amarna Period

There are many histories of the Amarna period and biographies of Akhenaten, including those listed below. Dominic Montserrat's book can be singled out for exploring the cultural milieu in which Akhenaten was "rediscovered" by modern scholars, while William Murnane's *Texts from the Amarna Period in Egypt* gives the chance to explore the voices of the Amarna period almost, if not quite, first-hand.

Arnold, D. 1996. *The Royal Women of Amarna: Images of Beauty from Ancient Egypt*. New York: Metropolitan Museum of Art.

Dodson, A. 2014. *Amarna Sunrise: From Golden Age to Age of Heresy*. Cairo: American University in Cairo Press.

Dodson, A. 2018. *Amarna Sunset: Nefertiti, Tutankhamun, Ay, Horemheb, and the Egyptian Counter Reformation*. Revised edition. Cairo: American University in Cairo Press.

Freed, R.E., Y.J. Markowitz, and S.H. D'Auria, eds. 1999. *Pharaohs of the Sun: Akhenaten, Nefertiti, Tutankhamen*. Boston: Museum of Fine Arts, Boston.

Gabolde, M. 2005. *Akhenaton: Du mystère à la lumière*. Paris: Découvertes Gallimard.

Kemp, B. 2012. *The City of Akhenaten and Nefertiti: Amarna and Its People*. London: Thames and Hudson.

Laboury, D. 2010. *Akhénaton: Les grands pharaons*. Paris: Pygmalion.

Montserrat, D. 2000. *Akhenaten: History, Fantasy and Ancient Egypt*. London: Routledge.

Murnane, W. 1995. *Texts from the Amarna Period in Egypt*. Atlanta: Society of Biblical Literature.

Seyfried, F. 2012. *In the Light of Amarna: 100 Years of the Discovery of Nefertiti*. Berlin: Michael Imhof.

The Archaeology of Amarna

In the last two centuries, there have been a number of archaeological projects at Amarna, the most of substantial of which have been:

1891–92: Fieldwork by Flinders Petrie, especially in and around the Central City.

1911–14: Excavations of the Deutsche Orient-Gesellschaft (DOG), primarily in the Main City.

1921–36: Widespread excavations of the Egypt Exploration Society (EES).

1960s onward: Excavations of the (now) Egyptian Ministry of Tourism and Antiquities at Kom al-Nana and in housing areas.

Since 1977: An international collaborative program of survey, excavation, and restoration lead by Barry Kemp (Amarna Project/University of Cambridge), under the auspices of the Egypt Exploration Society until 2006.

More information on this work and other fieldwork initiatives can be found in the readings below, although this is far from an exhaustive list. The website of the Amarna Project (www.amarnaproject.com) also provides details of specialist projects and publications, far too numerous to list here.

Survey

Fenwick, H. 2004. "Ancient Roads and GPS Survey: Modelling the Amarna Plain." *Antiquity* 78: 880–85.

Kemp, B., and S. Garfi. 1993. *A Survey of the Ancient City of el-'Amarna*. London: Egypt Exploration Society.

North and South Tombs

Davies, N. de G. 1903–1908 (reprinted 2004). *The Rock Tombs of el-Amarna*. Parts 1–6. London: Egypt Exploration Society.

Owen, G., and B. Kemp. 1994. "Craftsmen's Work Patterns in Unfinished Tombs at Amarna." *Cambridge Archaeological Journal* 4: 121–29.

Royal Tomb

The principal modern missions in the Royal Wadi are those of Geoffrey Martin and Ali al-Khouly in the 1970s and 1980s, and Marc Gabolde in the early 2000s. The Ministry of Tourism and Antiquities also runs a long-term conservation project in this and the other rock-cut tombs at Amarna.

Gabolde, M., and A. Dunsmore. 2004. "The Royal Necropolis at Tell el-Amarna." *Egyptian Archaeology* 25: 30–33.

el-Khouly, A., and G.T. Martin. 1987. *Excavations in the Royal Necropolis at el-'Amarna 1984*. Cairo: Institut français d'archéologie orientale.

Martin, G.T. 1974. *The Royal Tomb at el-'Amarna*. Vol. 1, *The Objects*. London: Egypt Exploration Society.

Martin, G.T. 1989. *The Royal Tomb at el-'Amarna*. Vol. 2, *The Reliefs, Inscriptions, and Architecture*. London: Egypt Exploration Society.

Boundary Stelae

Davies, N. de G. 1908 (reprinted 2004). *The Rock Tombs of El Amarna*. Vol. 5, *Smaller Tombs and Boundary Stelae*. London: Egypt Exploration Fund.

Murnane, W.J., and C.C. Van Siclen. 1993. *The Boundary Stelae of Akhenaten*. London: Kegan Paul International.

Central City

The Central City was excavated by the EES in the 1930s, following smaller-scale work by Petrie in the late 19th century. The EES/Amarna Project restarted work in this area in the 1980s.

Pendlebury, J.D.S. 1951. *The City of Akhenaten*. Part 3, *The Central City and the Official Quarters*. 2 vols. London: Egypt Exploration Society.

Petrie, W.M.F. 1894. *Tell El Amarna*. London: Methuen.

The Northern Palaces

The North Palace was excavated the early 1920s by the EES and re-cleared and restudied in the 1990s. The North Riverside Palace has seen only limited fieldwork, in the 1930s.

Spence, K. 1999. "The North Palace at Amarna." *Egyptian Archaeology* 15: 14–16.

Spence, K. 2009. "The Palaces of el-Amarna: Towards an Architectural Analysis." In *Egyptian Royal Residences*, edited by R. Gundlach and J.H. Taylor, 165–87. Wiesbaden: Harrassowitz.

The Southern Temples

The EES excavated briefly at the now-destroyed Maru-Aten in the 1920s. Osiris Gabriel worked on behalf of the (now) Ministry of Tourism and Antiquities at Kom al-Nana in the 1960s, and the EES/Amarna Project resumed work at this site in the 1990s.

Kemp, B.J. 1995. "Outlying Temples at Amarna." In *Amarna Reports* 6, edited by B.J. Kemp, 411–62. London: Egypt Exploration Society.

Peet, T.E., and C. Woolley. 1923. *The City of Akhenaten*. Vol. 1, *Excavations of 1921 and 1922 at el-'Amarna*. London: Egypt Exploration Society.

Williamson, J. 2016. *Nefertiti's Sun Temple: A New Cult Complex at Tell el-Amarna*. 2 vols. Leiden: Brill.

Desert Altars

Recorded by the EES in the 1930s and briefly by the EES/Amarna Project in the early 2000s.

Frankfort, H., and J.D.S. Pendlebury. 1933. *The City of Akhenaten*. Part 2, *The North Suburb and the Desert Altars: The Excavations at Tell el Amarna During the Seasons 1926–1932*. London: Egypt Exploration Society.

Kemp, B.J. 1995. "Outlying Temples at Amarna." In *Amarna Reports* 6, edited by B.J. Kemp, 411–62. London: Egypt Exploration Society.

Riverside Housing Areas

The DOG and the EES undertook widespread excavations in the Main City in the early part of the 20th century. The Ministry of Tourism and Antiquities and the EES/Amarna Project have also undertaken smaller-scale campaigns in recent decades. The North Suburb was extensively cleared by the EES from 1926 to 1931. Several workshops in the Main City have also seen targeted excavations.

Frankfort, H., and J.D.S. Pendlebury. 1933. *The City of Akhenaten*. Vol. 2, *The North Suburb and the Desert Altars: The Excavations at Tell el Amarna during the Seasons 1926–1932*. London: Egypt Exploration Society.

Hamza, M., and B. Kemp. 2000. "Report on a Large House at Amarna, Discovered near the Village of el-Hagg Qandil." *Journal of Egyptian Archaeology* 86: 161–65.

Kemp, B., and A. Stevens. 2010. *Busy Lives at Amarna: Excavations in the Main City (Grid 12 and the House of Ranefer, N49.18)*. 2 vols. London: Egypt Exploration Society and Amarna Trust.

Nicholson, P.T. 2007. *Brilliant Things for Akhenaten: The Production of Glass, Vitreous Materials and Pottery at Amarna Site O45.1*. London: Egypt Exploration Society.

Peet, T.E., and C. Woolley. 1923. *The City of Akhenaten*. Vol. 1, *Excavations of 1921 and 1922 at el-'Amarna*. London: Egypt Exploration Society.

Workers' Villages

The Workmen's Village was excavated by the EES in 1921 and 1922, and again by the EES/Amarna Project from 1979 to 1986. The Stone Village was the subject of a fieldwork campaign from 2005 to 2009.

Kemp, B.J. 1987. "The Amarna Workmen's Village in Retrospect." *Journal of Egyptian Archaeology* 72: 21–50.

Peet, T.E., and C. Woolley. 1923. *The City of Akhenaten*. Vol. 1, *Excavations of 1921 and 1922 at el-'Amarna*. London: Egypt Exploration Society.

Stevens, A. 2012. *Akhenaten's Workers: The Amarna Stone Village Survey, 2005–2009*. 2 vols. London: Egypt Exploration Society and Amarna Trust.

Amarna's Cemeteries

First located by surveyor Helen Fenwick in the early 2000s, the non-elite cemeteries were investigated from 2005 onward.

Dabbs, G.R., J.C. Rose, and M. Zabecki. 2015. "The Bioarchaeology of Akhetaten: Unexpected Results from a Capital City." In *Egyptian Bioarchaeology: Humans, Animals, and the Environment*, edited by S. Ikram, J. Kaiser, and R. Walker, 43–52. Leiden: Sidestone Press.

Kemp, B., A. Stevens, G.R. Dabbs, M. Zabecki, and J.C. Rose. 2013. "Life, Death and Beyond in Akhenaten's Egypt: Excavating the South Tombs Cemetery at Amarna." *Antiquity* 87: 64–78.

Stevens, A. 2018. "Death and the City: The Cemeteries of Amarna in Their Urban Context." *Cambridge Archaeological Journal* 28: 103–26.

Early Christian Occupation of Amarna

Much of the fieldwork undertaken by the EES/Amarna Project at Kom al-Nana in the 1990s and 2000s focused on its monastery and church. An extensive survey of the settlement at the North Tombs, and the Panehesy church, was undertaken in the 2000s as the North Tombs Settlement Project.

Kemp, B. 1993. "Amarna's Other Period." *Egyptian Archaeology* 3: 13–14.

Pyke, G. 2008. "A Christian Conversion: The Tomb of Panehsy at Amarna." *Egyptian Archaeology* 32: 8–10.

Pyke, G. 2010. "The Christian Settlement at the Amarna North Tombs." *Egyptian Archaeology* 37: 13–15.

On the Early Excavations (and Excavators) at Amarna

Brasch, C. 2007. *In Egypt*. Aotearoa: Steele Roberts.

Chubb, M. 1954. *Nefertiti Lived Here*. London: Libri Publications.

Grundon, I. 2007. *The Rash Adventurer: A Life of John Pendlebury*. London: Libri Publications.

Pendlebury, J. 1935. *Tell el-Amarna*. London: Lovat Dickson & Thompson.

Egyptian History in General

al-Sayyid Marsot, A.F. 2007. *A History of Egypt: From the Arab Conquest to the Present*. Cambridge: Cambridge University Press.

Thompson, J. 2008. *A History of Egypt: From Earliest Times to the Present*. New York: Vintage Books.

CONTRIBUTORS

AB: Andrew Bednarski (University of Cambridge)
AC: Alan Clapham (University of Cambridge)
AG: Anna Garnett (Petrie Museum, University College London)
AH: Anna Hodgkinson (Freie Universität Berlin)
AM: Amandine Mérat (independent researcher, France)
AS: Anna Stevens (University of Cambridge/Monash University)
AV: André Veldmeijer (American University in Cairo)
BK: Barry Kemp (University of Cambridge)
DD: Delphine Driaux (University of Vienna)
FA: Fathy Awad (Egyptian Ministry of Tourism and Antiquities)
GD: Gretchen Dabbs (Southern Illinois University)
GP: Gillian Pyke (Yale University)
GT: Gemma Tully (University of Cambridge)
HH: Helmi Hussein (Egyptian Ministry of Tourism and Antiquities)
HK: Hamada Kellawy (Egyptian Ministry of Tourism and Antiquities)
JB: Jolanda Bos (Archaeology and Heritage Consultancy Blikveld & Bos)
JW: Jacquelyn Williamson (George Mason University)
KS: Kate Spence (University of Cambridge)
KT: Kristin Thompson (University of Wisconsin)
MH: Marsha Hill (Metropolitan Museum of Art)
MS: Margaret Serpico (Institute of Archaeology, UCL)
PR: Pamela Rose (Austrian Archaeological Institute)

Tomb descriptions by BK; other site descriptions by AS in collaboration with GT; main text by AS.

ACKNOWLEDGMENTS

This work was supported by an Institutional Links grant, ID 261861975, under the Newton-Mosharafa Fund partnership awarded to the University of Cambridge and the Egyptian Ministry of Tourism and Antiquities (principal investigators Dr. Kate Spence and Dr. Yasmin El Shazly). The grant is funded by the UK Department for Business, Energy and Industrial Strategy and the Science and Technology Development Fund in Egypt and delivered by the British Council. For further information, please visit www.newtonfund.ac.uk. It is the result of international collaboration across researchers and caretakers of Amarna, and local community members. It is our hope that this book continues to inspire future collaborative efforts to protect both the site and local ways of life.

Management of Amarna is the responsibility of the Egyptian Ministry of Tourism and Antiquities, which oversees a wide range of initiatives to record and protect the site. The tireless work of local MoA staff in safeguarding Amarna, and their support during the development of this guidebook, must first be acknowledged. For their assistance during the completion of this book, particular thanks are due to Mr. Fathy Awad, Mr. Hamada Kellawy, Mr. Helmi Hussein, the staff of the Amarna Visitor Centre, and the staff of the Mallawi and Minya MoTA offices, particularly Mr. Gamal Abu Bakr and Mr. Mahmoud Salah. Thank you also to the excavation team from al-Hagg Qandil and al-Till for invaluable insights on life at Amarna today, and especially to Waleed Mohamed Omar for his help compiling this section of the guidebook.

The nucleus of this book was a guide to the rock-cut tombs and Central City initially written by Barry Kemp in the 1990s, and we are grateful to have been provided the opportunity to build upon this text. The information presented here also draws on the work of many other scholars, directly connected with Amarna and otherwise. We have kept citations to a minimum, but acknowledge the vast amount of research that underpins this book and hope that our decision to reference it lightly will be understood in the context of keeping the text accessible to a broad audience.

Many thanks are due to Mary Shepperson for so carefully and patiently developing illustrations and to Ferida Jawad and Adel Abdelmoneim for their meticulous preparation of the Arabic translation of this volume. Thanks also to the institutions and individuals who provided images for reproduction, and particularly to the Egypt Exploration Society for their generosity in sharing archival material from the early excavations at Amarna.

INDEX